RECORDS
Of The
REFORMED DUTCH CHURCH
Of
NEW PALTZ, NEW YORK

CONTAINING AN ACCOUNT OF THE ORGANIZATION
OF THE CHURCH AND THE
REGISTERS OF CONSISTORIES, MEMBERS,
MARRIAGES, AND BAPTISMS

Transcribed and Translated
BY DINGMAN VERSTEEG

CLEARFIELD COMPANY

Originally Published as
Volume III of
*Collections of The Holland Society
of New York* (1896)

Reprinted with permission
Genealogical Publishing Co., Inc.
Baltimore, 1977

**Reprinted for Clearfield Company, Inc.
by Genealogical Publishing Company Inc.
Baltimore, Maryland
1992**

Library of Congress Catalogue Card Number 77-77266
International Standard Book Number 0-8063-0772-2

Made in the United States of America

CONTENTS.

PAGE

ORGANIZATION OF THE CHURCH	1
FOUNDING OF THE SECOND CONGREGATION (CONFERENTIE)	6
CALL OF REV. J. M. GOETSCHIUS	10
CALL OF REV. RYNIER VAN NEST	13
CALL OF REV. STEPHANUS GOETSCHIUS . . .	16
BUILDING OF THE (CONFERENTIE) CHURCH, ON THE GREAT PIECE	20
SUBSCRIBERS TO THE ABOVE CHURCH	26
BUILDING OF THE NEW (COETUS) CHURCH . .	34
SUBSCRIBERS TO THE ABOVE CHURCH	40
CHURCH ACCOUNTS, ETC.	44
BAPTISMAL AND OTHER ENTRIES FROM THE FRENCH .	60
CONSISTORY	65
CONSISTORY OF THE SECOND CHURCH (CONFERENTIE) .	71
MEMBERSHIP	73
MEMBERSHIP OF THE SECOND CHURCH (CONFERENTIE)	79
MARRIAGES	80
BAPTISMS	93
INDEX	241
ERRATA	269

PREFACE.

One of the objects of The Holland Society of New York is defined by the Constitution to be to "collect and preserve information respecting the early history and settlement of the city and State of New York by the Dutch, and to discover, collect, and preserve all still existing documents, etc., relating to their genealogy and history."

In carrying out this object, the Society has sought to secure copies of all Dutch church records of the country antedating this century, and now has in its possession transcripts of nearly all such records now existing. Several years ago the Society published as its first volumes of collections the records of the Reformed Dutch churches of Hackensack and Schraalenburgh, New Jersey—including the registers of members, marriages, baptisms, and the consistories to the beginning of the nineteenth century. These volumes have proven to be of great assistance to many who were seeking to trace their lines of descent.

The present volume consists of all the records extant belonging to the church at New Paltz. This church was established in 1683 as a Huguenot church, and for some years the records were kept in the French language. The records from 1702 to 1730 are missing. Possibly no records for this period were kept at New Paltz, and the marriages and the baptisms may have been registered at Kingston. From 1730 until 1799 the records, with a few exceptions, were kept in Dutch, but in the latter year the Dutch was supplanted by the English language.

The translating and copying were done by Mr. D. Versteeg, who has done similar work for the Society in nearly all the church records now in possession of the Society. Mr. B. Fernow, of Albany, has also made a translation of these New Paltz church records, which is now in possession of the New York Genealogical and Biographical Society, and through the courtesy of that Society a comparison of these two transcripts has been made to promote accuracy.

THEODORE M. BANTA, Secretary.

THE NEW PALTZ CHURCH RECORDS

THE NEW PALTZ CHURCH RECORDS.

Volume I. of the records of the New Paltz Reformed Church is a small memorandum book of seventeen pages only, written in French with the exception of two items which are in Dutch. The record begins with an account of the organization of the church, January 22, 1683, and then follows the record of baptisms. Intermingled with these are a few items of records of marriages, membership, burials etc., which it has been deemed best to insert just as they appear in the original, rather than transfer them to the different appropriate records. The last continuous entry in this first volume is under date of February 21, 1702, after which there comes a gap extending to July 6, 1718, when the baptism of two children is recorded in Dutch. With these ends the first volume of the records. The second volume, as we have it, begins August 10, 1729, and it is evident that the book containing the records for the intervening years from 1702 to 1729, has been lost.

We have given a translation of the brief account of the organization of the church, and have followed it with an account of the history as it appears from the calls to the several Domines, the building of two or three church edifices, and such accounts as are found in the books of records. These items were scattered promiscuously through the volumes and have been collated and inserted as nearly as could be in chronological order.

The minutes of the Consistory are then given and the records of members, marriages, and baptisms.

THE ORGANIZATION OF THE CHURCH.

"1683, January 22. Mr. Pierre Daillie, Minister of the Word of God, arrived at New Paltz, preached twice on the

Sunday following, and proposed, at a social gathering of the families, to elect by a majority of votes of the heads of families, an elder and a deacon. This was done and the following named were elected :

Louis Dubois as elder, and
Hughe Frere as deacon,

to assist the minister in managing the affairs of the congregation assembled at New Paltz, and who were afterwards installed in the said office of elder and deacon—The present book has been made for the purpose of putting in writing what has taken place in the church."

The following three entries from book No. 2 are also in French :

Praised be God who has put it into our hearts to build Him a house to be therein worshipped and served, and through whose blessing we have finished it in the year eighteen (18) [probably 1718]. And may God grant that His Gospel may there be preached in this and following times (dean ce ciecle et dedan lautre [*sic*]) unto the day of eternity, Amen.

The names of those who have here built this house :

Mary, widow of Abraham Hasbrouck, now dead. Louy Bevier (deceased) and at present Samuel and Louy Bevier. Abraham Dubois,* Huge Frere, Salomon Duboys, Louys Du boys, Abraham Dóyo, Andres Le Fevre, Joseph Hasbrouck, Jacob Hasbrouck, Mary Du boys, now dead, and at present Daniel and Philip Du boys, Jean Le Fevre, Isaac Le Fevre, Ely Un, Chrestiane Doyo, Hanry Doyo, Abraham Frere, Jacob Frere.

Dec. 27, 1720.

Be it known to all christian people that the condition of this house is such, that all of us undersigned who have built this house here, do cede, and convey and transfer the one to the other, and to their heirs forever the place(s) which we have bought and paid for hereafter named, and the place(s) which shall be apportioned to us (a parteir) in this house of prayer. 1st the pew to the right of the pulpit on the east side : Abraham Duboy 2 seats and Jacob Hasbrouck 1 seat—further Joseph Hasbrouck 1 place, Louys Duboys one place, Mary,

---

* There will be observed much variation in the spelling of names. We have endeavored to follow the original verbatim.

widow of Abraham Hasbrouck, deceased, 2 places, and Chreistiane Doyo 1 place.

The 2d pew, behind the first pew: Heuge Frere 3 places, Louy Bevier (deceased) 2 places and at present Samuel and Louy Bevier, Mary Duboy (deceased) 2 places and at present Daniel and Felippe Duboys, Salomon Duboys 1 place.

The 3d pew Andre Le Feure 3 places, Isaac Le Feure 3 places, Jean Le Feure 3 places besides in the 4th pew 2 places in the corners—In the 4th pew Abraham Doyo 1 place, Louy Duboy 1 place, Louy Bevier, (deceased) and at present Andres Bevier 1 place, Jacob Frere 2 places—The 5th pew Abraham Doyo 2 places, Abraham Frere 2 places, Salomon Duboys 2 places, Jacob Hasbrouck 1 place, Heuge Frere Jr. 1 place.

The 6th pew Henry Doyo 2 places, Cristiane Doyo 1 place, Eli Un 2 places, Mary, widow of Abraham Hasbrouck, (deceased) 2 places.

Further the new places comprised in the corner near the small door, containing 4 seats on one side and 4 seats on the other: Abraham Duboys 2 places, Jacob Hasbrouck 2 places, Joseph Hasbrouck 2 places, Mary Dubois (deceased), Daniel and Fellippe Dubois 2 places.

The other new seats in front of the 5th pew:

Hugo Frere 3 places, Louy Duboys 1 place, Samuel —— 1 place, Hanry Doyo 1 place, Christiane Doyo 1 place.

All of us above mentioned approve and ratify these above named conditions, December 27, 1720.

(Also from Book No. 2.)

The following receipts show the salary paid to Reverend Johannes Van Driessen:

"I the undersigned acknowledge having received from the hands of the Consistory the amount of ten pounds New York money, and acknowledge to have been satisfied from the beginning of my ministry till this day.

Paltz, October 28, 1732.

(Signed) JOHANNES VAN DRIESSEN, V.D.M."

"I the undersigned acknowledge having received of the Reverend Consistory of the Paltz the amount of ten Pound and to be satisfied up to this date October 8, 1733.

(Signed) JOHANNES VAN DRIESSEN,"

August 23, 1753. Our installed preacher B. Vrooman arrived here with satisfactory proofs of his Ministry and delivered his introductory sermon at the Paltz on the 26th inst. To this we bear testimony.

(Signed) { JOHANNES HARDENBERGH.
DANIEL HASBROUCQ.
SAMUEL BEVIER.
JOHANN GEORGE RAND. }

August 27, 1753. The Consistory of New Paltz meeting in the fear of the Lord declare in regard to the members admitted among them by J. V. Driese, that they have professed to believe in the doctrines of the Reformed Church as expressed in the Heidelberg Catechism and in Article 37 of the Confession, and to submit to the Canons of said church and, as far as is known to them [the Consistory], still adhere to the same.

Thus given in our Consistory Meeting on the day and date as above.

Signed in the name of all,
B. VROOMAN, Praes.

(From Book No. 3.)

The following members of the Consistory of Shawangonk and New Paltz subscribed to a call extended to Reverend J. M. Goetschius, January 18, 1760.

ELDERS.
Matheus Terwilge.
Lourentz Alsdorf.
I. Bruyn.
Johannes Beviers.
Simon Dubois.
Jacobus Hasbrouk.
Johannes Hardenberg.
Abraham Lefefer.

DEACONS.
Benjamin Smedes Jr.
Hermanus Ostrander.
Hugo Terwilliger.
Sampson Sammons.
Johannes Dojou.
Petrus Ostrander.
Jacobus Bevier.

(From Book No. 2.)

March 15, 1762. The Congregation of New Paltz met together and elected by a majority of votes as overseers and builders of a new church building here, for the Congregation of New Paltz, and whom the Congregation promised to provide with the necessaries the following persons, viz :

Abraham Dojo. Jonas Freres.
Jacob Hasbroek. Hugo Freres Jr.
Cornelis Duboj. Abraham Hardenberg.
Simon Duboj.

(It appears that the plan was not carried out at that time.)

We the undersigned constituting the Consistory of the Reformed Church of Jesus Christ at New Paltz and Shawankonk unanimously appoint our Pastor and Instructor J. M. Goetchius and Jonas Freres our fellow brother, Elder, to appear in our name at the Ecclesiastical Assembly which is to be held at New York in order to treat in the fear of God concerning the well-being of God's church in this country, all in accordance with the Word of God and the Constitution of God's church in these regions, and to oppose everything not conforming to the same, all for the glory and upbuilding of God's church.

Thus given in our Consistory meeting held at New Paltz this 3d day of June, 1764.

1764, September 9. Acknowledge having then received of the Reverend Consistory of the Congregation at New Paltz the amount of twenty pounds, being full payment of my half year's salary now due. Say received by me

(Signed) JOH. MAURITIUS GOETCHIUS,
V. D. M.

On this 19th day of July at the house of Simon Duboy we held a meeting of the Consistory after having called upon God's name, and discussed the following point:

It was asked whether a member of the congregation at Schawankong may be admitted to the Lord's table here, without a written certificate?

The resolution and opinion of the Consistory in regard to this question is, that they do not see why they should require a certificate of the brethren of the Consistory of Schawankong for any God-fearing member of the congregation who might be desirous here to receive the Lord's Supper. This Consistory only resolves that such a person shall previously at the right time and place make known his desire either to the preacher or to the Consistory.

(From Book No. 4.)

Extracts from the minutes at the founding of the Second Church at New Paltz :

"On August 29, 1767, came together at the house of Henricus DuBoys, Domine Izaac Rysdyk with his Consistory and five members of the Reformed Nether Dutch Church who have heretofore belonged to the congregation of Kingston, viz. : Josia Eltinge, Noach Eltinge, Petrus Van Wagena, Jacob DuBoys, and Dirk D. Wynkoop, who, with some other members of the said Nether Dutch Church, have built a church here for the purpose of observing their most holy religion, and had requested Domine Isaac Rysdyk, Instructor at Pochkeepsie and Fishkill, as neighboring preacher, to be present at the organization and consecration of a Christian Reformed Nether Dutch congregation. (He) had been specially and in writing charged and authorized by his Consistory [to be present]." (See a translation of the whole on page 7.)

At the same time was read the following letter, in Dutch :

"We undersigned Consistory of Kingston having been requested by the after named members of our Church, living at the Paltz, and who have built a new church there, for the purpose of exercising by themselves all the rites of our Nether Dutch Reformed Church in the same, to legally dismiss them and to provide them with letters, have, after mature deliberation of the said request, been neither at liberty nor willing to refuse it, but hereby dismiss from among us the said members, viz. : Josia Eltinge, Noach Eltinge, Petrus Van Wagenen, Jacob Du Boys, Rebecka Van Wagenen, Dirk D. Wynkoop, Magdalena Du Boys, Jacomyntje Eltinge, and Sara Louw, under condition that from among the aforesaid members, within two months time, either by Domine Rysdyk or some other neighboring preacher belonging to the Classis of Amsterdam a Consistory shall be elected and thus a Nether Dutch Reformed congregation be formed, acknowledging the jurisdiction of the Reverend Classis of Amsterdam. Thus enacted by the Consistory of the Church of Kingston, August 3d, 1767.

(Below was written) :

In the name and by the authority of the Reverend Consistory of Kingston,

(Signed) { HEND. SLEGHT.
{ ABRAHAM LOW."

It was resolved to elect from among the said five members a Consistory of one Elder and one Deacon, and there were subsequently unanimously elected, as Elder Noach Eltinge and as Deacon Petrus Van Wagenen.

At the same time were admitted and acknowledged as members of this congregation :

Petrus Low.	Debora Van Vliet.
Henricus Du Boys.	Jannetye Hooghteyling.
Salomon Low.	Izaac Low.

Here follows the history of the founding of the Second Church at New Paltz.

On August 29 [1767] met together at the house of Henricus DuBois, Do. Izaac Rysdyk with his Consistory and five members of the Reformed Nether Dutch Church who previously belonged to the congregation of Kingston, viz. Josia Eltinge, Noach Eltinge, Petrus Van Wagena, Jacob DuBoys, Dirk D. Wynkoop who besides some other members of the said Nether Dutch Church have here built a church for the purpose of exercising their most holy religion and had requested as neighboring preacher Do. Isaac Rysdyk, Instructor at Poughkeepsie and Fishkill to assist at the organization and consecration of a Christian Reformed Nether Dutch congregation, and who had been specially and in writing authorised for the purpose by his Consistory.

After calling upon God's holy name for a blessing upon this important undertaking the aforesaid members, besides the others, communicated to Do. Rysdyk, upon his request, the reasons why they had here erected a church by themselves, and why, by leaving the congregation of Kingston and of the New Paltz, though the latter is situated close by here, they are desirous of founding a congregation by themselves ; viz :

First, because the congregation of the New Paltz and its preacher, Do. Mauritius Goetschius have separated from the orderly subordination to the Reverend Classis of Amsterdam under which the Nether Dutch Reformed congregations in this province have belonged from olden times and still ought to belong, and because all those preachers and congregations who call themselves Coetus, by the resolution of the Synod of 1765 and in accordance with the last letter of the Reverend Classis to the so-called Coetus, dated June 3, 1765, have been considered by the Reverend Synod of North Holland and by the Reverend Classis of Amsterdam as preachers and congregations which cannot be recognised as lawful, because they separated from the authority of the Reverend Classis, and wanted to organise here, in opposition to the ordinances of the Church an independent Classis, for which the said Classis declares to have neither might nor right, as is apparent from the following extracts of the Synodal Resolutions of 1763, as follows page 14, *Post quedam alia:*

I. "That those calling themselves Coetus, thus have become guilty of despicable ingratitude against their benefactors, who have so long labored for their well-being and have exerted so many efforts in behalf of the churches of New York, and that, acting in this manner and persevering in their actions, they give just cause to the Classis of Amsterdam and to the Synod of North Holland to break with them entirely and to stop all intercourse with them etc., etc."

In this aforesaid minute of the Synod can also be found the important reasons for this resolution, as well of the committee of investigation of the petition of the Coetus, as of the Classis of Amsterdam, pp. 8 and 9. See the Extract of the Minutes of the Synod held at Edam from July 26 till August 4, 1763, printed at New York by John Holt, 1765.

II. Of what the Reverend Classis writes in the letter to the so-called Coetus on the aforementioned date, where among the other matters it says:

"You say that you hope that the Classis will seize this opportunity, as being the last time that you will make the request.

"From the contents of this [letter] it appears that the classis, according to your opinion has not yielded, nor can do so.

"We therefore reply that whereas it is plain that you want to secede from us, we therefore in after times shall consider you as a body of preachers who have seceded from us, and consequently we are not in a condition from now on to treat you as such Brethren with whom we can live in amicable intercourse, as the nature of our union with you requires."

And in the end of the letter:

"Further, brethren, we commend you to God and his mercy who is mighty to build you up, and considering your decision as final, we shall, from now on, have no further communications with you." (See the said classical letter printed at New York by John Holt, 1765.)

For which and other reasons they cannot recognise the said preacher and congregation as lawful, because, since the arrival of the last named letter they persevered and are still persevering in their decision—so much the less because the above named persons consider the afore mentioned subordination as lawful, beneficial and necessary for the maintenance of the pure doctrine and discipline of our Reformed Nether Dutch Church, for the exercise whereof we have perfect liberty by virtue of the eighth article of the capitulation of 1664, ratified in the treaty of peace of 1667.

Whereby yet come the revilings and insults by the said Do. Goetschius and some of the so-called Coetus hurled at the Classis and Synod of Holland.

Secondly, the five members of the congregation of Kingston declared that they are living too far away from the church of Kingston to dutifully and statedly attend divine worship there, either for themselves, or to properly educate their children, according to their solemn promise at the holy baptism, in the pure doctrine of the truth, and to lead them to the communion of a Reformed (and to the Reverend Classis of Amsterdam subordinated) congregation. They, therefore, can neither be edified here, nor find a proper opportunity therein and for observing their precious religious duties.

Mr. Dirk D. Wynkoop gave for himself the following reasons: having, last spring, changed his place of residence from Kingston to this place, and now also living at too great a distance from the said church to observe his religious duties there, he therefore wanted to join this new congregation.

That they together for the above mentioned reasons had, in the fear of the Lord, undertaken the building of a church here which, being now almost completed, they requested might be solemnly dedicated by Do. Rysdyk as neighboring preacher. They consequently surrendered to Do. Isaac Rysdyk their letter of dismissal from the congregation of Kingston which having been read was approved, reading as follows:

[This letter appears on page 6.]

Do. Rysdyk and his Consistory having heard the afore mentioned reasons, and read the letter of dismissal, certified the same to be legal and reasonable; wherefore they also fully approved of the building of the church with good wishes for God's much needed blessing in the founding, increase and upbuilding of this church and congregation.

Copy of the Church certificate of Do. Joh. Mauritius Goetschius:

We the undersigned constituting the Consistory of the Reformed Church of Jesus Christ in the High and Nether Dutch language at Schoharey, attest and certify by the present that the Rev. Joh. Mauritius Goetschius has been for two years and a half our stated Pastor and Instructor, and has also during this time, faithfully, diligently and assiduously inculcated, according to the word of God our salutary and pure doctrines and articles of faith, at the same time illustrating and confirming them through a pious conversation and life. For these reasons we recommend him everywhere as a pious instructor, wishing him all hail and blessing.

Thus given at Schoharey in our Consistory meeting on this 6th day of August, 1760.

Barendt Vrooman.   Williem Enderson.
Pitter Schneyder.   George Rechtmeyer.
Johannes Bekker, Jr.   Joh. Hannese Becker.

Copy of letter of call to Domine Goetschius:

In the fear of God's holy name, amen.

Whereas the preaching of God's holy Word is the means ordained by him to lead men living upon this earth to salvation, therefore we the undersigned Elders and Deacons at present constituting the Consistories of the united Nether Dutch Reformed Churches at Shawangonk and New Paltz in the county of Ulster, province of New York, having learned about the gifts of the Rev. Johannes Mauritius Goetschius, preacher at Schoharey, and being satisfied with the same, and feel like calling "Come over and help us," have met together in the fear of the Lord for the purpose of extending this call, and after calling upon God's Holy Name we unanimously resolved to call the aforenamed Joh. Mauritius Goetschius, as we are by the present calling him, as our stated Overseer, Pastor and Instructor, to administer the holy office in our aforesaid congregations in conformity with God's Holy Word, and the Reformed doctrine and the discipline, adopted by the Christian Synod held at Dordregt, anno 1618 & 1619.

And we thus call his Reverence upon the following conditions:

1. That his Reverence through God's guidance and good government may come over to us and faithfully administer the holy offices in all portions as befits an orthodox Instructor and Pastor of the Reformed Church of Jesus Christ, publicly call upon the Name of God, preach the Word of God in its purity, administer the holy Sacraments according to the institution of Christ, and instruct the youth once a week in the congregation where his Reverence shall preach on the catechism, earnestly admonish, exercise the church discipline and in every respect as much as possible have a good supervision over the Church of Jesus Christ.

2. That his Reverence when in health and the weather permitting, shall, from Easter till the commencement of October, preach twice on every Lord's day in the Church of Shawankong and the succeeding Lord's day at New Paltz ; in the forenoon from some free text out of God's holy Word, in the afternoon from a topic in the Heidelberg catechism ; the remainder of the year, from the beginning of October till Easter, one sermon on each Lord's day will be sufficient, Shawankong and Pals each to have an equal share of the services.

3. That his Reverence shall conduct services on the Holy days as is customary in the Reformed Dutch Church, each place to receive an equal share.

4. That his Reverence, God willing, shall administer the Lord's holy supper four times per year, twice per year at Shawankong and twice at New Paltz, by turns, as Domine and his Consistory shall decide.

5. That his Reverence before administering each Supper, shall preach a preparatory sermon at the place where he is to administer the same, and to do the house visiting once per year in each congregation.

Upon these afore-named conditions we, the Consistories of the aforesaid congregations of Shawankong and New Paltz in our quality of elders and deacons for us and our successors who shall from time to time hold office after us, promise in all sincerity as long as his Reverence shall be our Pastor and Overseer the following salary or sum of money of eighty pounds current money of the province of New York to be paid annually and every year, each congregation its just half, and whether the salary of £80 shall be paid out in a single payment, or £40 each half year, we shall agree about with your Reverence when coming over to us.

Each Elder and Deacon before being installed in their office shall sign this letter of call, while your salary shall commence as soon as your Reverence shall come among us.

We shall provide your Reverence with a decent house, barn, garden, and ninety acres of land besides a good spring near the house, the same to be provided in and by the congregation of Shawankong, near the church where your Reverence will live, as long as your Reverence shall be with or among us as our Overseer, Pastor, and Instructor.

His Reverence while conducting the services at New Paltz

shall be provided by the New Paltz congregation with quarters, board and bed.

His Reverence is to find his own fire wood as there is enough of it on the land where he will live.

These promises we, the undersigned Elders and Deacons and our successors, shall pay in the fear of the Lord annually and every year the amount of £80, New York money. [Literal translation of this clause.]

We, then, the Consistories of the aforesaid congregations dedicate this call to and deliver it into the hands of the aforesaid Joh. Mauritius Goetschius, desiring and praying that he may accept the same in the fear of the Lord and come over to us with a rich blessing of the Gospel as a member of the Reverend Coetus.

And to show that this our action is sincere and well-intentioned we affix our signatures on this 18th of January in the year of our Lord 1760.

ELDERS.	DEACONS.
Matheus Terwilge.	Benjamin Smedes, Jr.
Lourenz Alsdorf.	Hermanus Ostrander.
I. Bruyn.	Hugo Terwilliger.
Johannes Beviers.	Sampson Sammons.
Simon Dubois.	Johannes Dojou.
Jacobus Hasbrouk.	Petrus Ostrander.
Johannes Hardenberg.	Jacobus Bevier.
Abraham Lefefer.	

APPROBATION.

The Reverend Assembly of the Coetus finds this call correct, and approves the same, in accordance with the desire of the Consistory.

New York, May 6, 1760.

(Signed) { B. Vrooman, p. t. Praes.
{ David Marinus, p. t. Scriba.

March 17, 1771. The Reverend J. Mauritius Goetschius, Helvitio Figurinus, Instructor of the congregation at New Paltz and Shawenkonk died in the Lord, Sunday afternoon at 4 o'clock in his house at Shawenkonk, and was buried on the 19th inst. in the church at Shawenkonk in the baptistry, aged 47 years.

Receipt by the widow of Rev. J. M. Goetschius for salary due to her deceased husband.

New Paltz, March 14, 1772. Then received of the Rev. Consistory of this congregation the amount of three pounds four shillings, and some time ago the amount of twenty-two pounds six shillings, being my deceased husband's salary in full, and also in full of all accounts up to the present day. I say received by me. (Signed) CATHRINA GOETSCHIUS.

£ 3-4.
22-6.
_____
£25-10.

(Translated from Book No. 4.)

Ds. Rynier Van Nest's call [to the Second church of New Paltz].

In the Name and Fear of the Most High Triune God, Amen.

Whereas the preaching of God's Holy Writ in its purity is the God-ordained means to lead men from misery to eternal salvation ;

Therefore, we the undersigned Elders and Deacons at present constituting the Reverend Consistory of the two united Nether Dutch Reformed Congregations of Jesus Christ at Shawengonk, and the Second Church at New Paltz in the County of Ulster and Province of New York, having with much pleasure, heard the laudable gifts of the pious Mr. Rynier Van Nest, Jr., S.S.M.Cand. to whom the inclination and desire of the aforesaid Congregations are calling " Come over, and help us," having met together in the fear of the Lord for the purpose of seriously considering the matter of a call, have unanimously resolved after calling upon God's Name to call, and consequently call by these presents, the aforesaid Mr. Rynier Van Nest, Jr., for our stated Pastor and Instructor, to faithfully administer the holy office among us, in accordance with God's holy Word and the accepted doctrine and discipline of the Nether Dutch Reformed Church adopted in and by the National Synod held at Dordrecht, A.D., 1618 and 1619.

And we extend our call to his Reverence on the following conditions :

1. That his Reverence as soon as possible shall submit to a peremptory examination by the Very Reverend General Assembly of the Nether Dutch Reformed Church of New York

and New Jersey to be set apart to the holy office with the laying on of hands according to apostolic Reformed usage, and to be confirmed before our congregations.

 2. That his Reverence thus having come to us through God's government shall observe all parts of the holy office as befits an orthodox Overseer, Pastor and Instructor of the Reformed Church of Jesus Christ; publicly call upon the God of heaven, preach the word of God in its purity; administer the sacraments of salvation (heyl-Sacramenten) according to the institution by Christ; [a word left out in the original] the keys of heaven diligently and prudently besides, and with the Consistory, visit the sick, and in every way as much as possible exercise a good supervision over the church of Jesus Christ.

 3. His Reverence shall, God willing, from Easter to the beginning of October, preach twice on every Lord's day in one of the aforenamed congregations, in the forenoon from some text out of God's holy Word, in the afternoon according to the topics contained in the Heidelberg Catechism; during the remainder of the year one sermon shall be sufficient. After the sermon his Reverence shall, in the place where it is his turn to preach, teach the youth and others who need it through catechetical exercises. Further catechetical instruction shall be given on such a day during the week as shall be approved of by his Reverence and the Reverend Consistory. The congregation of the Second Church at New Paltz is to enjoy every fourth turn of preaching, the remainder of the time the preaching service shall take place in the congregation of Shawengonk; on the holydays there will be services according to Reformed usage.

 4. His Reverence shall twice per year administer the Lord's Holy Supper in each of the aforenamed congregations, at such a time as shall be approved of by his Reverence and the Reverend Consistory, and God willing, once a year the house visiting shall take place in both congregations.

Upon these conditions we the Reverend Consistories of the two aforesaid congregations in our quality of Elders and Deacons promise for us and our successors who shall from time to time come in after us, as long as his Reverence shall be our stated Pastor and Instructor, the following:

 1. We promise to provide his Reverence from the congregation of Shawengonk with a good and commodious dwelling, barn, cistern, garden and ninety acres of land situated close to the church in the congregation of Shawengonk, and the Reverend Consistory of the Second Church at New Paltz

promises his Reverence decent lodgings and board at the time when the turn to preach there shall come.

2. We promise to pay his Reverence annually and each year by itself the amount of eighty pounds New York current money. By the congregation of Shawengonk the amount of sixty pounds and by the congregation of the Second Church at New Paltz the amount of twenty pounds, so that each congregation shall be responsible for its own share, to be paid annually in two payments, *i. e.* the twenty pounds of the Congregation of the Second Church at New Paltz in the spring and the sixty pounds of the church at Shawengonk in the fall, which salary shall commence from the day when his Reverence shall deliver his first sermon in one of the aforesaid congregations, after having accepted this call.

3. We promise to allow six Sundays in the year to his Reverence to be spent as his Reverence may please, up to the time that the said congregations shall feel able to increase the salary to the amount of one hundred pounds, when the Reverend Consistories expect that his Reverence shall spend the six aforesaid Sundays among the two calling congregations.

4. We promise that every newly elected Elder and Deacon shall sign this call, or an authentic copy of the same, before being installed in their respective offices.

We, therefore, dedicate this call to his Reverence and deliver it up into the hands of the aforesaid Mr. Rynier Van Nest, hoping that his Reverence may accept the same in the fear of the Lord, with a cordial prayer that the good God, the governor of the World, the appointer of his Ministers, may be pleased to send him to us with a rich blessing of the Gospel.

That we are sincere and well-meaning in this our Act we certify by our own signatures on this 26th day of April, Anno Domini 1774.

SHAWANKONK.   SECOND CHURCH, NEW PALTZ.

Elders.   Elders.

Jacobus Bruyn.   Roelof Jos. Eltinge.
Dirk Roosa.   Jacob Dubois.
Benjamin Van Keure.
Jacob Smedes.

Deacons.   Deacons.

Benjamin Terwilliger.   Isaak Low.
Joseph Dekker.   Dirk D. Wynkoop.
Cornelius Schonmaker.
Thomas Jansen, Jr.

These following persons have affixed their signatures to the call in behalf of the Second Church at New Paltz:

(Signed) { SALOMON LOW.
{ SALOMON ELTINGE.

We promise to carry out the conditions of the above call, for the Second Congregation at New Paltz.

(Signed) { ABRAHAM ELTINGE.
{ HENDRICUS DUBOIS, Jr.

(Translated from Book No. 3.)

Stephanus Goetchius, son of J. H., born October 25, 1752, having undergone his preparatory examination October, 1775, has accepted the call of the New Paltz in the fear of God, on November 1, 1775.

The call reads as follows:

Whereas, the whole world on account of sin has become condemned before God, and it has pleased God in His infinite mercy to reveal a road to salvation, and to lead the poor sinner to believe in Him through the truth of preaching;

Therefore, we, the undersigned Elders and Deacons constituting the Consistories of the two united congregations of Jesus Christ at New Paltz and New Hurly, in the County of Ulster and province of New York, having heard with great pleasure the laudable gifts of the Reverend and pious Mr. Stephanus Goetschius, at present licentiate and living just now at Schralenburg, and whom it is the unanimous wish and desire of our congregations to call "Come over and help us," having met in the fear of the Lord for the purpose of conscientiously considering the matter of a call, unanimously resolved, after calling upon God's name, to call the aforesaid Mr. Stephanus Goetschius as our stated Pastor and Instructor, to faithfully administer among us the holy office, in accordance with God's Holy Word, and the formulas of unity and discipline established in the Nether Dutch Reformed Church at and by the National Synod, held at Dordrecht, A.D. 1618 and 1619, as by the present we immediately call his Reverence (Zyn E.) upon the following conditions, viz.:

First. His Reverence shall assiduously and faithfully observe all parts of the holy religion as it befits an orthodox Overseer, Pastor and Instructor of the Church of Jesus Christ; publicly call upon the God of heaven; preach the Word of God in its purity; administer the holy sacraments in accordance with the institution of Christ; impart necessary instruction in the catechism to the youth, on each day where it shall be his Reverence's turn to preach; therebesides his Reverence shall, as often as possible, catechise during week days in both congregations, and thus, in every way, as much as possible, shall exercise due supervision over the church of Jesus Christ.

Second. His Reverence, when in good health and with the will of God, from Easter till the end of September shall preach twice per day on each Lord's day in one of the aforenamed places; in the forenoon upon some text from the Word of God, in the afternoon according to the topics suggested by the Heidelberg Catechism; the remaining time preaching once on every preaching day shall suffice, with the proviso that his Reverence is required by the present to preach only once on every Lord's day or other preaching days during the first year of his Reverence's ministry as aforementioned.

New Paltz shall receive twice as much service as New Hurley, so that New Hurley shall only receive one third portion of the service, which service shall be performed by turns in the congregations in such a manner that not on three successive Sundays services shall take place in one congregation. On the holy days services shall be held according to Reformed custom.

Third. His Reverence shall administer the Lord's holy Supper twice per year in each of the two aforesaid congregations, and shall do the house visiting once per year in both congregations.

Upon these conditions we, the Consistories of the abovenamed congregations, in our quality of elders and deacons, promise for ourselves and our successors, who from time to time shall come in after us, as long as his Reverence shall be our regular Overseer, Pastor and Instructor, the following, viz.:

Firstly. We promise to provide his Reverence with a good dwelling fit for a preacher with kitchen, barn, cistern, garden and sixty acres of land; the house, barn, and larger portion of the land being situated near the church in the congregation of New Paltz. His Reverence will also be provided with fit lodgings and refreshments at New Hurley by the said congregation at the time of his turn to preach there.

Secondly. We promise to give his Reverence six Sundays in the year to do with as he pleases, from the share of the congregation at New Paltz, to be spent where his Reverence shall deem it necessary. This the Consistory of New Paltz alone promises.

Thirdly. We promise to pay your Reverence annually and all years the amount of ninety pounds of money current in

New York, viz., the congregation of New Paltz the amount of fifty-six pounds ten shillings, and the congregation of New Hurley the amount of thirty-three pounds ten shillings, so that each congregation is responsible for its share, to be paid annually in two installments, *i. e.*, one of the said congregations to pay in the spring, the other in the fall, and the whole of this salary shall commence from the day that he shall deliver his introductory sermon in the abovenamed congregations.

We, therefore, dedicate this call to his Reverence and deliver the same into the hands of the said Mr. Stephanus Goetchius, wishing that his Reverence may accept the same in the fear of the Lord, with the heartfelt prayer that the good God, the governor of the world, the appointer of his servants, may be pleased to send him to us with a rich blessing of the Gospel.

That this is our sincere and cordial opinion we confirm by affixing our seals and own signatures this 24th day of September, 1775.

Actum at New Paltz.

CONSISTORY OF NEW HURLEY.	CONSISTORY OF NEW PALTZ.
Dirk Teerpenning,	Johannes Hardenberg,
Petrus Ostrander,	Andries Lefever,
Hermanus Ostrander,	Jacob Hasbrouck, Jr.,
Jacobus Roos, Jr.,	Jacob Frere, Jr.,
Teunis Teerpenning,	John Terwilger,
Cornelius Masten,	Johannes Frere, Jr.,
Jan Teerpenning,	Benjamin Doio.
Johannes Parleman.	

Executed in the presence of me as Moderator (Consulent), September 24, 1775, at Schawangong.

RYNIER VAN NEST, JR., V.D.M.

The above call has been approved by the Reverend particular Assembly of Dutchess and Ulster Counties, on this 26th day of May, 1777.

Ds. RYSDYK,
Ds. RYNIER VAN NEST.

Addition to, or Revision of, his Reverence's letter of call made on September 1, 1784.

In the name of the Triune God, Amen.

Whereas the whole world is condemned before God, and it has nevertheless pleased Him in His infinite mercy through the preaching of the Gospel of Jesus Christ to urge the sinner to believe and to lead him to salvation.

Therefore, we Elders and Deacons constituting the Consistory of the Collegiate Reformed congregations of Jesus Christ at New Paltz and New Hurley in Ulster County and State of New York, well knowing the laudable gifts of our present Pastor and Instructor, Stephanus Goetschius, fearing his Reverence's departure and the sad consequences of a pastorless condition, being met together and having considered the matter in the fear of the Lord, join our voices to those of the congregation, and call out to him :

"*Remain with us, and help us.*"

And in order to show this to be our sincere opinion we promise in our quality of consistories of the aforesaid congregations, for us and our successors, to pay his Reverence annually and each year besides the amount stipulated in his Reverence's letter of call the amount of twenty-four Pounds New York current money, viz., from the Congregation at New Paltz sixteen pounds, and from the Congregation of New Hurley eight pounds.

Upon the following conditions :

1. In case his Reverence, having been called by Meniscenc, shall remain with us, and observe the church services in every part as is required in the office of a faithful Pastor and Instructor, as has been stipulated in the call.

2. Nor shall the Consistory be responsible after the date of these presents for the losses in his Reverence's call through death or his removal up to the present time.

[The above is very obscure in the original ; it may mean that death or removal of those who subscribed towards the salary may affect the minister's salary.]

3. The aforenamed amount shall be payable on November 1, 1785, and so in every year besides the money mentioned in the call.

4. The money shall be collected by the aforenamed Consistories, and the persons having subscribed corn shall be notified to annually deliver the same at his Reverence's house.

That this is our sincere intention we certify through our seals and with our signatures this September 1, 1784.

CONSISTORY OF NEW PALTZ.	CONSISTORY OF NEW HURLEY.
Abram Lefever.	Johannes Bovier.
Jacob Hasbrouck.	David Ostrander.
Daniel Lefever.	Cornelius Vernoy, Jr.
Dirk Wynkoop, Jr.	Jacob Terwilger.
Dr. George Wirtz.	Lawrence Alsdorph, Jr.
Hugo Frere, Jr.	Ezechiel Masten.
Jacob I. Frere.	Abram Steenberg.

The Reverend Stephen Goetchius removed later on to Marbletown, and the congregations of New Paltz and New Hurley on March 23, 1799, called the Rev. John H. Meier, Cand. Sac. Min. to the pastoral care of said congregations. The call is in English and copied in Book 3 of the original.

The following entries were translated from a book, labelled "Account Book":

In the year of our Lord 1766, the 29th day of August, some Christian inhabitants of the village of New Paltz and the neighborhood thereunto belonging, assembled together and resolved to build a church on the southern extremity of the land of Noach Eltinge, named the Great Piece on the "Hoogtentje" to the West of the Royal road and near the Great Parcel gate (Stuck heck), viz.: A church or house of *Bintwerck* * and thirty feet square, the walls to be drawn up with clay and wood and to be covered with boards on the outside, a shingle roof, and with room enough to make a gallery in the same if necessary, and further to finish the whole in a becoming manner. And in order to finish this work we have thought fit to systematically proceed until the work shall be completed.

1. A subscription list shall be drawn up of what every one will give towards the building of this church, whether money or anything else.

2. And after the list shall have been made up, those who have given promises shall select three men for managing this work. They shall have authority to build the aforesaid church as they think fit, according to the aforesaid subscriptions, but in conformity with this order. In case the subscriptions are insufficient they shall send out men for the purpose of getting more for the building of that house or church, and in case they cannot get enough to finish it, the aforenamed three men shall finish it, and each subscriber to the list shall be obliged to pay in proportion to his promise until the church shall be completed.

3. And these aforenamed three men shall choose an overseer for this work and shall from time to time as they see fit give him written instructions about what to do in building the aforesaid church.

This overseer shall be obliged to execute the orders given him by these men in building the aforesaid church, and after having executed the orders he shall, from time to time, send in his accounts to them. And thus they shall give orders, and he shall render account from time to time until the work shall be completed.

* A *bint* is a joint or cross beam.

4. And in case this overseer should happen to die or move away, or not submit correct accounts, the aforesaid men shall select another, and the former overseer shall be obliged to account to the newly appointed overseer, and to surrender all things belonging to the aforesaid church to the newly elected overseer, and this shall be adhered to from time to time, at the appointment of new overseers.

5. These three men shall also have power to make regulations in the church after the same shall be completed, providing always that those regulations are not contrary to the regulations of the Christian Reformed Churches, adopted by the National Synod last held at Dordrecht, in the years 1618 and 1619. And after the work shall have been completed the above named three men shall audit all the overseer's accounts and he shall be obliged to fully account for everything and to surrender to them everything belonging to the aforesaid church, and thereupon they shall discharge him.

6. When they know the total expense, they shall put the total cost equally upon the seats, and shall invite those whose names are on the subscription list to appear on a fixed day and hour in the aforesaid church, and shall then be just to whomsoever they owe places or to their heirs, and shall sell the places at vendue. Those having given much shall be repaid in places and in no other manner, and those having given little shall add thereto in case they buy a seat or seats which cost more than they have subscribed. But no place shall be sold at less than the estimated cost.

7. The aforesaid men shall also be obliged to acknowledge the rights of every person who assisted in building the aforesaid church, and further to faithfully perform the duties in accordance with these instructions and in case it can be proved against them that they are negligent in this respect, they shall be obliged to make reparation with the expense incurred out of their own pockets.

They shall further allot to everyone their place or places in the church in a manner similar to the practice in the Church of Kingston.

The aforesaid men shall further make or buy a book in which the entire instructions shall be entered, and the subscription list shall also be entered therein, and the instructions to the overseer and the overseer's accounts shall also from time to time be entered in the same, and further everything concerning the building of the church and the regulations.

And after the seats shall have been distributed they shall also enter into this book to whom and where they are located.

And after the above named men shall have completed the work they shall elect other churchmasters in accordance with the stipulations in the charter or grant of the Church of Kingston. And after the others shall have been elected the above named men shall be held to render an account to the newly elected churchmasters, and to surrender to them everything belonging to the aforesaid church. And it shall remain for the use of the said church, and thereupon they shall be discharged from their office.

And in order to oblige the above named three men who may be elected, to act in accordance with these instructions, and to execute everything required of them in the same, they shall, after having been elected, subscribe to these instructions.

         HENDRICUS DUBOIS,
(Signed) JOSIA ELTINGE,
         NOACH ELTINGE.

Be it known to everybody by these presents that we, Hendriecus Dubois, Josia Eltinge, and Noach Eltinge, the three elected men in conformity with the previous instructions, elect Philip Dubois as overseer of the said work. And in order to oblige him to act and work according to the aforenamed instructions, in everything as is required of him by the same, he shall sign these presents.

     (Signed) PHILIPPUS DUBOIS.

Be it known to everyone by these presents that the promised amounts here below pledged by the subscribers of this list shall be expended in erecting the church building in conformity with the agreement and instructions of some of the inhabitants of the New Paltz and its vicinity.

Dated the 29th day of August in the year of our Lord 1766. And everyone shall put down what he promises opposite his name whether money or anything else.

	£.	s.		£.	s.
Hendricus Dubois	20.		Roelof Josias Eltinge	5.	
Josia Eltinge	20.		Isack Louw	2.	
Noach Eltinge	16.		James Huey	3.	10
Peterus Louw	6.		Jacob Duboies	5.	
Peterus Van Wagenen	5.		Abraham Een	1.	
Abraham Eltinge	6.				
Salomon Louw	5.		Total,	£99.	10
Philip Dubois	5.				

New Paltz, September 2, 1766.

We, Josiah Eltinge, Hendricus Dubois and Noach Eltinge met in our capacity of supervisors or managers for erecting the church building and resolved commencing to build the said edifice. And we order you Philip Dubois as overseer of the work, to frame and prepare the timber piled on the spot, and to build, and put on the slats and shingles.

(Signed) Hendricus Dubois,
Josia Elting,
Noach Eltinge.

October 28, 1766.

On the above date we order Philip Dubois overseer of our work on the church building as follows: to finish the roof, and to wall in the house with boards and to lay the floor and to finish the door and windows, also the seats.

(Signed) Hendricus Dubois,
Josia Eltinge,
Noach Eltinge.

December 12, 1766.

On this date Philip Dubois, as overseer of the work on the church building completed his task in accordance with the two foregoing orders and submitted his accounts to us undersigned. The total expense amounts to £107–18–10 wherewith we credit in this book every body in particular (as they have earned it, or contributed in money) opposite their subscriptions.

(Signed) Hendricus Dubois,
Josia Eltinge,
Noach Eltinge.

1770, August 10.

We, the undersigned, rendered account to each other of the expenditures on the church, from December 12, 1766 to this date. The total amount is £41.3.1. The money we have collected, and the sums received for the boards and nails which we did not use amount to £23.9.7, so that the balance for the builders amounts to £17.13.6 wherewith we have credited in this book everybody in particular (as they have earned or contributed it) opposite their subscriptions.

(Signed) Hendricus Dubois,
Josia Eltinge,
Noach Eltinge.

1770 August 24.

We, Hendriecus Dubois, Josia Eltinge, and Noach Eltinge

equally distributed the cost over 140 seat, so that each place costs 18 shillings. We also numbered the pews, viz.:

No.	Seats:		No.	Seats:	
1		8	2		8
3		8	4		8
5		8	6		8
7		6	8		8
9		8	10		8
11		8	12		8
13		8	14		8
15		5	16		5
17		5	18		5
19		5	20		5
	69 seats			71 seats	

And sold those seats at public auction viz.:

No.		£ s d
3 to Josia Eltinge for		9. 5
4 " Hendriekus Dubois for		10.
12 " Noach Eltinge for		9.10
11 " Abraham Eltinge for		8. 1
17 " Josia Eltinge for		5.11
16 " Roelof Josies Eltinge for		5.11
15 " Jacob Dubois for		5.
18 " Noach Eltinge for		5.14
19 " Josia Eltinge for		5. 5
20 " Salomon Louw "		4.13
13 " The heirs of Philip Dubois for		8.
14 " James Heuy for		7.10
1 " Hendricus Dubois for		7. 8
2 " Petrus Van Waege and Salomon Louw for		7. 9
Viz. 6 seats for Peetrus Van Wagene, and 2 for Salomon Louw		
10 " Josia Eltinge (5), Jacob Dubois (2), Roelof Josias (1) for		8.13
9 to Noach Eltinge for		7.13
5 " Petrus Louw for		7. 5
From No. 6 to Isaac Louw (3 places at 18 shillings per 1 place) for		2.14
8 " Hendriekus Dubois, for		7. 4
From No. 6, 2 places to Hendriekus Dubois in behalf of Abraham Een, at 18 shillings per place, for		1.16
From No. 6, 2 places to Hendricus Dubois at 19 shillings, for		1.18
From No. 6, 1 place to Noach Eltinge at 20 shillings, for		1. 0
From No. 7, 2 places to Hendrikus Dubois, for		1.16
Total,		£138.16

A list of those who bought more places than they contributed for, and of how much they are yet indebted, viz. :

	£ s. d.		£ s. d.
Hendrikus Dubois	3. 1.	Brought forward	14. 4. 7
Josia Eltinge	4. 1½	Isaac Louw Debit	
Noach Eltinge	3.13.	8 sh. of Jan Van	
Abraham Eltinge	9. 6.	Deuse	8.
Roelof Josias El-			£14.12. 7½
tinge	6. 4½		
Jacob Dubois	17.	Aug. 28, 1770. Paid	
Salomon Louw	4.	to Hendricus	
The heirs of Philip		Dubois lock for	
Dubois (Anna		church, 12 sh.	
Dubois)	1.13. 9.	Roelof Josias El-	
James Huey	3. 1. 7½	tinge, entering	
Isaac Louw	3. 6.	account in this	
Abraham Een	10. 9.	book, 12 sh. (8?)	1.
	£14. 4. 7½	Total, £13.12. 7½	

1770, August 24. We, Hendriekus Dubois, Josia Eltinge and Noach Eltinge elected as churchmasters Salomon Eltinge and Isaac Louw, and on August 28, we, Hendriekus Dubois, Josia Eltinge and Noach Eltinge rendered account to the above named newly elected churchmasters, and surrendered everything to them, viz. : This book and a list therein containing the names of those yet indebted for the places they have bought. Also 8 shillings of Isaac Louw, and £2.11.6 in money, amounting altogether to £13.12.7½.

1770, August 24. We, Hendrikus Dubois, Josia Eltinge and Petrus Van Wagene and Salomon Louw make Roelof Josias Eltinge custodian of Noach Eltinge's bond for the church.

1772, June 20. Hendriecus Dubois, Jr., was Churchmaster.

1775, January 2. David Low was Church Master.

1770, December 3. Paid to Noach Eltinge, 11 shillings.

December 8. Paid for liquor, 9 pence.

1771, February 11. Paid to Isaac Low the amount of £1.16.11¼.

May 20. Paid to Jacobus Vanderlyn, £5.

CREDIT TO THE CHURCHMASTERS OF THE CHURCH ON THE "GROOTSTUK" OR GREAT PIECE.

	£. s. d.
1770, October 20. Noach Eltinge, for boarding Jacobus Vanderleyn for 11 days at 1 shilling per day	0. 11.
October 20. Jacobus Vanderlyn, for painting the Church	7. 16. 5.

December 8. Isaak Low, ironwork for the little
 beam in the church   1. 4. 11¼
December 8. Isaac Low, for making scaffold
 and carting little beam, etc.   12.
December 8. Hendricus Dubois for work on the
 little beam   8.
December 8. Salomon Eltinge, for liquor   0. 9.
1772, June 19. Isaak Low, for cleaning the
 church   2. 6.
1772, June 19. Salomon Eltinge paid to Jacobus
 Vanderlyn   8. 8¼
1772, October 27. Isack Low, clamps and for
 fixing the windows   2.
1772, October 27. Noach Eltinge, lime   3. 6.
1772, October 27. Hendericus Dubois Sr. 3
 window panes   1. 6.

1770, November 3. Noach Eltinge and Petrus Van Wage exchanged seats in the Church on the "Grootstuk," as follows: Noach Eltinge gave 2 seats in No. 9 for 2 of Petrus Van Wage in No. 2.

HENDRICUS DUBOIS.

Debit.		Credit.	
1766, August 29.		1766, December 12.	
Subscription	£20.	17¾ days labor at 5 shillings	£4. 8.9
1769 October 21.		½ days carting at 8 shillings per day	4.
A workbench	2.		
His proportion according to promise	5. 5.	Carting 4 loads of boards at 12 shillings per load	2. 8.0
1770. August 24.		Money paid for boards	8.19.5
In money	2. 3.3		
A note of Jacob Dubois	6. 6.3	Drying boards	3.
To receive of Abraham Een	0.15.3	½ day's work at 4 shillings per day	2.
		9¾ lbs. putty at 1 shilling per lb.	9.9
Carried forward	£34.11.9	Set 24 panes at 1 pence per pane	2.0
		Slats for one side of the house	12.6
		Timber for the church	4.18.0
		800 shingles at 5 shillings per 100	2.

HENDRICUS DUBOIS—Continued.

Debit.		Credit.	
	1767, July 16.		
	Work by Samuel Schoonmaker at 5 sh. (16½ days)	£ 4.	2.6
	Paid for Spriggs 5/3		5.3
	Board for Spriggs		16.6
	11 boards at 10/1		10.1
	¾ days' work for 3 men at 4 sh. per day		9.
	3 days' work for 5 men at 4 sh. per day		3.
	For horses and wagon		12.
	Carting boards for the pulpit		3.
	3 days' work for whitewashing wall		6.
Brought forward £34.11.9		£34.11.9	

JACOB DUBOIS.

Debit.		Credit.	
1766, August 29.		1770, August 24.	
Subscription £5.		Paid in money	£6.6.3
His proportion according to promise	1.6.3		
£6.6.3			

JOSIA ELTINGE.

Debit.		Credit.	
1766, August 29.		1766, December 12.	
Subscription £20.		35¾ days' work at 5 shillings per day	£8.18.9
From Niekus Krom	8.	Lumber for the church	5. 7. 0
1768, May 6.		800 shingles at 5 shillings per 100	2. 0. 0
Received money collected by Isaac Louw	20.18.	for carting 3 loads of boards at 12 shillings per load	1.16. 0
1770.		1 day driving, looking up boards	5. 0
From John Winckoop for nails	9.4¼		
His proportion according to promise	5. 5.0	Slats for 1 side of the house	0.12. 6

JOSIA ELTINGE—Continued.

	Debit.			Credit.	
1770, August 29.			270 lbs. of nails,		
Money paid	£— 9.3		freight and carting	8.10.	3
			1 Flour barrel	0. 2.	0
			1767, July....		
			3¾ days' work 2 men at 4 shillings per day	1.10.	0
			3¼ days for horse and wagon	13.	0
			Carting the lime	0. 7.	6
			Hair for plastering	0. 2.	0
			August 31.		
			Paid for the church book	0.13.	0
			3 boards for the pulpit	0. 7.	6
			1¾ days' labor	0. 7.	0
			¼ day for horse and wagon	0. 2.	0
			1768, May 7.		
			Paid James Huey	7. 8.10	
			Paid Anna Dubois	7.10.	0
			Paid Dirk Wynkoop for boards at Aert Van Wage's	0.16.	0
			1 thick plank	1.	3
	£47. 9.7½			£47. 9. 7	

JAMES HUEY.

	Debit.			Credit.	
1766, August 29.			1766, December 12.		
Subscription	£3.10. 0		34¼ days' work at 6 shillings per day	£10. 5.	3
Proportion according to promise	0.18. 4½		66 lights at— per light	1.15.	0
1768, May 7.			20 panes put in	0. 1.	8
Money paid by Josia Eltinge	7. 8.10				
August 24.					
Money paid	0. 4. 8½				
	£12. 1.11			£12. 1.11	

ISACK LOUW.

Debit.		Credit.	
1766, August 29. Subscription Proportion according to promise	£2. 0.10.6 —— £2.10.6	1766, December 12. 2¾ days' labor at 6 shillings per day 10 lbs. nails at 10 shillings per lb. 16 window panes put in 2¾ days' work at 6 shillings per day 1770, August 9.	£0.16. 6 0. 8. 4 0. 1. 4 0.16. 6 7.10 —— £2.10.6

NOACH ELTINGE

Debit.		Credit.	
1766, August 29. Subscription 1769, October 21. Boards November. Money of I. Van Kampen, C. K. and W. E. 14 lbs. nails at 9 pence per lb. His proportion according to promise 1770, August 24. Money Note of Petrus Van Wagene	£16. 0.0 2.3 16.0 0.10.6 4. 4.0 8. 5.8 2.18.9 ——	1766, December 12. Lumber for the Church Carting 2 loads of boards Paid 25 boards 18/9 ¼ day driving and chopping wood 1 load of boards carted from Jonathan Terwilger's 800 shingles at 5 shillings per 100 2 loads of brick 1/6 per load 7 oak boards, 1/6 per board 3 knoohoute, 1 shilling per piece 24 thick knoohoute, 1/6 per piece 1 box of glass 25 window panes of 4 pence per pane	£4.18.0 1. 4.0 0.18.9 0. 3.0 0. 3.0 2. 0.0 0. 3.0 0.10.6 0. 3.0 1.16.0 1.16.0 0. 8.4

NOACH ELTINGE—Continued.

Debit.		Credit.
1767, July.		
8 days' work, paper hanging at 4 shillings per day		1.12.0
4½ days' work plastering at 4 shillings per day		0.18.0
26 Scheepel of lime		1. 1.9
2 days' washing the wall at 2 shillings per day		0. 4.0
1 day's work for 1 horse carting lime		0. 1.6
1768, May.		
½ day driving with horse and wagon		5.00.
3 pillars		0. 1.6
1 load of boards fetched from Aert Van Wage's		0.10.0
October.		
12 thick knoohoudt boards		0.15.0
November.		
Two pewter beakers at 3 shillings a piece		0. 6.0
1769, October.		
Timber for the beams of the gallery		0. 4.0
A large ceiling board		0 .1.6
October 21.		
A Scheepel of lime		0. 1.0
November.		
A Scheepel of lime		0. 1.0
1770, June 22.		
Paid Thomas Schoonmaker for 27 boards		1. 4.9

NOACH ELTINGE—Continued.

Debit.		Credit.
	Paid Samuel Schoonmaker 6.16.6	
	Paid Wilhelmus Schoonmaker 2.15.1	11. 6.7
	Paid Hendricus Dubois, Jr. 1.15.0	
	£32.17.2	£32.17.2

PETERUS LOUW.

Debit.		Credit.	
1766, August 29. Subscription Proportion according to promise	£6. 1.11.0	1766, December 12. 800 shingles, 5 shillings per 100	£2.
		1 day's labor at 3 shillings	3.
		1¼ day's drive, 8 shillings per day	12.
		Carting and chopping wood	6.
		Carting 2 loads of boards	1. 4.
		4 loads of lumber, 3 shillings per load	0.12.0
		18 window panes put in	0. 1.6
		December 19. Iron work for the door	0. 4.0
		1767, June 11. 2¼ days' paper hanging	9.0
		July 2. 2 hinges for the pulpit	0. 4.0
		4 large nails	0. 2.0
		July 10. Iron work for the pulpit	0.10.0

PETERUS LOUW—Continued.

Debit.		Credit.
	1769, October 21.	
	Iron work	0.14.3
	1770, August 24.	
	Money	0. 9.3
£7.11.0		£7.11.0

ROELOF JOSIAS ELTINGE.

Debit.		Credit.	
1766, August 29.		1766, December 12.	
Subscription £5.		14¾ days' work at 5 shillings per day	£3.13. 9
1769, October 21.			
Boards and supports	0. 3.6	For writing the instructions and bond	1. 0. 0
Proportion according to promise	1. 6.3	Paid to Mathewes Canteyn	0. 1. 6
1770, August 29.		1 day, going to Mormel	0. 5.
In money	0.15.5	1767.	
		1 church book	0. 3.
		For writing instructions, keeping accounts, and books	0.14. 0
		1768, May 13.	
		3 lbs. nails at 10½	0. 2. 7½
		2 pairs of hinges H 1/6	0. 3. 0
		32 little nails	0. 0. 4
		1769, October 17.	
		4 pairs of hinges 3/2	0.12. 8
		2 pairs of hinges 2/6	0. 5. 0
		4 lbs. of nails 10 1/2	0. 3. 6
		October 21.	
		Flour barrel for nails	0. 0.10
£7. 5.2		£7. 5. 2	

PETRUS VAN WAGENEN.

Debit.		Credit.	
1766, August 29.		1766, December 12.	
Subscription	£5.0.0	Lumber for the church	£1.16.0
Proportion according to promise	1.6.3	1767, July 5. 5 days' work plastering, at 6 sh.	1.10.0
		Wages for his negro, Tam	0. 1.6
		1770, August 24. Note to Noach Eltinge	2.18.9
	£6.6.3		£6. 6.3

PHILIP DUBOIS.

Debit.		Credit.	
1766, August 29.		1766, December 12.	
Subscription	£ 5. 0.0	37¾ days' work at 6 shillings per day	£11. 6.6
Proportion according to promise	1. 6.3	Making 72 lights, 0/7 per light	2. 2.0
Paid by Josia Eltinge	7.10.0	Putting in 54 window panes 1 pence	4.6
1770, August 24. Money	0. 6.9	2 gallons of rum, 5 shillings a gallon	10.0
	£14. 3.0		£14. 3.0

ABRAHAM ELTINGE.

Debit.		Credit.	
1766, August 29.		1767, July.	
Subscription	£6. 0.0	4½ days' paper hanging, 4 shillings per day	£0.18.0
Proportion according to promise	1.11.6	1769, October. 5 heavy boards	0. 6.3
		1770, August 24. In money	6. 7.3
	£7.11.6		£7.11.6

SALOMON LOUW.

	Debit.		Credit.
1766, August 29.		1766, December 12.	
Subscription	£5.0.0	1 load of brick, at	
Proportion according to promise	1.6.3	1/6	£0. 1.6
		Carting a load of boards	0.12.0
		Making 4 hinges, etc.	0.12.0
		1770, August 24.	
		Money	5. 0.9
	£6.6.3		£6. 6.3

CORNELIUS LOUW.

	Debit.		Credit.
—	—	1766, December 12.	
		25 boards	£1.4.6

ABRAHAM EEN.

	Debit.		Credit.
Subscription	£1.	For carting 1 load of boards	£0.10.0
Proportion according to promise	0.5.3	To pay to Hendriecus Dubois	0.15.3
	£1.5.3		£1. 5.3

The following translations were made from Book 5.

In the year of our Lord 1771, October 25th, the Christian Reformed Nether Dutch congregation at New Paltz met, and discussed the fact that their present church is no longer sufficient to hold religious meetings in.

They therefore resolved to build a new church in the village of New Paltz on a piece of ground bought of Petronella Lefever, located on the west side of the street and opposite the north side of Colonel Abraham Hasbrouck's house lot. And the same to be built in the manner as described below :

Primo. The Consistory of our congregation shall visit the members of the congregation to request each in particular to contribute or promise a certain amount, to be paid in such a manner as is here below stipulated, for the building of the aforesaid new church. A list shall be kept of how much and what every one promises whether money or labor or anything else in erecting the said church.

And after the Consistory shall have visited the members, and made up the subscription list, and judges that the subscriptions are sufficient for building the church, four advertisements shall be nailed up in the most public places of our precinct whereby all persons having subscribed towards erecting the aforesaid church shall be requested to appear at a certain day, hour and place for the purpose of electing seven men from among them, and to constitute them a committee in the following manner :

The aforesaid seven men after having been elected on the aforesaid day by a majority of the votes of those who have subscribed for the church, shall have absolute power to dispose of the money, the labor and anything else promised on the above mentioned list, for the purpose of here building the church. They are also empowered, after the church shall have been completed, to make rules and regulations for the same in such a manner that they shall not be contrary to the Christian Reformed Church order. They shall also have power to determine the size of the building, but in such a manner that they shall erect the aforesaid church on the plot of ground in the aforesaid village mentioned above.

And eight days after the seven men shall have been elected and been qualified they shall meet at a certain place and hour in the aforesaid village, and then the aforesaid seven men shall elect one from among themselves as overseer or builder of the church, and also to receive the money and labor promised upon the list, and to dispose of the same for what shall be wanted in building the church in conformity with the instruction of all seven or any four of them. And the person who shall be elected overseer or master builder shall be appointed after the other six shall first have agreed with him about the amount he is willing to do it for, the said amount not to exceed fifteen pounds.

And after this one man shall have been elected and commissioned by the other six he shall make a memorandum book in which the whole of these instructions by the congregation shall be entered, and the seven men also shall sign their names, besides the one man who shall be elected by or from among the seven and further also the time when. (sic)

And the above named subscription list shall also be copied in the book, every one's subscription specially, and after the subscription shall have been paid or discharged the same shall be credited on the side opposite.

But the man who shall have been elected by the other six for the purpose of receiving the money and labor and to be overseer shall be obliged to deposit a bond with the other six before being allowed to enter upon his functions, and with such security as the other six shall deem proper, viz. of any amount not less than five hundred pounds.

And after the seven men shall have resolved to commence operations they shall meet and discuss about the best methods to be followed and write them down, and thereupon the one man from among the seven who shall have been elected for the purpose shall take the plan and work according to it, and after it shall have been completed all seven shall meet again, and the man who supervised the work according to the plan shall then render his accounts to the other six, containing a report of how and at what expense the work has been performed. And at this same meeting they shall again work out a plan about what is most advisable to be done in erecting the aforesaid church, and the master builder shall again proceed according to it, and thus it shall be done from time to time until the church shall have been completed.

And in case the Director of the work should happen to die or move away, or that his accounts should not be straight, the other six shall be qualified to elect from their number another master or overseer. After the election of this new overseer or master the retiring one shall be obliged according to his bond, either by himself or through his heirs, to deliver to the new overseer or master of the work all the money, and the book, the papers and everything further related to it, and shall also render a correct account of the same to the remaining six, or have to forfeit the aforesaid bond. And the new overseer or master shall also first procure a bond as above explained, and shall have the same power as the former overseer. And this shall take place from time to time as long as it shall be necessary to elect new overseers.

And all the above instructions and plans and accountings and whatever more shall be done by the seven men in building the aforesaid church shall be entered in the above named book.

And in case the promised money or labor or other things should not suffice in building the Church, the aforesaid seven men or any four of them shall be authorised to again visit the members of the congregation for the purpose of receiving money or other necessaries for building the church. And in case this should not yet be sufficient the above named seven men or any four among them shall be authorised to take up as much money as they judge will be necessary for completing the church, wherever they can find it, and in case it cannot be had in any other manner, to give interest for the same, and thus complete the church. And in order to pay back the borrowed money it shall be distributed over all the seats in the Church, as a rent laid equally upon every place. But the places for Consistory, the minister's place and the common pews shall be exempt from the aforesaid rent. All of those claiming their seat or seats shall be obliged first to pay the said rent to the aforesaid seven men or any four among them before they shall receive their title to the seat.

And before the seven men or any four among them shall distribute the places in the church, they shall figure out how much the church shall have cost or is to cost; and after having done this they shall take an inventory of the number of seats in the church except, as was said before, the seats reserved for the Consistory, the domine and the poor (gemeene Banken). And when they have learned the cost of the church and also know the number of seats to be distributed in the church, the above said seven men or any four among them shall divide the cost by all seats in the church which are to be distributed, an equal share upon every place. And the calculation or division shall be made in such a manner that the above named amount is exactly covered [by the tax] on the above named seats.

And then they shall invite the congregation to appear on a certain day and hour in the aforesaid church, and in order to render justice to every body and to satisfy those to whom they owe places, (or their heirs), they shall publicly dispose of the places to the highest bidder; and this shall be subsequently done with all places to be distributed.

And the money, labor or anything else which any body has contributed to the said church shall be regarded as payment for his or her seat or seats in the church, as far as it will reach.

And those having contributed much towards the church will be repaid in seats but in no other manner; but those having contributed little to the church shall be held to add to it in case they purchased a seat or seats which cost more than the amount of their contribution, provided always that nobody shall buy more seats in the church than he is entitled to for what he paid or did for the church, until all those who took a share in building the church shall have received their seat or seats in exchange.

But in case any money contributed towards building the said church, shall remain unexpended and not be required for building the aforenamed church that same money or anything else not used, shall remain the property of the church.

But no places shall be granted at a less price than has been fixed at the above mentioned calculation. And the aforesaid seven men shall be obliged by these instruction to secure to every person who has contributed towards the cost of this church, an undisputed right and just title for the seats which every one shall receive in the church, "to him and his heirs and assigns forever." And the aforesaid seven men are also obliged, in accordance with these instructions, to do justice without discrimination to every person who has contributed towards building the church, and further to perform their duties in accordance with these instructions. And in case they shall be negligent each one of the aforesaid seven men shall be obliged, if it can be proved against them, to repair the wrong or injustice they have done, and to defray the expense consequent upon it out of their own pocket to every one having assisted in building the church and who shall have suffered in consequence of said neglect.

And in order to bind the seven men they shall upon their election, sign these instructions. And after the church shall be completed they shall show to everybody his or her seat or seats in return for the money or the work that has been given or done, but in such a manner that it be not contrary to the regulations of the neighboring Christian Reformed Churches.

And after the places shall have been conveyed it shall also be entered in the above named book to whom and even where the place or places are located. And after the above named work shall have been completed by the above named seven men, other church masters shall be elected at the same time that there shall be an election of members of the Consistory in conformity with the rules of neighboring churches.

And thereupon the above named seven men shall render account of all they have done in building the aforesaid church, and in case any money shall have remained they shall hand it over to the new church masters and it is to be used to the benefit of the church; and also the above named book, and whatever else they have to deliver they shall deliver to the new churchmasters, and thus they shall be discharged from their office.

(Signed)
{
ABRAHAM DOIAU,
JACOB HASBROUCK, JR.,
SIMON DUBOIS,
NATHANIEL LEFEVER,
GERRIT FREER, JR.,
ABRAHAM LEFEVER,
HUGO FREER.
}

According to an order or instructions by the **Reformed Dutch Congregation** at New Paltz, dated October 25, 1771, the aforesaid congregation met on this ninth day of November in the same year at the house of Abraham Doiau to elect by virtue of the aforesaid instructions from among the aforesaid congregation, upon a majority of votes, seven men. Consequently the following persons were chosen, viz. Abraham Doiau, Jacob Hasbrouck, Jr., Simon Dubois, Nathaniel Lefever, Gerrit Freer, Jr., Abraham Lefever, and Hugo Freer.

In the year 1771 on the 16th day of November, we Jacob Hasbrouck Jr., Simon Dubois, Nathaniel Lefever, Gerret Freer Jr., Abraham Lefever and Hugo Freer, in accordance with the instructions made by our congregation, contracted with Abraham Doiau to be Director or Overseer of the work in building the church for fifteen pounds, under condition that in case he should die, or move away or be deposed by the other six before the completion of the church, he shall be proportionately paid for his trouble and labor, and not the full amount of fifteen pounds. And according to the aforesaid order and the above conditions we have chosen and authorised the aforesaid Abraham Doiau to be Overseer and Director of the work, and to receive the money and the labor, and to employ the same in the building of the church, according to the aforesaid regulations.

In witness whereof we have affixed our signatures herebelow on the day and date as above.

(Signed)
{
JACOB HASBROUCK, JR.,
SIMON DUBOIS,
NATHANIEL LEFEVER,
GERRET FREER, JR.,
ABRAHAM LEFEVER,
HUGO FREER.
}

In the year 1771 on the 16th day of November, we Jacob Hasbrouck Jr. etc. have given order and authority to the overseer Abraham Doiau to order and cart the boards and kaphout and further all the lumber needed in building the church, and also to have the bricks carted, and also to engage and contract with masons and carpenters. And we further give orders to Abraham Doiau to collect from the subscribed money and promised labor as much as is necessary for the above, and also to pay for the book and to allow for horses and sleigh and driver for one day for carting the bricks 8 shilling per diem;

and for a day's work for one man, he boarding himself, till next spring, 3 shillings and 3 pence per diem, and to enter this in the book, and also to enter these instructions in the book. In witness whereof we have hereunto affixed our signatures, dated as above.

In the year 1772, on the 8th day of April, we, Jacob Hasbrouck Jr. etc. ordered and authorised Abraham Doiau the Overseer to allow for chopping and carting of the timbers for the roof (kaphout) for the church 10 shillings for each rafter ; and for each beam (stukhout) for Wormtens 2 shillings 6 pence a piece and 2 shillings a piece for floor-beams (grondhouten) 33 feet long, and for breaking lime stone, the chopping of the wood for burning lime and for building the lime-oven, 4 shillings per diem, and for horses and wagon and man for carting the lime stone to the oven, and for carting the wood 10 shillings per diem, and for carting a load of lime 9 shillings per diem ; for the mason's helpers, they boarding themselves, 4 shillings per diem. For carting a load of boards from Leggewech 20 shillings. For carting load of boards from Marbletown 9 shillings. For carting a load of 500 shingles and a load of 350 stone (klinkers) 7 shillings. For boarding the workingmen 1 shilling per diem. Also to order beer and a barrel of rum for the workingmen. For carting sand 6 shillings per day, and also to order loaf sugar. In witness whereof etc.

On this 5th day of September 1772 the Overseer Abraham Doiau has rendered account to us the six churchmasters according to the instructions of our congregation of the expenses up to now incurred in building the church, which expenses amount to £479.8.11. We audited the said account and found the same to be correct and full. And we further order and authorise the overseer to order from New York all the paint and oil that shall be needed for painting the church.

SUBSCRIPTIONS FOR BUILDING THE NEW CHURCH AT NEW PALTZ, 1771 and 1772.

NAMES OF THE SUBSCRIBERS.

Abraham Doiaa,	Money, £30.,	Work, £15.,	Total, £45.
Nathaniel Lefever,	9.	9.	18.
Lowis J. Dubois,	10.	3.	13.
Andries Lefever,	10.	5.	15.
Nathaniel Lefever, Jr.,	3.	2.	5.

	Money, £	Work, £	Total, £
Daniel Doiau,	5.	3.	8.
John York,	5.		5.
Wilhelmus Ostrander,	2.		2.
Johannes A. Hardenbergh,	9.	3.	12.
Jonathan Terwilger,	6.	6.	12.
Christophel Ostrander,	1.		1.
David Ostrander,	2.		2.
Petrus Ostrander,	3.		3.
Marcus Ostrander,	1.10		1.10
Johannis Freer, Jr.,	6.		6.
Daniel Freer, Jr.,	5.	5.	10.
Joseph Freer,	7.	6.	13.
John Terwilger,	6.	6.	12.
Isaac Freer,	9.	6.	15.
Teunis Van Vliet,	1.	1.	2.
Gerret Freer, Jr.,	11.	7.	18.
Jacobus Bevier,	12.	8.	20.
Jacobus Hasbrouck,	15.	5.	20.
Daniel Dubois,	7.	2.	9.
Jacob Freer, Jr.,	12.	6.	18.
Johannis Freer, 5.4, Through his wife Agetta, 3.	8. 4		8. 4
Hugo Freer,	20. 5	5.	25. 5
Benjamin Freer,	6.		6.
Christophel Doyo,	11.	6.	17.
Christian Doyo,	10.		10.
Claartje Doyo, widow,	2.		2.
Paulus Freer,	1.	1.	2.
Jacob J. Freer,	3.10	1.	4.10
Benjamin Doyo,	7.	3.	10.
Daniel Freer,	1.15	1.	2.15
Petrus J. Schoonmaker,	2.	1.	3.
Johannis M. Louw,	12.		12.
AbrahamVan der Merken, 10. Through Isaac Hasbrouck, 5.	15.	5.	20.
Petronella Lefever,	6.		6.
Andries Lefever, Jr.,	5.	5.	10.
Simon Dubois,	17.	10.	27.
Wyntje Hasbrouck,	23.	10.	33.
Johannis Doyo, Jr.,	5.		5.
Nathaniel Dubois,	5.		5.
Petrus Van der Merken,	7.		7.
Dennee Relyee,	2.		2.
Daniel Lefever,	9.18.6	6.	15.18.6

Petrus Hasbrouck, Money, £11.		Work, £5.	Total, £16.
Jonas Freer, Jr.,	10.16		10.16
Abraham Ein,	4. 8		4. 8
Margrietje Bevier,	12. 1.8	8.	20. 1.8
Joseph Terwilger,	4.	4.	8.
Jacob Hasbrouck, Jr.,	45.	10.	55.
Benjamin Dubois,	11.	4.	15.
Joseph Coddington, Money and Administrative work,			9.
Johannis Hardenbergh,	17.		17.
Abraham Lefever,	10.	7.	17.
Simon Freer,	8.16	2.	10.16
Petrus Freer,	5.	1.	6.
Solomon Bevier,	2.		2.
Isaac Lefever,	6.	4.	10.
Petrus Lefever,	13.	8.	21.
Simeon Low,	3.		3.
George Wirtz,	3.		3.
Matthew Lefever,	12.		12.
Christian Auchmoedy,	2.10		2.10
Benjamin I. Freer,	2.10		2.10
Elisa Freer,	8.		8.
Petrus Smedes, Jr.,	6.	2.	8.
John Dowden, Jr.,	2.10		2.10
Louis Bevier, Esq.,	15.		15.
Wilhelmus Schoonmaker,	8. 8		8. 8
Col. Abraham Hasbrouck,	30.		30.
Geesje Een,	3.		3.
Johannis Walron,	4.		4.
Cornelius Dubois, Jr.,	8. 8		8. 8
Josaphat Hasbrouck,	6.		6.
Mary Hardenbergh, Widow,	3.		3.
Cornelius Hasbrouck,	3.		3.
Peter Doyo,	10.		10.
Executors of John Hasbrouck, deceased,	5.		5.
Lewis Brodhead,	4.		4.
Sophia Teerpenningh,	5.		5.
Johannis Eckerd,	2.10		2.10
Michel Devoe,	2.10		2.10
			£546. 1.0

For the purpose of showing the scope of the administrative work at the time of the building of the church, Joseph Coddington's credit follows below :

1771.
Oct. 25.	Writing the instructions,	£0.16.
	" " 2 headings of subscription list,	0. 4.
Nov. 4.	" 4 advertisements for inviting the congregation to meet for electing the 7 men,	0. 2.
" 9.	Serving the congregation as clerk in electing the 7 men, and for writing the minutes,	0. 4.
" 16.	Minutes of the election by the 7 men of an overseer and writing out their orders to him,	0. 4.
" "	Writing the Overseer's bond,	0. 3.

1772.
March.	Drawing the columns in the church book (for entering the L. S. D.),	0. 2.
	For making alphabet index in the same,	0. 4.
	Copying the aforesaid instructions in this book,	0.16.
	For copying in this book the minutes of the meeting of the congregation and of the 7 men (9 and 16 November) mentioned above,	0. 4.
	Copying in this book the subscription list, viz. every one's name and promise in particular,	0.10.
April 7.	Writing out 4 advertisements, etc.,	0. 3.
" 8.	Writing the orders of the 6 men to the overseer, concerning wages for carting, working, etc.,	0. 4.
May 13.	Writing 4 advertisements, etc.,	0. 2.
	Copying in this book the order of the 6 men to the overseer, on April 8,	0. 2.
Sept. 5.	Assisting the 6 church masters in auditing the overseer's account and writing out the same,	0.10.
Nov. 20.	Writing a heading for subscription for gallery, etc.,	0. 2.

1773.
Oct. 23.	Copying in this book second subscription list,	0. 5.
Nov. 8.	Writing 5 advertisements,	0. 2.6

1774.
April 18.	Writing 5 advertisements,	0. 2.6

May 7.	By £3.10 taken over from Abraham Doiaa,	£3.10
" 12.	Two days clerking at the vendue for selling the seats in the church, and writing a copy of the list,	1.
	Copying the order of September 5, 1772 of the 6 men to the overseer,	0. 2.
From June 27, 1774, till Feb. 13. 1783.	Writing several documents concerning church lands and other services rendered the trustees, the Consistory, and the church builders,	3. 5.0
		£12.19.0

The following was in English:

Account of what the church sold for, June 23, 1787, by Ezekiel Eltinge as per the vendue list	£34.19.9
Allowing the said Ezekiel Eltinge for taking down and selling the same	6.18.0
Balance	£28. 1.9

Shares of the different owners of the money accrued by the sale in proportion to their subscription for building of the aforesaid church.

Hendricus Dubois	£ 6. 0. 5	Philip Dubois	£1. 6. 9
Josiah Eltinge	5. 6.11	James Huey	18. 8
Noah Eltinge	5. 1. 7	Petrus Van Wagene	1. 3. 9
Abraham Eltinge	1.12. 4	Petrus Low	1.10.10
Roelof Eltinge	1. 7.10	Isaac Low	11. 5
Jacob Dubois	1. 6. 2	Abraham Ein	5. 4
Solomon Low	1. 7. 6		
			£27.19. 6

Petrus Van Wagene, debit, bought at vendue	£1. 5. 8
Credit by his share of the sale	1. 3. 9
Balance,	£0. 1.11
To Ezekiel Elting, for settling the business of the vendue which he gave to all the owners	£1. 1. 4½
(It is evident some item has been omitted.)	
	£5. 6.11½

Petrus Low, debit, paid Schut, 15.5, paid David, 15.5 £1.10.10
" " credit, by his share of the sale 1.10.10

Isaac Low, Debtor, settled his share with account he owed to the church.

Abraham Ein's share paid to Mathusalem Dubois, as Hendricus Dubois paid his subscription as they told me.

Methusalem Dubois, debit, bought at vendue £3.14. 6
Paid to him by account of Roelof I. Elting 2. 5.11

£6. 0. 5

Methusalem Dubois, credit by his father's share of the sale 6. 0. 5

Josiah Eltinge, debit, paid his heirs :
 To Roelof I. Eltinge £1.1.4½
 To Abraham Eltinge 1.1.4½
          £2. 2. 9
To Solomon Low, the shares of Cornelius Elting and Jacobus Hardenbergh 2. 2. 9

To Noah Eltinge, debit,
 Derick Wynkoop, bought at vendue £3. 1. 9
 Paid Derick Wynkoop in cash 1.19.10
       £5. 1. 7
Credit by his share of the sale 5. 1. 7

Abraham Eltinge, Debtor, bought at vendue £3.16. 9

Credit by his share of the sale £1.12.4
" by one share of his father 1. 1.4
" by account of his father 1. 3.1
         £3.16. 9

Roelof Eltinge, Debit, bought at vendue £3.12. 8
Credit by his share of the sale 1. 7.10

 His balance £2. 4.10
Together with £6.18.0
 and Solomon Elting's share 1. 1.4
        7.19. 4

I have left in his hands £10. 4. 2

Jacobus Dubois, Credit by the sale £1.6.2
Brought to his credit on his account to Roelof I.
  Eltinge   1.6.2

Solomon Low, Debtor, bought at vendue   £2. 2.11
To Cash paid him   1. 7. 4
                                              ─────────
                                              £3.10. 3
Credit by his share of the sale   £1. 7. 6
By 2 shares of Josiah Elting   2. 2. 9
                                  ─────────
                                   3.10. 3
Philip Dubois, Credit by his share of the sale   1. 6. 9
Paid on account of Ann Hardenbergh to the Estate
  of Roelof I. Elting
James Huey, Credit by his share of the sale   0.18.8

Account of sale at Public Vendue of the pews in the New Paltz Church, by the seven managers chosen by the congregation to build the said church, etc., pursuant to an òrder of the said congregation made for that purpose, May 11, 1774.

FIRST, THE PEWS ON THE FLOOR.

Appraisement of the pews.	Number of the pews.	Seats in each pew.	Purchasers' Names.		Purchase money.
£ 10. 5. 5	1	5	Abraham Doiau, 4 seats,	£ 8. 2	£ 10.12
			John Dowden, Jr., 1 seat,	2.10	
12. 6. 6	2	6	Hugo Freer,		16. 4
12. 6. 6	3	6	Gerrit Freer, Jr.,		18. 1
12. 6. 6	4	6	John Lefever, 3 seats,	£ 9. 5	18.10
			Simon Dubois, 3 seats,	9. 5	
12. 6. 6	5	6	Petrus Hasbrouck, 2 seats,	£ 6.18	20.14
			Wyntje Hasbrouck, 4 seats,	13.16	
£ 59.11. 5					£ 84.01

Appraisement of the pews.	Number of the pews.	Seats in each pew.	Purchasers' Names.	Purchase money.
£ 59.11. 5				£ 84.01
16. 8. 8	6	8	Jacob Hasbrouck, Jr., 2 seats, £ 5. 3. 9 George Wirtz, 2 seats, 5. 3. 9 Solomon Van Wagenen, 2 seats, 5. 3. 9 Isaac Hasbrouck, Jr., 2 seats, 5. 3. 9	20.15
16. 8. 8	7	8	Johannis M. Low, 4 seats, £ 10. 0. 3 Petrus Lefever, 2 seats, 5. 0. 1½ Isaac Lefever, 2 seats, 5. 0. 1½	20. 0. 6
16. 8. 8	8	8	Hugo Freer, 7 seats, £ 14. 9. 7½ Benjamin I. Freer, 1 seat, 2. 1. 4½	16.11
8. 4. 4	9	4	Andries Lefever, 2 seats, £ 4. 9 Nathaniel Lefever, Jr., 2 seats, 5. 7	9.16
8. 4. 4	10	4	Peter Doyo,	10.11
8. 4. 4	11	4	Margrietje Bevier,	10. 4. 6
8. 4. 4	12	4	Christian Doyo,	8. 8
8. 4. 4	13	4	Abraham Doiau,	8.19
8. 4. 4	14	4	Joseph Coddington,	9.14
8. 4. 4	15	4	Samuel Bevier, 2 seats, £ 4.18 Christophel Doyo, 1 seat, 2. 9 Jacob Freer, Jr., 1 seat, 2. 9	9.16
6. 3. 3	16	3	Petrus Van der Merken,	6.18
8. 4. 4	17	4	Cornelius Dubois, Jr.,	8. 5
8. 4. 4	18	4	Daniel Doyo,	8.12
£188.19. 8				£232.11

Appraisement of the pews.	Number of the pews.	Seats in each pew.	Purchasers' Names.	Purchase money.
£188.19. 8				£232 11
8. 4. 4	19	4	Nathaniel Dubois, 2 seats, £ 4. 2. 6 Samuel Schoonmaker, 1 seat, 2. 1. 3 Jacobus Bruyn, 1 seat, 2. 1. 3	8. 5
6. 3. 3	20	3	Hendrick Smit, 1 seat, £ 2. 3. 6 Petrus Bevier, 1 seat, 2. 1. 1 Jan. 28, 1799, Petrus Bevier sold his seat as above to Johannes York, £2.1.1.	
6. 3. 3	21	3	Christophel Ostrander, 2 seats,	3.14
8. 4. 4	22	4	Wilhelmus Schoonmaker,	8. 5
8. 4. 4	23	4	Jacob J. Freer,	8.16
8. 4. 4	24	4	Isaac Freer,	9.19
8. 4. 4	25	4	Lewis J. Dubois, 3 seats, £ 7.13 Lewis Brodhead, 1 seat, 2.11	10. 4
8. 4. 4	26	4	Petrus Lefever,	11. 3
8. 4. 4	27	4	Joseph Freer,	13
8. 4. 4	28	4	David Bevier, 1 seat, £ 3.10. 3 Esther Bevier, 1 seat, 3.10. 3 Philip D. B. Bevier, 2 seats, 7. 0. 6	14. 1
8. 4. 4	29	4	Col. Abraham Hasbrouck,	14.16
8. 4. 4	30	4	Jacob Hasbrouck, Jr., 2 seats, 7.10. 6 Isaac Hasbrouck, Jr., 2 seats, 7.10. 6	15. 1
8. 4. 4	31	4	Abraham Doiau,	14
8. 4. 4	32	4	The Church,	10.10
8. 4. 4	33	4	Johannis A. Hardenbergh,	12.16
£308. 3. 6				£387.01

Appraisement of the pews.	Number of the pews.	Seats in each pew.	Purchasers' Names.		Purchase money.
£308. 3. 6					£387.01
8. 4. 4	34	4	Wyntje Hasbrouck, 2 seats, £	7. 2	14. 4
			Petrus Smedes, Jr., 2 seats,	7. 2	
8. 4. 4	35	4	Col. Johannis Hardenbergh,		15. 1
8. 4. 4	36	4	Johannis Freer,		15. 3
8. 4. 4	37	4	Margrietje Bevier,		15. 1
8. 4. 4	38	4	Jacob Hasbrouck, 1 seat, £	3. 9. 4	13.17. 4
			Petronella Lefever, 3 seats,	10. 8	
8. 4. 4	39	4	Andries Lefever, Jr.,		15. 1
8. 4. 4	40	4	Benjamin Doyo, 2 seats, £	7	14.
			Dennee Ralyea, 1 seat,	3.10	
			Wilhelmus Oostrander, 1 seat,	3.10	
8. 4. 4	41	4	Jacob Freer, Jr.,		13.10
8. 4. 4	42	4	Simon Freer, 2 seats,	6. 0. 6	12. 1
			Petrus Freer, 2 seats,	6. 0. 6	
8. 4. 4	43	4	Abraham Lefever, 2 seats,	5. 3	10. 6
			Benjamin Dubois, 2 seats,	5. 3	
6. 3. 3	44	3	Abraham Vander Merken,		6. 3. 6
8. 4. 4	45	4	Daniel Dubois,		10. 1
8. 4. 4	46	4	Jonas Freer, Jr.,		9. 1
6. 3. 3	47	3	Josaphat Hasbrouck,		6. 4. 3
8. 4. 4	48	4	Johannis Freer, Jr.,		9. 1
8. 4. 4	49	4	Petrus Hasbrouck, 1 seat, £	2. 8. 9	9.15
			Heirs of John Hasbrouck, 2 seats,	4.17. 6	
			Christian Auchmoedie, 1 seat,	2. 8. 9	
£435. 9. 8					£575.11. 1

Appraisement of the pews.	Number of the pews.	Seats in each pew.	Purchasers' Names.		Purchase money.
£435. 9. 8					£575.11. 1
8. 4. 4	50	4	Daniel Freer, Jr.,		9.10
6. 3. 3	51	3	Joseph Terwilger,		7.17
8. 4. 4	52	4	John Lefever,		13
8. 4. 4	53	4	Benjamin Freer, 1 seat,	£3.12. 9	
			Abraham Ein, 2 seats,	7. 5. 6	14.11
			Sophia Teerpenning, 1 seat,	3.12. 9	
8. 4. 4	54	4	Daniel Lefever,		15. 7
8. 4. 4	55	4	Andries Lefever,		11.12
8. 4. 4	56	4	Claartje Doyo, widow, 1 seat,	3.19. 9	
			Christian Doyo, 1 seat,	3.19. 9	15.19
			Johannis Doyo, Jr., 2 seats,	7.19. 6	
8. 4. 4	57	4	Christophel Doyo, 2 seats,	8. 1. 6	16. 3
			Jacobus Hasbrouck, 2 seats,	8. 1. 6	
8. 4. 4	58	4	Johannis M. Low, 2 seats,	8. 0. 6	16. 1
			Petrus Hasbrouck, 2 seats,	8. 0. 6	
10. 5. 5	59	5	Samuel Bevier,		15. 1
			Samuel Elias Bevier sold to Peter Lefever.		
12. 6. 6	60	6	Abraham Lefever, 2 seats,	5.14. 4	
			Michael Devoe, 1 seat,	2.17. 2	17. 3
			Benjamin Dubois, 3 seats,	8.11. 6	
12. 6. 6.	61	6	Jacob Hasbrouck, Jr.,		18.16
£542. 6					£746.11. 1

Appraisement of the pews.	Number of the pews.	Seats in each pew.	Purchasers' Names.		Purchase money.
£542. 6.					£746.11. 1
12. 6. 6	62	6	Col. Johannis Hardenbergh, 3 seats,	£ 8.11	17. 2
			Matthew Lefever, 3 seats,	8.11	
12. 6. 6	63	6	Abraham Vander Merken, 3 seats,	9.10	19.
			Simon Dubois, 3 seats,	9.10	
16. 8. 8	64	8	Col. Abraham Hasbrouck, 4 seats,	10.15	21.10
			Jacob Hasbrouck, Jr., 1 seat,	2.13. 9	
			David and Philip D. B. Bevier, 2 seats,	5. 7. 6	
			Abraham Doiau, 1 seat,	2.13. 9	
16. 8. 8	65	8	Benjamin Freer, 1; Sophia Teerpenning, 1; Benjamin Doyo, 1, 3 each	2.16. 4½	22.11
			Jacobus Hasbrouck, 2 seats,	5.12. 9	
			Johannis Eckerd, 1; Christophel Doyo, 1; Jonathan Terwilger, 1, 3 each	2.16. 4½	
16. 8. 8	66	8	Benjamin I. Freer, 1 seat,	2. 6	18. 8
			Jonathan Terwilger, 5 seats,	11.10	
			Petrus J. Schoonmaker, 2 seats,	4.12	
£616. 5					£845. 2. 1

Appraisement of the pews.	Number of the pews.	Seats in each pew.	Purchasers' Names.		Purchase money.	
£616. 5.					£845. 2. 1	
8. 4. 4	67	4	Isaac Freer, 2 seats,	£ 4.12		
			Gerrit Freer, Jr., 1 seat,	2. 6	9. 4	
			Teunis Van Vliet, 1 seat,	2. 6		
8. 4. 4	68	4	John Terwilger, 3 seats,	6.18	9. 4	
			Daniel Diver, 1 seat,	2. 6		

This seat of Daniel Diver was set up again in vendue, and bought by Dr. Andries De Witt, February 21, 1787, for £ 3. 0. 6.

£632.13. 8	308				£863.10. 1

SECONDLY, THE PEWS ON THE GALLERY.

£ 12. 6. 6	1	6	Johannis Waldron, 4 seats,	£10. 1. 4		
			Petrus Hasbrouck, 1 seat,	2.10. 4	15. 2	
			Josaphat Hasbrouck, 1 seat,	2.10. 4		
12. 6. 6	2	6	Simon Freer, 1 seat,	2. 1. 1⅛		
			Benjamin Freer, 1 seat,	2. 1. 1⅛		
			Abraham Ein, 1 seat,	2. 1. 1⅛	12. 6. 7	
			Petrus Lefever, 2 seats,	4. 2. 2⅝		
			* Daniel Diver, 1 seat,	2. 1. 1⅛		
£657. 6. 8					£890.18. 8	

* This was crossed out later on, and in a different handwriting "Christophel Ostrander, £1.16" substituted for it.

Appraisement of the pews.	Number of the pews.	Seats in each pew.	Purchasers' Names.		Purchase money.
£657. 6. 8					£891. 7. 8
12. 6. 6	3	6	Abraham Doiau, 4 seats,	£11.13. 4	17.10
			Benjamin Dubois, 2 seats,	5.16. 8	
12. 6. 6	4	6	Abraham Doiau, 2 seats,	4. 2. 4	
			Col. Abraham Hasbrouck, 2 seats,	4. 2. 4	12. 7
			Andries Lefever, 1 seat,	2. 1. 2	
			Nathaniel Lefever, Jr., 1 seat,	2. 1. 2	
12. 6. 6	5	6	Samuel Bevier, 1 seat,	2. 3. 8	
			Daniel Lefever, 1 seat,	2. 3. 8	13 2
			Petrus Lefever, 2 seats,	4. 7. 4	
			Isaac Lefever, 2 seats,	4. 7. 4	
12. 6. 6	6	6	Hugo Freer, 2 seats,	4. 2. 6	
			Gerrit Freer, Jr., 1 seat,	2. 1. 3	12. 7. 6
			Benjamin Doyo, 1 seat,	2. 1. 3	
			John York, 2 seats,	4. 2. 6	
12. 6. 6	7	6	John York, 1 seat,	2. 1. 7	
			Hugo Freer, 2 seats,	4. 3. 2	12. 9. 6
			Abraham Lefever, 3 seats,	6. 4. 9	
12. 6. 6	8	6	Margrietje Bevier, 2 seats,	4. 3. 1	
			Christian Auchmoedie, 1 seat,	2. 1. 1	
£718.19. 2					£958.14. 8

Appraisement of the pews.	Number of the pews.	Seats in each pew.	Purchasers' Names.		Purchase money.
£718.19. 2					£958.14. 8
			Jacobus Auchmoedie, 1 seat, £	2. 1. 1	
			Isaac Bodine, 1 seat,	1.13	These were entered later on in a different handwriting.
			Johannes York, 2 seats,	3	
10. 5. 5	9	5	Lewis Dubois, 1 seat,	1. 6	
			Mathusalem Dubois, 1 seat,	1. 6	
			Lucas Van Wagenen, 1 seat,	1. 6. 6	
12. 6. 6	10	6	Jonathan Van Wagen, 1 seat,	18. 6	
			Mathusalem Dubois, 1 seat,	1. 0	
12. 6. 6	11	6	Simon Freer, 2 seats,	4. 2.10	£12. 8. 6
			Lewis J. Dubois, 3 seats,	6. 4. 3	
			Petrus Freer, 1 seat,	2. 1. 5	
12. 6. 6	12	6	John Terwilger, 3 seats,	6. 3. 6	
			Jonas Freer, Jr., 1 seat,	2. 1. 2	12. 7
			Daniel Freer, Jr., 1 seat,	2. 1. 2	
			Isaac Freer, 1 seat,	2. 1. 2	
14. 7. 7	13	7			
20.10.10	14	10			
12. 6. 6	15	6	Jacobus Hasbrouck, 3 seats,	6. 3. 6	
			Christophel Doyo, 2 seats,	4. 2. 4	12. 7
			Jacob Freer, Jr., 1 seat,	2. 1. 2	
12. 6. 6	16	6	Jonathan Van Wagenen, 1 seat,	1. 8	
£838. 2.					£995.17. 2

Appraisement of the pews.	Number of the pews.	Seats in each pew.	Purchasers' Names.		Purchase money.	
£838. 2.					£995.17. 2	
			Mathusalem Dubois, 3 seats,	£4. 2		
			[The above two names were entered later on in a different handwriting.]			
12. 6. 6	17	6	Wyntje Hasbrouck, 4 seats,	£10. 2		
			Jacob Hasbrouck, Jr., 1 seat,	2.10. 6	15. 3	
			Petrus Smedes, Jr., 1 seat,	2.10. 6		
12. 6. 6	18	6	Christian Doyo, 2 seats,	4.13. 4		
			Nathaniel Dubois, Esq., 3 seats. Transferred to Lewis J. Dubois and Daniel Graham.	7	14	
			Simeon Low, 1 seat,	2. 6. 8		
12. 6. 6	19	6	Jacob Hasbrouck, Jr., 2 seats,	5.13. 8		
			Isaac Hasbrouck, Sr., 2 seats,	5.13. 8	17. 1	
			Cornelius Hasbrouck, 1 seat,	2.16.10		
			Johannis A. Hardenbergh, 1 seat,	2.16.10		
12. 6. 6	20	6	Simon Freer, 1 seat,	2.13. 6		
			Christophel Doyo, 2 seats,	5. 7	16. 1	
			Jacobus Hasbrouck, 1 seat,	2.13. 6		
			John Lefever, Jr., 2 seats,	5. 7		
£887. 8					£1058. 2. 2	

Appraisement of the pews.	Number of the pews.	Seats in each pew.	Purchasers' Names.		Purchase money.
£887. 8					£1058. 2. 2
12. 6. 6	21	6	Simon Dubois, 4 seats,	£10.10. 8	
			Mathew Lefever, 2 seats,	5. 5. 4	15.16
12. 6. 6	22	6	Gerrit Freer, Jr., 2 seats,	4.10	
			Samuel Bevier, 2 seats,	4.10	
			Jacob Freer, Jr., 1 seat,	2. 5	13.10
			Joseph Coddington, 1 seat,	2. 5	
£912.1	444				£1073.14. 1
$2280.12½					$2684.26.00

NOTE.—It will be observed that in a number of cases above, the amounts of sales for seats have not been carried out in the column headed "Purchase Money," the explanation of which is doubtless found in the following, which is translated from a loose paper without date, found in the book.—TRANSLATOR.

Pews sold and not paid for.

Daniel Diver { Pew 68, floor, £2. 6.0
Pew 2, Gallery, 2. 1.1

1 seat bought of Daniel Diver, £2. 6.0
Also bought by Daniel Diver, 2 seats, 2. 1.1

Petrus Schoonmaker, 2 seats in pew 66, yet due, 1.12.0
2 seats formerly bought by Christian and Jacobus Achmoedy, 4. 2.2

Theuniss Van Fleet, 0.18.9
1 seat to Cornelius Dubois, 3. 3.3

John York, 2. 0.1
Isaac Frere, 2. 4.0
1 seat to Cornelius Dubois, 3.12.0

Simon Low, 2. 6.8
Simon Frere, 2.13.6
1 seat to Philip Cooper, 1.12.0
1 seat to George Wertz, 1.13.0

2 seats bought of Petrus Frere, 6. 0.6
4 seats bought by Hendrick Smith, 6. 3.6
1 seat to Lucas Van Wagenen, 1.12.0

1 seat to Christopher Ostrander,	£1.16.0	1 seat to Jonathan Van Waganen,	£1. 8.0
2 seats to Christopher Ostrander,	{ 1.18.0 { 1.16.0	1 seat to Methusalem Dubois,	1.10.0
1 seat to Isaac Bodyne,	1.13.0	1 seat to Methusalem Dubois,	1. 6.0
1 seat to Johannes York,	1.10.0	1 seat to Lucas Van Waganen,	1. 6.6
1 seat to Johannes York,	1.10.0		
1 seat to Matheusalem Dubois,	1.10.0	1 seat to Methusalem Dubois,	1. 0.0
1 seat to John Eltinge,	1.10.0		
1 seat to Daniel Van Waganen,	2. 2.0	1 seat to Jonathan Van Weganen,	0.18.6
1 seat to Lewis I. Dubois,	1. 6.0	1 seat to Roelof Eltinge,	0.18.0
2 seats to Roelof Eltinge,	2.19.6	1 seat to Lucas Van Waganen,	0.17.0
2 seats to Methusalem Dubois,	{ 1. 7.0 { 1. 7.0	1 seat to Methusalem Dubois,	0.18.0

Translated from a loose piece of paper :

NEW PALTZ, Nov. 1, 1782.

Whereas reading and singing during religious service are not only beautiful (een zierraedt) but also in accordance with the word of God and the canons of the church, therefore the Reverend Consistory, after Mr. Coddington for sufficient reasons had resigned, have unanimously elected Mr. Simeon Low, and contracted with him for the amount of £3 annually. For which reason, in order to satisfy the aforesaid person, we earnestly request the congregation to assist us, and to subscribe in order to annually pay him, as long as he shall faithfully perform his service. The surplus shall be carefully saved until the needs of the church shall require it.

John A. Hardenbergh,	£0.2.0	Cristian Doyoo,	£0.1.0
Simon Freer,	0.1.0	Jacobus	
Cristophel Doyoo,	0.1.6	(Rest of paper destroyed.)	

Copied from another loose piece of paper without date :

Jesse Wood,	$2.10	Henry D. B. Freer,	$1.10
Rachel Wood,	1.10	Jane Freer,	0.50
Eltie Deyo,	1.10	Catharintje Elting,	5.10
Abraham Ean,	2.10	Mathusalah Elting,	5.10
William W. Dyo,	5.10	Josiah P. Lefever,	3.10
Charles Elting,	3.10	Jacob J. Housbrouck,	5.10
Mrs. Peter Ean,	1.10	Ralph Deyo,	1.00

John S. Dubois,	$2.10	Rulof Dubois,	$3.00
S. L. Dubois,	2.10	Abraham Achmoody,	3.00
John W. Schooncher,	2.10	Abraham J. Dejo,	4.00
Maria Weerts,	5.10	Jonathan Freer,	2.10
Christopher Lefever,	3.10	Isaac Abrams,	1.50
Jacob Lefever,	1.10	Elias Schoonmaker,	0.50
Stephen Stilwell,	1.10	Roelof S. Elting,	2.10
John N. Terwilliger,	1.10	Getty Lefever,	0.50
Elenor Dubois,	1.10	Margaret Housbrouck,	0.50
Abraham Steen,	0.50	Catharin C. ? Freer,	2.10
John H. Schoonmaker,	1.10	Jacob Reljea,	2.10
John E. Munster,	1.10	David Soper,	1.10
Louis Lefever,	1.10	Wessel Dubois,	2.10
Maria Lefever,	1.10	John Vredenbergh,	1.00
John Freer, ?	1.10	Andries Dubois,	5.00
Sarah Dubois,	0.50	Lewis L. Dubois,	2.10
Joshua Freer,	0.25	John J. Terwilliger,	1.00
Stephen Freer,	0.25	Sarah Elting,	1.10
Philip Deyo,	1.10	Henry I. Dubois, .	3.10
Mrs. Louis ? Eltig,	0.50	Alfred Dejo,	2.10
Elias Freer,	1.00	Gerloin ? Ackerman,	2.10
Gilbert Elting,	1.10	Mary Vredenbergh,	0.50
John Schoonmaker, Jr.,	2.00	Cornelius Weerts,	3.10
Peter S. Dubois,	2.00	Maria Weerts,	1.10
Abraham W. Deyo,	4.00	Peter Dejo,	1.10
Matthew J. Lefever,	5.00	Cornelia Housbrouck,	3.10
Cornelius Dejo,	3.00	Maria Elting,	1.10
Rachel N. Lefever,	3.00		

(No object for subscription stated.)

Translated from another loose piece of paper (no date)—Dutch—

Hend. Dubois,	£34.11. 9	Cornelius Louw, for boards,	£1. 4. 6
Josia Elting,	32.10. 9	Auction money and for boards, nails and work bench,	24.14. 1
James Huey,	12. 1.11		
Noach Elting,	21.10. 7		
Isaac Louw,	2. 2. 8		
Petrus Louw,	7. 2. 3	Samuel Schoonmaker,	6.16. 6
Roelof Josias Eltinge,	7. 5. 2	Wilhelmus Schoonmaker,	2.15. 1
Petrus Van Wagne,	3. 7. 6		
P. Dubois,	14. 3. 0	Hendk Dubois, Jr.,	1.15. 0
Abraham Eltinge,	1. 4. 3	(The above may be wages, etc.)	
Salomon Louw,	1. 5. 6		
Jacob Dubois,	—	The cost of the church,	
Abraham Een,	0.10. 0		£124.7.10

RESOLUTION OF THE CONSISTORY.

(Entered among the Baptismal records in Book 3, and probably refers to the registering of the names of children for baptism.)

Whereas, there are many people who do not contribute towards the salary, or so little that it does not pay for the registration and the book, let alone a proportionate contribution for the annual service ; THEREFORE, we, the Consistory, resolve that whosoever contributes nothing, or below three shillings, towards the salary, shall pay his three shillings, one half for the Registrar, the rest shall be put away in the box (koffertje) for general expenses. The Quæstor shall be

Q. T. STEPHS. GOETSCHIUS, V.D.M.

April 12, 1783.

(From Book 3.)

THE SUBSCRIPTION MONEY RECEIVED AND OWING.

No year	s.	d.		s.	d.
May 25. 2 children,	6.		Hendric Snyder,	2.	9
1 chd.,	3.		Thomas Klarwater,	3.	
John Lemonjon,	2.		Joseph Klarwater,	3.	
William Wood,	3.		John Barret,	3.	
Edward Wood,	3.		Samuel Corson,	3.	
Joseph Coddington,	3.		John C. Hardenberg,	3.	
Willem Smith,	3.		Edward Wood,	3.	3
Israel Wering,	2.	5	Henry Harp,	3.	
Salomon Wering,	3.		Elias Davis,	3.	
Isack Herres,	2.		Laurence Hendricks,	3.	
David Etkins,	3.		Marcus Wekman,	3.	
Teunis Sammons,	3.		Benjamin Wood,	3.	
Abram Hess,	3.		Cornelius Brink,	3.	
Hendric Wakman,	3.		Nath. Wells,	3.	
Abram Hog,	3.		Zacharias Hofman,	2.	9
Newman (?) Wering,	3.		Fred. Hopensted,	2.	9
William Hood,	3.		John Hofman,	3.	
Johs. Rosekrans,	3.		Numan Wering,	2.	
Fredric Schonmaker,	3.		Isack Hardenberg,	3.	
Isack Vañ Wagen,	3.		John Stooks,	3.	
Petrus Dewitt,	2.10		Daniel Klarwater,	3.	
Hermanus Osterhout,	3.		John Sort,	3.	
Gerret Devenport,	3.		Mathew Kontryman,	3.	
John McNeel,	3.		Daniel Kerny (?)	3.	

No year.	s. d.		s. d.
Hendric Doio,	3.	Simeon Skurigan (?)	2.
Jacob Green,	3.	Ann Byk (?)	3.
Simon Helm,	3.	Jer. Hasbrook,	8.
Thomas Klarwater,	3.	Step. Forter (?)	3.
Peter Wood,	3.	I. Van Wag,	3.
Richard Stoks,	3.	E. Terwilliger,	3.
Steps. Scryver,	2.	William McDonald,	3.
John C. Hardenberg,	3.	Is. Dubois,	3.
John Alliger,	2. 9	Wm. Smith,	3.
Daniel Klaerwater,	3.	Peter Yurk,	3.
John Replie,	3.		

(From Book 1. In French.)
BAPTISMAL AND OTHER ENTRIES.

Oct. 23, 1698. Richard Viltfil and Madelin Chut, his wife, had a child baptized. Its name is Mannette. (This is rather obscure in the original and possibly should be Marianet.) Lovye Bayvier, Godfather; Marian ——, Godmother.

Oct. 23, 1698. Abraham Frere and Achye, his wife, had a child baptized. Its name is Salomon. Moyse Quntin, Godfather; Rachal Hasbrouq, Godmother.

July 2, 1699. Jacob Clarvater and Mary, his wife, had a child baptized. Its name is Abraham. Abraham Hasbrouque and Salomon Dubois, Godfathers; Mary Doio, Godmother.

May 19, 1700. Richar Viltfil and his wife, Madelin Chut, had a son baptized. His name is Daniel. Huge Frere is Godfather, and Maryam Leroy Godmother. By Mr. Bonrepo, Minister of the Word of God.

Isaac Dubois, son of Louys du Bois and of Caterien Blancon, was married by the minister after having been announced three Sundays previously, to Marie Hasbrouck, daughter of Jan Hasbrouck and Anne doieie.

(No date, but in the same handwriting as the first entry, referring to the organization of the Church, dated Jan. 22, 1683, and probably took place prior to Oct. 14, 1683.)

Oct. 14, 1683. Baptized two children of Pierre Doieie and Haghe Mkel, named the one Pierre, and the other Margerit. Godfather, Abraham Rutan, and Godmother, Marie Petilon ; of the other, Godfather, Abraham Dubois ; Godmother, Margerit Doioie.

Oct. 21, 1683. Baptized a child of Lymon Le Febvre and Lysbet Doieie, named Isaac. Godfather, Isaac Duboys, and Godmother, Marie Hasbrouck.

Oct. 23, 1684. Baptized a child of Abraham Hasbrouck and Marie Doieie, named Josef. Godfather, Jacob Dubois ; Godmother, Marie Doieie.

Sept. 23. Baptized a child of Abraham Rutan and Marie Petilon, named Daniel. Godfather, Louys Dubois ; Godmother, Caterien Blancon.

April 28, 1684. Baptized a child of Isaac Dubois and Marie Hasbrouck, named Daniel. Godfather, Louis Dubois, and Godmother, Caterien Blancon.

April 4, 1685. Baptized a child of Jan Hasbrouck and Anne Doieie, named Lysbet. Godfather, Pierre Doieie ; Godmother, Lysbet Doieie.

April 6. Baptized a child of Louis Bevier and Marie Le Blan, named Louis. Godfather, Abraham Hasbrouck ; Godmother, Marie Doieie.

April 17. Baptized a child of Abraham Dubois and Margeret Doioie, named Abraham. Godfather, Louys Dubois ; Godmother, Caterien Blancon.

Oct. 28. Baptized a child of Symon Le Febvre and Lysbet Doioie, named Jan. Godfather, Pierre Doioie ; Godmother, Marie Doioie.

March 20, 168⅚. Baptized a child of Abraham Rutan, named Paul. Godfather, Hughe Frere ; Godmother, Agaer Mckel.

Oct. 17, 1686. Was baptized a child of Abraham Hasbrouck and Mary Doyo, a son, his name is Salomon. Godfather, Louys Bayvier ; Godmother, Estel LaToynelle.

April 15, 1688. Jan Hasbrouc and Anne Doyo had a child baptized named Jacobe. Godfather, Lovys Baivyer ; Godmother, Mary Leblan.

April 17, 1688. Abraham Rutan and Mari Petilion had a child baptized called Davide. Godfather, Pier Doye ; Godmother, Genne Vybau or Vylar.

April 16, 1687. Pier Doyo and Agite had a child baptized, a daughter. Her name is Madeleine. Godfather, Yan Hasbrouck ; Godmother, Margerite Doyo.

April 16, 1687. Louys Baivyer and Mari Leblan had a daughter baptized named Ester. Godfather, Yan Hasbrouque ; Godmother, Estere LaToinelle.

April 16, 1687. Ysaque Duboy and Marie Hasbrouque had a son baptized, named Benjamin. Godfather, Abraham Duboy ; Godmother, Anne Doyo.

Oct. 16, 1687. Abraham Duboi and Margerite Doyo had a daughter baptized named Leya. Godfather, Salomon Duboi ; Godmother, Mari Leblan.

This is the way these two entries appear in the original. They seem to refer to one person.
/ Jacob Ruth, his wife Marie.
Abraham Assebroucq, godfather, Jean Blecker ?
Catherine Ruth, Peronne Quantin.
On April 27, 1689, was born, and baptized the son of Jacob Ruth named Jacob, nine (9) days old.

Children.	Parents.	Witnesses.	
Jacob	Henderik Dekker	Jacob Dekker	
July 6, 1718	Jannetjen Kortregt	Zara Minten	These entries are in Dutch, and entered in the manner as here shown.
Ester	Philip Duboy	Jacob Haasbroek	
	Ester Gemaar	Ester Bevier	

Oct. 13, 1689. Louis Bayvier had his son baptized, named Salomon. Godfather, Isaque Duboy ; Godmother, Ann Doyo.

Oct. 13, 1689. Abraham Duboy and Margerite Doio had a daughter baptized named Rachel. Godfather, Abraham Hasbrouc ; Godmother, Mari Doyo.

May 14, 1690. Isaac Dubois and Marie Hasbrouq his wife, had a son baptized named Phillipe. Godfather, Jean Hasbrouq ; Godmother, Ester Hasbrouq.

May 14, 1690. Abraham Rutamt and Marie Petilion, his wife, had a daughter baptized named Ester. Godfather, Abraham Hasbrouq ; Godmother, Ester Hasbrouq.

June 7, 1690. Hugue Frere, son of Hugue Frere, his father, and Marie Haye, his mother, was married by Mr. Dailliez to Marie LeRoy.

Oct. 12, 1690. Mr. Dailliez baptized a boy of Pierre Doyaux, named Henry. Godfather, Jean Cottin ; Godmother, Ester Hasbroucq.

Oct. 17, 1691. Hugue Frere, the son, and Marie LeRoy, his wife, had a boy baptized called Hugue. Godfather, Abraham Frere; Godmother, Maria Frere.

Oct. 24, 1691. Abraham Hasbroucq and Marie Doyaux, his wife, had a boy baptized called Sonas (or Jonas). Abraham, son of Jean Hasbroucq, Godfather; Anne Hasbroucq, Godmother.

Oct. 24, 1691. Abraham Rutemp and Marie Petilion, his wife, had a boy baptized named Pierre. Godfather, Pierre Quimar; Godmother, Ester Hasbrouc.

On June 9, 1690, the members of the Consistory of the Paltz placed in my hands two sealed bags, saying that in the one there are one hundred and forty-three (143) francs, so in Zewannes [Seewan; wampum] as in silver. In the other bag they say there are four hundred francs (400), so in Zewannes as in silver money.

     Mark of X HUGUE FRERE,
           Elder.

  ABRAHAM HASBROUCK, } Witnesses.
   LOVYS BAYVYER, }

April 18, 1692. Mr. Dailliez married: Pierre Guimar, born at Moize, in Saintonge, France; son of Pierre Guimar and Anne D'Amour (his father and mother), and Ester Hasbroucq, born in the Palatinate, Germany, daughter of Jean Hasbroucq and of Anne D'Oyaux.

May 21, 1693. Abraham Dubois and Margueritte D'Oyaeux, his wife, had a daughter baptized named Catherine. Godfather, Louis Dubois, the son, and Trinque (Trintie?), wife of Salomon Dubois, Godmother.

May 21, 1693. Hugue Frere and Marie Anne Le Roy, his wife, had a son baptized named Isaac. Godfather, Denis Reille; Godmother, Haguette.

May 21, 1693. Moyse Quentin and Lisbette D'Oyaux, his wife, had a son baptized named ———. Godfather, Pierre Guimar; Godmother, Rachel Hasbroucq.

Dec. 8, 1693. The wife of Hugue Frere died in the Lord.

April 28, 1694. Abraham Frere married Haiquiez Titesorte.

Jan. 19, 1701. Lovyse Duboy married Racel Hasbrouc. {This entry was in a different handwriting from those immediately preceding and following it. It was at foot of page in original.}

May 5, 1694. Anne D'Oyau died in the Lord, aged 50 years.

May 31, 1696. Mr. Bon Repos baptized a daughter of Hugue Frere and Marie Le Roy, her father and mother. She came into the world May 5, 1696. Her name is Marie. Abraham Hasbroucq, Jr., Godfather, and Rachel Hasbroucq, Godmother.

May 31, 1696. Mr. Bonrepos baptized a daughter of Abraham Frere and Haiquiez Titesorte, her father and mother. She came into the world on May 15, 1696, and is named Nilletiez. Godfather, Louis Dubois ; Godmother, Elisabet Titesorte.

May 31, 1696. Mr. Bonrepos baptized a son of Abraham Hasbrouq and Marie Doyaux, his father and mother. His name is Benjamin. Godfather, Abraham Doyaux ; Godmother, Marie Frere.

Oct. 15, 1699. Mr. Bonrepo baptized a daughter of Huge Frere and Marian Le Roy. Her name is Ester. Godfather, Yan Tebenin ; Godmother, Exgye Titesorte.

Feb. 21, 1702. Cristian Doyo and Mary Le Conte were married in this town of Paltz (Pals, sometimes also called Le Palle).

No date to the following entries, and had been crossed out in original :

Daniel Duboy has paid 5 francs 10 tenure too much.
Jean Le Fevre owes 3 francs.
Louy Duboy had paid 88 francs 5 tenure too much.
Henry Doyo has paid 22 francs 15 tenure too much.
Joseph Heuge Frere has paid 3 francs 5 tenure too much.
Joseph ——— has paid 3 francs 5 tenure too much.
Abraham Doyo has paid 5 francs 15 tenure too much.

July 3, 1699. Yan Bayvyer, Abraham Bayvyer, Isaque Hasbrouq, Crystyan Doio, Yacob Frere, Rachel Hasbrouq, Sara Duboy, were received at the table of the Lord in the congregation of the Paltz, by Mr. Bonrepos, Minister of the Word of God.

Oct. 22, 1699. Lovys Deboy was received at the Lord's table in the congregation of the Paltz, by Mr. Bonrepos, Minister of the Word of God.

June (?) 19, 1700. Andre Le Feve and Sammuel Baivyer were received at the Lord's table in the Paltz, by Mr. Bonrepos, Minister of the Word of God.

June 28, 1690. Isaac Dubois died in his house at the Paltz (au Palle).

Aug. 5, 1690. A daughter of Abraham Rutemps died, aged about 6 months.

Aug. 9, 1690. Isaac Frere, son of Hugue Frere, died, aged about 18 years.

CONSISTORY.

(From Book 2.)

1730–1, March 11. Elected—Elders: Nicolaas Roos, Andries Le Fever. Deacons: Sammuel Bevier, Salomon Haasbroek.

1733, Sept. 22. Elder: Luys Du Boy. Deacon: Christyiaan Do Joy.

1734, Oct. 13. Elder: Nicolaas Roos. Deacon: Jacob Haasbroek.

1736, May 22. Elder: Sammuel Bevier. Deacon: Daniel Haasbroek.

1750, Oct. 19. Elder: Daniel DuBois. Deacon: Hans Jury Rang.

1751, Aug. 24. Elder: Johannes Hardenbergh. Deacon: Evert Terwilge.

1752, May 18. The Monday of Pentecost. After calling upon God's name were unanimously elected by the Great Consistory of the congregation of this place in the presence of me, J. H. Goetschius: As Elder in the place of Daniel Dubois, Daniel HaasBouk. As Deacons in the place of Hans Jory Rang, Simon duBois. Installed May 28.

1752, Nov. 1. After calling upon the Lord's name the Consistory met in my presence and it was unanimously resolved to elect, besides the governing Elders and Deacons, two more Elders and Deacons, and were elected as such—Elders: Samuel Bevie, Hans Yory Rang. Deacons: Abraham Lefeber, Jacob

Haasbroek, Jr. After three publications they were installed without objections on Nov. 25 by me
(Signed)   J. H. Goetschius.

1756, Aug. 22. After calling upon the Lord's name the Great Consistory at New Paltz met at the house of Jacob Hasbroek and resolved with a sufficient majority of votes to wait for some time with the election of a new Consistory. In presence of me   (Signed)   J. H. Goetschius.

1757, Nov. 20. Elected—Elders: Simon DeBoy, Jacobus Haasbroek, Jr., in place of the retiring Johannes Hardenberg, Hans Jori Rang. Deacons: Johannes DeJo, Petrus Oostrander, in place of the retiring Jacob Haasbroek, Abraham Lefeber.

1759, March 3. Elected—Elders: Johannes Hardenbergh, Abraham Levever, in place of Abraham De Joo, Abraham Hardenbergh. Deacons: Johannes Freer, Jacobus Bovie, in place of Abraham Bovie, Nathaniel Lefever.

1761, Apr. 25. Elected—Elders: Andres Lefefer, Abraham Dioo. Deacons: Hugo Freres, Jr., Johannes Lefefer. Installed May 11, 1761.

1762, March 27. Elected—Elders: Abraham Hardenbergh, Jonas Freer. Deacons: Benjamin Dubois, Lowis J. Dubois. Installed Apr. 25.

1763, May 12. Elected—Elders: Nathaniel Le Fever, Jacob Hasbrouck, Jr. Deacons: John Terwilger, Benyamen Freer. Installed June 5.

1764, June 3. Elected—Elders: Johannis Matyse Low, Abraham Bevier. Deacons: Gerrit Freer, Jr., Christofphel Doyo. Installed June 24.

1765, Apr. 27. Elected—Elders: Simon Dubois, Abr. Lefefer. Deacons: Christiaan Dojou, Abraham Vander Merke.

1766, Apr. 12. Elected—Elders: Johannes Hardenbergh, Abraham Doiau. Deacons: Jan Hasbrouck, Benyamen Dojo. Installed May 25.

1767, May 9. Elected at the house of Mr. Abraham Dojou, at N. Paltz.—Elders: Andries Lefever, Johannis Lefever. Deacons: Jacob Freer, Jr., Joannis Freer, Jr.

1768, May 12. Elected—Elders: Jacob Hasbrouck, Jr., Jacobus Bevier. Deacons: Petrus Vandemerken, Marcus Ostrander.

1769, May 27. Elected Elders and Deacons : Abraham Bevier, Huge Freer, Daniel Lefever and Christofphel Doyo.

1771, May 26. Elected—Elders : Abraham DeYo, Natanael Feber, in place of Abraham Bevier, decd., Jacob Haesbroek, Gerret Vreer, in place of Jacobus Bevie. Deacons : Lowis DuBoi, Johannis Vreer, Jr., in place of Petrus Van de Merken, Marcus Oostrander.

1772, July 8. Elected—Elders : Simon Deboys, Jacobus Hasbrouck, in place of Abram De Yoo, Hugo Freer, retiring. Deacons : Christiaan De Yoo, Benjamen Freer, in place of Daniel Le Fever, Christofel DoYoo.

1773, Oct. 3. Elected—Elders : Jonas Freer, Andreas Leffeber, in place of Nataniel Leffeber, Garret Freer. Deacons : Jacob Freer, Jan Terwillgen, in place of Johannes Freer, Jr., Lewis DeBois.

1774, - - - - Elected—Elders : Col. Johannes Hardenberg, Jacob Hasbrouck, Jr., in place of Simon Dubois, Jacobus Hasbrouck. Deacons : Benjamin Doyo, Johannes Frere in place of Christaan Doyo, Benjamin Frere.

1775, Oct. 8. Elected—Elders : Abraham Doyo, Hugo Frere, in place of Andries Lefever, Esq., Jonas Frere, decd. Deacons : Daniel Lefever, Lowis Dubois, in place of Jacob Frere, Jan Terwilliger.

1776, Dec. 8. Elected—Elders : Abraham Lefever, Gerret Frere, in place of Col. Johannes Hardenberg, Jacob Hasbrouck, Jr. Deacons : Dr. Georgius Wirtz, Christian Doyo, in place of Benjamin Doio, Johannes Frere.

1777, Nov. 30. Elected—Elders : Simon Dubois, Jacobus Hasbrouck, in place of Hugo Frere, Abraham Doio. Deacons : Hugo (?) Frere, Benjamin Frere, in place of Lowis Dubois, Daniel Lefever. Churchmaster : Abraham Doio in place of his deceased father.

1778, November 20. Elected—Elders : Jacob Hasbrouck, Petrus Lefever, in place of Abram Lefever, Gerret Frere. Deacons: Daniel Graham, Abraham Doio, in place of Georgius Wirtz, Christian Doio.

1779, Nov. 10. Elected—Elders : Christoffel Doio, Andries Lefevour, in place of Simon Dubois, Jacobus Hasbrouck. Deacons : Nathaniel Dubois, Samuel Bavier, in place of Hugo Frere, Benjamin Frere. Petrus Frere in place of Daniel Graham, who left the town.

1780, Nov. 6. Elected—Elders: Lois Dubois, Benjamin Doio, in place of Jacob Hasbrouck, Petrus Lefever. Deacons: David Hasbrouck, Petrus Frere, in place of Abraham Doio, Petrus Frere (continued).

1781, Nov. 2. Elected—Elders: Abraham Vander Merken, Johannis Frere, in place of Christoffel Doio, Andries Lefever. Deacons: Johannes Hardenberg, Petrus Hasbrouck, in place of Nathanel Dubois, Samuel Bevier.

1782, Oct. 15. Elected—Elders: Daniel Lefever, Abraham Lefever, in place of Lowis Dubois, Benjamin Doio. Deacons: Joseph Hasbrouck, Jacob I. Frere, in place of David Hasbrouck, Petrus Frere.

1783, Oct. 10. Elected—Elders: Jacob Hasbrouck, Dirk Wynkop, Jr., in place of Abram Van de Merk, Johannes Frere. Deacons: Hugo Frere, Jr., George Wertz, in place of Petrus Hasbrouck, Johannes Hardenberg.

1785, Apr. 30. Elected—Elders: Johannes Frere, Benjamin Frere, in place of Daniel Lefever, Abraham Lefever. Deacons: David Low, Jonas Frere, in place of Joseph Hasbrouck, Jacob I. Frere.

1786, May 10. Elected—Elders: Petrus Lefever, Salomon Low, in place of Jacob Hasbrouck, Dirk Wynkop. Deacons: Petrus Bovier, Jonathan Doio, in place of George Wirtz, Hugo Frere, Jr.

1787, May 15, Elected—Elders: Lowis Dubois, Dr. Andries Dewitt, in place of Benjamin Frere, Johannes Frere. Deacons: Johannes B. Doio, Matheus Lefever, in place of David Low, Jonas Frere. Churchmaster, Jacob Low with Abram Doio, remaining.

1788, May 20. Elected—Elders: Christoffel Doio, Abram Elting, in place of Petrus Lefever, Salomon Low. Deacons: David Hasbrouck, Jacob Bovier, in place of Petrus Bovier, Jonathan Doio.

1789, July 20. Elected—Elders: Andries Lefever, Esq., Daniel Lefever, in place of Lowis Dubois, Andries De Witt, Esq. Deacons: Cornelius Dubois, Jeremias Frere, in place of Johannes B. Doio, Matheus Lefever.

1790, Aug. - -. Elected — Elders: Jacobus Hasbrouck, Benjamin Frere, in place of Christoffel Doio, Abram Elting. Deacons: Methusalem Dubois, Jeremias Frere, in place of David Hasbrouck, Jacob Bovier.

1791, Aug. - -. Elected—Elders : Christian Doio, Johannes Frere, in place of Andries Lefever, Esq., Daniel Lefever. Deacons : Jonathan Doio, Elias Bovier, in place of Cornelius Dubois, Jeremias Frere.

1792, Aug. - -. Elected—Elders : Christian Doio, Cornelius Dubois, in place of Jacobus Hasbrouck, Benjamin Frere. Deacons : Elisa Frere, Hendric Smitt, in place of Methusalem Dubois, Jeremias Frere.

1793, Aug. - -. Elected—Elders : Nathaneel Dubois, Benjamin Doio, in place of Christian Doio, Johannes Frere. Deacons : Jacob Low, Simon Lefever, in place of Jonathan Doio, Elias Bovier.

1794, Aug. - -. Elected—Elders : Jacob Hasbrouck, Andries Dewitt, in place of Christian Doio, Cornelius Dubois. Deacons : Petrus Lefever, Esq.,David Raljie, in place of Elisa Frere, Hendric Smitt.

1795, Aug. - -. Elected—Elders : Dinie Raljie, Jeremias Frere, in place of Nathaneel Dubois, Benjamin Doio. Deacons ; Jonathan Vanwagene, Andries Lefever, in place of Jacob Low, Simon Lefever.

1796, June - -. Elected—Elders : Benjamin Frere, Abraham Dojo, in place of Jacob Hasbrouck, Jr., Andreas D. Witt. Deacons : Elias Ean, Jacob Lefever, in place of Petrus Lefever, Jr., David Relyea.

1797, Sept. 2. Elected—Elders : George Wirtz, Lewis Dubois, in place of Jeremia Frere, Dine Relyea. Deacons : Johannes York, Johannes B. Dojo, in place of Andrew Lefever, Jr., Jonathan Van Wagene.

1798, Aug. 22. Elected—Elders : Petrus Hasbrouck, Methusalem Dubois, in place of Benjamin Frere, Abram Doio. Deacons : Philip Lefever, David Doio, in place of Elias Ean, Jacob Lefever.

1799, Dec. 28. Elected—Elders : Christian Deyo, Jonathan Deyo, Mathew Lefevre, in place of Petrus Hasbrook, deceased, Lewis I. Dubois, George Wirtz. Deacons : Peter Lefevre, Jr., Jonathan Van Wagenen, in place of John B. Deyo, Johannes York. Ordained January 12, 1800.

1801, Jan. 17. Elected—Elders : Benjamin Freeres, Jacob Lowe, in place of Christian Dojo, Methusalem Dubois. Deacons : Simeon Lowe, Simeon Rose, in place of David Dojo, Philip Lefever. Ordained February 15.

1802, Jan. 1. Elected—Elders : Garrit Freer, Derick Wynkoop, in place of Jonathan Dojo, Mathew Lefever. Deacons : John Low, Ezekiel Elting, in place of Petrus Lefever, Jr., Jonathan V. Wagenen. Ordained January 24.

1803, Jan. 24. Elected—Elders : Jeremiah Freer, Methuselah Dubois, in place of Benjamin Freere, Jacob Lowe. Deacons : Josiah R. Eltinge, Philip Lefever, Elias Een, in place of Simon Rose, Simon Lowe, I. C. Lowe, deceased. Ordained March 20.

1804, Jan. 28. Elected—Elders : Mathew Lefever, Andries Lefever, Jr., in place of Derick Wynkoop, Garrit Freer. Deacons : Peter Lefever, Jonathan Van Wagenen, in place of Elias Een, Ezekiel Elting. Ordained April 15.

1805, Jan. - -. Elected—Elders : Benjamin Frere, Louis Dubois, in place of Jeremias Frere, Methusalem Dubois. Deacons, Jacob Lefever, Peter Eltinge, in place of Philip Lefever, Josia R. Eltinge. January 23. Colonel Josiah Hasbrouck chosen Churchmaster by Consistory.

1806, April - -. Elected—Elders : Jonathan Doio, Simeon Low, instead of Andries Lefever, Mathew Lefever. Deacons : John Elting, Simon Roos, instead of Peter Lefever, Jr., Jonathan Van Wagenen.

1807, June 28. Elected—Elders : Peter Lefever, Jacob Low, in place of Benjamin Freer, Lewis Dubois. Deacons : Philip Lefever, Elias Ean, in place of Peter Eltinge, Jacob Lefever. Ordained same day by Moses Freligh.

1808, April 29. Elected—Elders : Methuselah Dubois, Mathew Lefever, in place of Jonathan Deyoo, Simeon Low. Deacons : John B. Deyoo, Josiah R. Eltinge, in place of John Eltinge, Simon Roos. Ordained May 22.

1809, April 28. Elected—Elders : Dirk Wynkoop, Jeremiah Freer, in place of Jacob Louw, Peter Lefever. Deacons : Isaac Bodine, Elias Bovier, in place of Philip Lefever, Elias Ean. Ordained May 23.

1810, April 28. Elected—Elders : Cornelius Dubois, Jr., Ezekiel Eltinge, in place of Methusalem Dubois, Mathew Lefever. Deacons : Jacobus Roose, Jr., William Deyoo, in place of Josiah R. Eltinge, John B. Deyoo. Ordained May 11.

1811, April 22. Elected—Elders : Jacob Lefever, Elias Ean, in place of Dirck Wynkoop, Jeremiah Freer. Deacons :

Cornelius B. Dubois, Mathew I. Blenchan, in place of Isaac Bodine, Elias Bovier. Ordained May 11.

1812, April 28. Elected—Elders : Jonathan Deyoo, Peter Lefever, in place of Cornelius Dubois, Ezekiel Eltinge. Deacons : Jonathan Van Wagenen, Roelif Eltinge, in place of Jacobus Roose, Jr., William Deyoo. Ordained May 19.

1813, April 27. Elected—Elders : Methusalem Dubois, Josiah R. Eltinge, in place of Elias Ean, Jacob Lefever. Deacons : Garrit Dubois, Abraham Agmoedy, in place of Cornelius B. Dubois, Mathew I. Blenchan. Ordained May 20, except Mr. A. Agmoedy, who not being present was ordained to his office June 21.

1814, May 7. Elected—Elders : Isaac Bodine, Elias Ean, in place of Jonathan Deyoo, Peter Lafever. Deacons : Simon Roose, John Eltinge, in place of Jonathan Van Wagen, Roelif Eltinge. Ordained May 22.

Nov. 9. With submission to the holy and righteous will of God which removed by death one of the members of the Consistory, the remaining members elected Peleg Stevans a deacon in the room of Garrit Dubois, deceased.

1814, Nov. 27. Mr. Peleg Stevans was ordained to his office.

1815, April 27. Elected—Elders : Philip Lefever, William Deyoo, in place of Methusalem Dubois, Josiah R. Eltinge. Deacons : Philip Eltinge, Moses Lefever, in place of Abraham Agmoedy, Peleg Stevans. Ordained May 24.

1816, June 23. Elected—Elders : Peter Lefever, Jacob Lefever, in place of Elias Ean, Isaac Bodine. Deacons : Charles Dubois, Peter Elting, in place of John Eltinge, Simon Rose.

CONSISTORY OF THE SECOND CHURCH.

1768, May 23. Minute of the Rev. Consistory of New Paltz.

After calling upon God's name, the annual change of the Consistory in accordance with the laws of the Church took place, and it was resolved to add to the partial Consistory which had been elected last year, another Elder and Deacon, for the purpose of thus forming a complete Consistory, and subsequently, under God's blessing, to elect annually.

Were unanimously elected—As Elder : Henricus Du Boys. As Deacon : Roelof Josiah Eltinge.

On Aug. 1, following the above named persons were installed in office by D°. Gerhard Daniel Cock, Pastor in Camp, etc.

1769, Aug. 23. Were elected in the fear of God—As Elder: Salomon Louw, in place of the retiring Noach Eltinge, Esq. As Deacon : Jacob Du Boys, in place of the retiring Petrus Van Wagena.

The above named brethren were subsequently installed in their offices by me, Isaac Rysdyk, on November 8, 1769.

1770, Oct. 12. Elected as Elder : Noach Eltinge, in place of the retiring Henricus Du Boys. Deacon : Abraham Eltinge, in place of the retiring one, Roelof Josia Eltinge.

Oct. 29. Installed in their offices by D°. Cock.

1771, Nov. 14. Unanimously elected in place of the retiring brethren, Salomon Louw and Jacob Du Boys. As Elder : Roelof Eltinge. As Deacon : Isaak Louw.

May 21, 1772. Installed by Rev. Izaak Rysdyk.

1772, Sept. 2. Unanimously elected in place of the retiring brethren, Noa Eltinge and Abraham Eltinge. As Elder : Jacob Du Boys. As Deacon : Dirk Dirkse Wynkoop.

1773, Feb. 24. Installed by D°. Gerhard Daniel Cock, V.D.M., at Camp and Rhinebeck.

1774, Feb. 2. Elected as Elder : Salomon Louw, in place of Rulof Josia Eltinge. Deacon : Salomon Elting, in place of Isac Louw.

1774, Dec. 11. Installed by Rev. Rynier Van Nest, Jr., V.D.M.

Acta or Minutes of the Collegiate Churches of Shawengonk and the Second Church at New Paltz, under the ministry of Dom. Ryneir Van Nest, who entered upon his ministry at Shawengonk on November 6, 1774, and on the following Sunday in the Second Church at New Paltz.

1775, May 1. Consistory meeting at New Paltz at the house of Jacobus Bruyn. After calling upon the Lord's name the following business was done :

1. Elected Dirk Rosa, besides their preacher, to attend the next special meeting, which is to convene the fourth Tuesday in May, 1775, at Poughkeepsie.

2. Concerning Easter and Pentecost Monday, it was resolved to have services on that day, at the place where services were held the previous Sunday.

3. Ascension Day shall count as a turn.

4. Concerning Christmas and New Year's Day, if that day falls on Saturday, the service shall be held at the place whose turn comes the following Sunday. If on Monday, the service shall take place where service was held on the previous Sunday, but on other days it shall count as a turn.

MEMBERSHIP RECORD.

(From Book No. 2.)

1733, Sept. 30. Jacob Haasbroeck, Maria Hardenbergh, Elizabeth Duboys, Jonathan Dubois, Sara Haasbroeck, Catharina Du Boys.

1734, June 21. Daniel Du Boys, Johannes Hardenbergh, Pieter Symonsz, Magdalena Beuvier, Mareytie Du Boys, Mareytie and Elzie De Joy.

1736, May 22. Wyntje Haasbroek, Petronella Lefever, Elizabeth Do Joy, Margrietje Lefever, Sara Lefever, Margareta Do Joy.

1750, Apr. - - Received with Letters as members at N. Paltz : Johan George Rauck and Lorantz Altsdorf, and wife Maria.

On this Apr. 19, 1751 the following persons by approbation of the Rev. Consistory made a confession before me, J. H. Goetschius, V.D.M., and were admitted as members of the Congregation at Paltz : Evardt Ter Wilgen, Henderik Van der Merken, Johannes Hardenberg, Jr., Simon De Bois, and wife Catryntje, Abraham Van der Merken, Abraham Le Feber, and wife Maria, Janetje, wife of Hugo Ter Wilgen, Margret, wife of Jacobus Hofman, Andreas Le Feber, Jakomyntje Van der Merke, Y.D., Catrina Van der Merke, Y.D., Lea Van der Merke, Y.D., Rachel Van der Merke, Y.D., Margrita, wife of Abraham Bevier, Ester Bevie, Y.D.

Upon Certificate : Johan Jacob Roggen.

1751, Dec. 8. Upon Confession : Johannes Bevier, Petrus Van der Merken, Y.M., Jacobus Haasbrouque, Y.M., Jacob Haasbrouque, Jr., Nathanael Lefeber, and wife Marytje, Abraham Duyo, Abraham Bevier.

1752, May 30. Upon Confession: Moses Dejo, and wife Clara Stokraed, Jonas Vreer, and wife Catryna Stokkraed, Gerrit Vreer, Jr., and wife Maria Vreer, Eleanor Wood, Y.D.

1752, May 31. Upon Certificate: Hans Yory Niess and his mother Margriet, Madlena Bevier, wife of Johannes Bevier, Adrian Newkerk.

1752, Nov. 25. Upon Confession: Hugo Freer, Marytje, wife of Isaac Freer, Abraham Hardenberg, Hugo Freer, and wife Hester, Moses York, and wife Maria, Jacobus Bevier, and wife Antje, Daniel Lefeber, Charles Hardenberg, Jacob Rutse Hardenberg, Benjamin DuBois, and wife Maria, Benjamin Freer, Maria, wife of Hans Hardenberg, Jr. Upon Certificate: Catrina, wife of Daniel Lefeber, Elsje, widow of Joseph Haasbroek, Maria, widow of Isaac Lefeber, Maria, wife of Abraham Hardenberg, Janetje, wife of Jacob Haesbroek, Jr.

1753, July 1. Upon Confession: Wessel Broadhead, Ester, wife of Samuel Bevie, Clara, wife of Jory Rauck. With Letters from Kingston: Hendrick Dojo, Petrus Louw and wife Debora Van Vliet, Jonathan Louw, Sarah Louw, Philippus Bevier and wife Treyntje Louw, James, Maria, and Magdalena Auchmutie, Henricus DuBois and wife Jannetje Hoogteling.

1754, April 3. Upon Confession: Johannes Louw and wife Rebecca Freer, Johannes Freer and wife Agetta Dojo, Jacob Freer, Jr., and wife Sarah Freer, Benjamin Dojo and wife Jennekie Van Vliet, Jan Hasbrouk, Simon Hasbrouk, Pieter Jork, Majerie Van Leuven, Isaack Louw, Jannetje Louw, Johannes Le Fever, Rachel Hardenbergh, Christoffel, David and Christejaan Dojo, Sarah Le Fever, Jan Terwillegen, Margareta and Catharina Dojo.

1754, Dec. 26. Upon Confession: Lisabeth Helm, wife of Pieter De Yoo. With Letters: Yanatje Freer, Y.D.

1756, Aug. 28. Upon Certificate: Jacob Rutse Hardenberg, and wife Dina.

1757, Nov. 20. With Letters: Petrus Oostrander.

1757, Nov. 27. With Letters: Divertje Van Wagenen, wife of Jacobus Haasbroek.

1758, Sept. 3. With Letters: Michel Sax and wife, Johanna Bevier.

1761, — —. Upon Confession: Louwis Jonathan Dubois, and wife Cathrina. With Letters from Burbach, Germany:

Anna Maria Rippinghausen. With Letters from Wawarsing: Elizabeth Vernoy, wife of Petrus Lefefer.

1762, March 28. Upon Confession: Martynes Freres, Johannes Freres, Jr., Sarah Bever, wife of Johannes Freres, Jr.

— —, Aug. 29. Upon Confession: Margritt Lefefer, wife of Daniel Dojau.

1764, April 21. With Letters from Kingston: Henerik Ostrander, and wife Elizabeth Van Bommele. With Letters from Wawarsink: Sarah, wife of Johannes Lefever.

1765, July 6. Upon Confession: Magdalena Beviers. See further in the New Church book.

1771, Oct. 5. Upon Confession: Denie Relje, and wife Maria Van Vliet, Hugho Vreer, Jr., Catrina Bevier.

BY REV. J. H. GOETSCHIUS.

The following list of membership was copied from Book III.

1780, — —. Admitted upon Confession: Petrus Hasbrouck, Eva Ekker, Elizabeth Van Wagene, wife of Paulus Frere, Jackemyntje, wife of Matheus Bovier, Jacob I. Frere.

1765, July 6. Upon Confession and with Certificate: Magdalena Beviers, Y.D., Sarah Beviers, Y.D., daughters of Abraham Beviers; Cathrina VanderMerke, wife of Joseph Coddington. With Letters from Poghkeepsy: Marcus Ostrander. From Reynbeek: Catharina Eversbach, wife of Georg Huber.

1778, Feb. 19. Upon Confession: Petrus Lefever, Abraham Doio, Petrus Frere, Nathaniel Dubois, Esq., Samuel Bavier, Daniel Graham, Esq., David Hasbrouck, and wife Maria Hogelandt, Lowrence Alsdorp, and wife Rachel Teerpenning, Josaphat Hasbrouck and wife Cornelia Dubois, Johannes A. Hardenberg.

1779, Feb. 2. With Letters from Wawarsing: Annatje De Witt, Margrietje Lefever, widow of Jonathan Vernoy.

1782, Oct. 21. Upon Confession baptized and admitted into membership: Ester and Lise Buyker (?). At the same time upon Confession: Joseph Hasbrouck, Col.

1783, March 2. Baptized after Confession: Maria Jee.

1776, (?) — —. With Letters from Schawangong: George Wertz, Dr.

1783, May 25. The Second Church of the Paltz after preliminary deliberation and discharge by the Reverend particular (byzondere) assembly held at Mormelton, the second Tuesday of May in the year 1783, was in the fear of God in love and mutual friendship united to the old congregation of the New Paltz.

The members come in through the foregoing consolidation are : Dirk Wynkop, Jr., and wife (Sara Elting), Abraham Elting, David Low, Henry Dubois and wife (Rebecca Van Wagenen), Jacob Dubois and wife, Salomon Low and wife, Magdalena Dubois, wife of Josia Elting, Margarita Hue, wife of William Patterson, Maria Low, wife of Rolof Elting, Cornelius Elting, Jacobus Achmody, Ann Dubois, Annatje Hoogteling, widow of Hendricus Dubois, Petrus Van Wagene and wife (Sara Low).

P.S.—The names between (parenthesis) were added in a different (modern) handwriting.

1784, Sept. 2. With Letters : Andries Dewitt and wife, and daughter Maria, Rachel Achmoedy, wife of Samuel Bavier.

Same date, upon Confession : Jonas Frere, Jacob Bavier and wife, Jonathan Doio and wife, Petrus Bavier and wife, Elizabeth Dubois, wife of Stephanus Goetschius, V.D.M., Sara Low, wife of Abram Bavier, Jr., Ester Hasbrouck, wife of George Wertz, Elizabeth Lefever, wife of Matheus Lefever.

1786, June 10. With Letters from Kingston : Sara Van Wagenen, wife of Hendrick Smitt. With Letters from Mormelton : Elizabeth Bovier, wife of Joseph Hasbrouck. Upon Confession : Johannes York, Simeon Low, Rachel Delemeter, wife of David Low.

1786, July 23. Upon Confession, baptized and admitted as member : Maria Wells.

1787, Jan. 21. Upon Confession : Matheus Lefever, Johannes B. Doio and wife, Catrina Kritzinger.

1787, June 9. Upon Confession, baptized, and admitted : Syntje Buiker.

1788, May 25. Upon Confession : Cornelius Dubois, Jr., Methusalem Dubois, Jeremias Frere.

1790, Feb. 23. With Certificate : Sara Van Steenberg, wife of Stephanus Schryver.

1791, July 9. Upon Confession : Denie Raljie and wife, Anatje Vanvliet, Elias Bovier and wife Sara Lefever, David

Raljie, Maria Lefever, widow of Isack Lefever, Hendric Smitt, Zacharias Sluiter.

1792, July 1. Upon Confession: Petrus Lefever, Jr., Jacob Lefever, Eliza Frere, Jacob Low, Syntje Strickland, wife of Jeremia Wesmuller.

1793, May 11. With Letters from N. Hurly: Laura Ostrander, wife of David Raljie, Petrus P. Terwilger and wife, Wilhelmus Schonmaker and wife.

1793, May 11. Upon Confession: Simon Lefever, Elias Ein, Andries Lefever, Daniel Van Wagene, Jonathan Van Wagene and wife, Maria Doio, wife of Ambrosius Elmore.

1795, Nov. 7. Upon Confession: Levi Van Wagene and wife Elizabeth Low, Gertruyt Bruin, wife of Cornelius Dubois, Maria Van Wagen, wife of Simon Roos. With Letters: Benjamin Terwilger and daughter; Jannetje, wife of Johannes Terwilger, Jr.

No year. Jan. 29. With Letters from N. Hamsted: Jacobus Demorest.

1798, Aug. 12. Upon Confession: David Doio and Philip Lefever.

1800, Nov. 2. Upon Confession: Johannis Dojo, Jr., Ezechiel Eltinge, Simon Rose, Jacobus Rose and wife Sarah Van Wagenen, Catharine Van Wagenen, wife of Thomas Owens. Upon Certificate from Ramapough: William Jenkens; from Warwasing: Catharine Dewitt, wife of Daniel Dojo; from Shawangunk: Maria Terwilliger, wife of Joseph Dojo.

1801, Aug. 16. Upon Confession: John I. Freer. Upon Certificate from Kingston: John Louw.

1801, Oct. 16. Upon Confession: Josia R. Eltinge and wife Sarah Lefever, John Eltinge, Catryntje Eltinge, wife of Philip Eltinge, Catryntje Lowe, wife of Daniel Van Wagener, Magdalen Eltinge, wife of Peter Lefever, Jr.

1803, March 20. Upon Confession, baptized and admitted as a member: Henry Linus, a negro, belonging to Garret Freer.

1803, Apr. 10. Isaac, a negro, belonging to David Doyo, Samuel, a negro, belonging to Jacobus Hasbrook.

1803, Apr. 10. Upon Confession: Peter Elting and wife, and Cornelia Wynkoop.

1808, Nov. 11. Upon Confession: William Deyoo and wife Sarah Eltinge, Roelof Eltinge, Isaac Bodine, Mathew I. Blanchan, Lanah Eltinge, wife of Ezekiel Eltinge, William Erwin. Upon Certificate from Klein Esopus R. D. Church: Anny Turk, wife of Mathew I. Blenchan.

1808, Dec. 25. Upon Confession: Abraham Halstead and wife Magdalanah Schryver.

1809, Aug. 12. Upon Confession: Catrina Van Wagenen, widow of Abraham Ean, Elschie Dubois, wife of Philip Lefever, William Hood, Cornelius B. Dubois, and wife Rebecah Dubois.

1810, Feb. 25. Upon Confession: Abraham Aughmoedy, Jr.

1810, May 11. Upon Certificate: Catherine Low, widow of Solomon Eltinge.

1810, June 8. Admitted to Baptism and church Membership: Anny Simmons, wife of William Hood.

1810, Dec. 25. Upon Confession: Peleg Stevans.

1811, Feb. 10. Upon Confession: Jacob Halstead.

1811, Feb. 24. Upon Confession: Jonas Freer.

1811, March 13. Baptized and admitted: Jemimy Trubridge, wife of John Wilkelow.

1811, April 12. Upon Confession: Pheebe Coe, wife of Lewis B. Dubois. From D. R. congregation of Warwick: Isaac Halsted and wife Caroline. From the R. D. congregation of Middleton: Gideon Van Aker and wife Elizabeth.

1811, Oct. 27. Upon Certificate from the R. D. church of Kingston: Ann Beesimere. Upon Confession: Margaret Steenbergh, wife of John Beesimere; Catryntye D——, wife of Jacob Wertz; Maria Bovier, wife of Benjamin Hasbrouck; Maria Freer, wife of Peter Ean.

1812, May 15. Upon Confession: Jane Moore, widow of James McCollagh; Ruth Terwilliger, wife of Simon Roose; Deborah Louw, wife of Ezekiel Deyoo.

1812, Oct. 29. Upon Confession: Garrit Dubois, and wife Maria Eltinge, Catherine Ean, the wife of Jon. Deyoo.

1813, May 21. Upon Confession: Philip Eltinge.

1814, Feb. 13. Upon Confession: Maria Wintfield.

1814, May 8. Upon Confession: Moses Lefever, and wife Margaret Vernoy.

1814, June 25. Upon Confession : Jane Hardenbergh, wife of William Delemater.

1814, Sept. 18. Admitted to Baptism and Membership : Mary Geer, wife of Zacariah York.

1814, Nov. 9. Upon Confession : Nelly Bogart, wife of Peter D. Fraligh, Isaac Bovier, and wife Mary York.

1815, April 12. Admitted to Baptism and Membership : Dolly Geer, wife of Elias York.

1815, May 5. Upon Confession : Charles Dubois, and wife Maria.

List of Members copied from Vol. IV. of the original :

Register of the members of the newly founded Congregation at the New Paltz.

1767. On August 29th were acknowledged and accepted as members of this congregation upon dismissal from the Consistory of Kingston, to be seen in the commencement of this book : Josia Eltinge, Noach Eltinge, Petrus Van Wagenen, Jacob DuBoys, Rebecka Van Wagenen, Dirk D. Wynkoop, Magdalena DuBoys, Jacomyntje Eltinge, Sarah Low.

On the same day were also accepted as members : Petrus Low, Henricus DuBoys, Salomon Low, Isaac Low, Debora Van Vliet, Jannetje Hooghteiling.

1768, May 2. Were admitted as members of this Congregation by Do. Gerhard Daniel Cock, after a previous confession of their faith : Rulof Josia Eltinge, Jacobus Achtmoethe, Abraham Eltinge, Salomon Eltinge, Cornelius Eltinge, David Louw, Hendricus Dubois, Jr., Maria Louw, wife of Rulof Josia Eltinge, Sarah Elting, wife of Dirk Wynkoop, Catharyntien Eltinge, Lea Duboys, Elizabeth Louw, Annatien Elting, Dina Duboys, wife of Abraham Eltinge, Margaretha Lucy, or Huey, Rachel Duboys.

1768, May 22. Upon Certificate from Kingston, Judith Van Vliet, wife of Salomon Low.

1770, May 14. Upon Confession : Ann Huy, Rebecca Van Wagenen, wife of Hendricus DuBoys, Jr.

1776, Sept. 28. With Letters : Sarah Bosch, wife of Salomon Louw.

Found among the Consistory Records.

1775, June 2. Consistory of congregation at Shawengonk met at the house belonging to the congregation now occupied by Jacobus Van de Lyn, and after calling upon God's name, admitted the following persons as members of this congregation : Jacob Reynhart, Maria Winfield, wife of Abram Dekker ; Maria Terwilliger, wife of Jacob Dekker.

1775, Oct. 30. Elected at the house of Cornelius Dubois, New Paltz : As Elder : Abram Elting, in place of Jacob Dubois. As Deacon : Henry Dubois, Jr., in place of Dirck Wyncoop.

1776, Dec. 16. Elected at the house of Cornelius Dubois, at New Paltz : As Elder : Dirck Wynkoop, in place of Salomon Low. As Deacon : David Low, in place of Solomon Elting.

MARRIAGES.

(From Book No. 2 in Dutch.)

The following three items are translations from entries in French, found among the baptismal records in Vol. II.

1731, Oct. 8. Gemes Acmoidec married Mari Doyo, daughter of Christianne Doyo and Mary LeConte.

1732, Aug. 25. Jonatan DuBoy married Elisabet LeFeuer.

1733-4, Jan. 25. Wessel Brades married Caterine DuBois.

1733-4, Jan. 25. Married, after three previous publications : Wessel Broadhead and Catherina Du Boy.

1734, April 2. Married by me, Johannes Van Driessen, V.D.M.. and after three previous publications in our French Church : Daniel Haasbroek and Wyntie De Joy.

1734, Oct. 14. After three publications : Jan Gasherie, widower, and Maria Haasbroek.

1735, June 24. After three publications : Simon LeFever and Petronella Haasbroek.

1735, Oct. 30. After three publications : Abraham DuBoy and Elizabeth DuBoy.

1735, Dec. 19. After three publications : Joannes Lau and Rebecca Frere.

1737, June 17. After three publications : Matheus Lefever and Margerita Bevier.

1742, Oct. 7. Married by Zacharias Hoffman, Esq., after three publications, by Daniel Haasbrouque: Simon DuBois, Y.M., and Catrina Lefevre, Y.D.

1745, Oct. 20. After three proclamations : Andrias Le Fever and Rachel DuBois, in our French Church at New Paltz.

1749, Sept 2. Married by Cornelius DeBois, Esq., after three publications by Daniel Hasbrouque : Johannes Beviere, Y.M., and Magdalena Le Febre, Y.D.

1751, April 12. After three publications : Johannes Hardenberg, Jr., Y.M., and Maria Le Fevre, Y.D.

April 14. After three publications : Jacob Haasbrouque, Y.M., and Janetje DuBoys, Y.D.

April 16. After three publications. At Bontekoe : Hugo Terwilge, Y.M., and Janetje Freer, Y.D.

April 21. After three publications. In church : Benjamin Terwilge, Y.M., and Elsje Freer, Y.D.

March —. Daniel Lefebre, Y.M., and Catryntje Cantyn, Y.D.

Nov. 1. Edward Woed, Y.M., and Catrina Van der Merke, Y.D.

Those married in 1751 were united by Rev. J. Henry Goetschius.

1752, May 29. After three publications : Johanes Lefeber, Y.M., and Sara Vernoy, Y.D.

1752, June 1. After three publications : Abraham Hardenberg, widower, and Mary Chasherje, widow.

1752, Nov. 27. After three publications : Benjamin Haasbroek, Y.M., and Lidia Schoonmaeker, Y.D.

1753, Nov. 17. Jan Teerpenning and Elizabeth Aalsdorf.

1761, Dec. 20. Registered : Daniel Dojo, Y.M., and Margritt Lefefer, Y.D., both born and living at New Paltz.

1760. Registered. Married by J. Mauritius Goetschius : Jonathan Freres Terwilliger or Terwilliger Freres, Y.M., born at Shaw, living at New Paltz, and Maria Freres, widow, born and living at New Paltz.

1750, Aug. 5. By Fryenmoet, John Mounin, Y.M., born in Rhode Island, and Elizabeth Clark, Y.D., born at Kleyn Esopus, both living near Paltz.

1755, Aug. 25. After three proclamations : Benjamin Freer, Y.M., born and living at Paltz, and Elisabeth Terwilgen, Y.D., born at Shawenkonk, living at Paltz.

The following entry was taken from Book No. 2, and found by itself between several blank leaves :

1761, Jan. 18. Married : Jonathan Terwilligen, Y.M., born at Shawenkonk, and Maria Freres, widow, born at New Paltz, both living at New Paltz.

1762, Sept. 12. Registered : Williem Lits, Y.M., born at Kinderhoek, living at Kingston, and Deborah Shmith, Y.D., born and living at Hoorley. Married last Wednesday in September.

1763, Jan. 1. Registered : Zacharius Sluyter, Y.M., living at Horely, and Breggie York, Y.D., living at New Paltz, both born at Hoorley.

1764, Feb. 1–12. Registered. Married February 26 at Nath. Lefever's : Henry Green, Y.M., born at New York, living at Hoorley, and Maria Dojou, Y.D. of Mr. Isaak Dojou, born and living at New Paltz.

1764, Oct. 26. Abraham Dojou, Jr., Y.M., and Elsjie Lefever, Y.D., both born and living at New Paltz.

1765, Aug. . . Jonas Hasbroek, Y.M., born and living at New Paltz, and Cathrina Dubois, Y.D., born and living at Rochester.

The entry below was found in Book 3, between several blank leaves :

1765, Aug. 3. Registered : Jonas Haasbroek, Y.M., born and living at New Paltz, and Cathrina Dubois, Y.D., born and living at Rochester.

The following entries were taken from Book No. 4 :

1767, Aug. 30. License. Married by Do. Isaac Rysdyk : Peter Swart, Y.M., and Jannetje Persen, Y.D., both born and living at Kingston.

1768, Nov. 1. Married by Do. G. D. Cock, Hendricus Du Boys, Jr., Y.M., and Rebecca Van Wagenen, Y.D.

The following marriages were taken from Book No. 3 :

1765, Oct. 25. Daniel Freres, Y.M., and Annatie Dojou, Y. D., both born and living at New Paltz.

1765, Oct. 26. Petrus Hasbroek, Y.M., and Sarah Bevirs, Y.D., both born and living at New Paltz.

1766, Jan. 19. Registered. Married February 17 : Johannes Walderaan, Y.M., living at Keyserryk, and Elisabeth Eyn, Y.D., living at New Paltz, both born at New Paltz.

Jan. 19. Registered : Francis Kain, Y.M., born and living at Shawankong, and Elisabeth Graham, Y.D., born and living at Walekill.

Jan. 19. Registered : Jacob De Wit Schoonmaker, Y.M., and Jacomeyntie Van Wagene, Y.D.

Feb. 23. Registered. Married March 9 : Josaphat Haasbroek, Y.M., and Cornelia Dubois, Y.D., both born and living at New Paltz.

June 25. Registered. Married July 3 : Joseph Don, Y. M., born in Pennsylvania, and Mary Wikem, Y.D., born at Newburg, both living at New Paltz.

Sept. 7. Registered. Married October 17 : Joseph Freres, Y.M., born and living at New Paltz, and Saartie Terwilliger, Y.D., born and living at Shawankong.

Oct. 25. Registered. Married November 9, 1766. Matheus Decker, Y.M., born and living at Shawankong, and Magdalena Bevirs, Y.D., born and living at New Paltz.

Same date. Registered. Married November 9 : Petrus Ancton, Y. M., born at Paris, France, and Margritta Dojou, Y. D., born at New Paltz, both living at New Paltz.

Same date. Registered : Married November 17 : Daniel Freres, Y.M., and Maria Helm, Y.D., both born and living at Horely.

Same date. Registered. Married November 21, by Abraham Hardenberg, Esq. : Willem Whehler, Y. M., and Paggy Killy, Y. D., both born at Horely and living at New Paltz.

Same date. Registered. Married, December 25 at New Paltz : Jeremiah Johnston, Y.M., born on Staten Island, living at Shawankong, and Phebe Brouwn, Y.D., born in New Jersey, living at Newburg.

Dec. 28. Registered. George Harding, Y.M., and Elisabeth Cassman, Y.D. Married I don't know where. (Remark of the registrar in original.)

1767.
Mar. 13. Johannes Alsdorf, Y.M., and Agetta Dojou, Y.D.
Apr. 12. Johannes Dojou, Jr., Y.M., and Lea Vandermerken, Y.D.
May 21. George Ervin, Y.M., and Rachel Dotting, Y.D.

Aug. 18.	Daniel Dubois, Y.M., and Catreyntie Lefefer, Y.D.
Sept. 14.	Coenrad Burger, and Rachel Dojou, Y.D.
Nov. 22.	Petrus Smedes, Jr., Y.M., and Elsjie Hasbroek, Y.D.
1768.	
Jan. 13.	Abraham Bevirs, Jr., Y.M., and Maria Dubois, Y.D.
Oct. (?) 22.	Jacob Jacobse Freres, Y.M., and Margriet Een.
March 17.	Jonathan Ostrander, Y.M., from the Paltz, and Lydia Terwilliger, Y.D., from Shawankong.
— —.	Hendrik Dojou and Anetie Schut, married by an Esquire.
Nov. 25.	Elysa Freres, Y.M., and Martha Everit, Y.D.
1769.	
March 9.	Nathanael Lefefer, Y.M., and Maria Dojouw, Y.D.
June 10.	Benjamin Sluyter, Y.M., and Margritt Berner, Y.D.
Oct. 14.	Jonas Freres, Y.M , and Madlena Bevirs, Y.D.
Nov. 25.	Petrus Burger, Y.M., and Cathrina Dojou, Y.D.
Dec. 2.	Matheus Bevir, Y.M. and Jacomeyntie Bevir, Y.D.
1770.	
Jan. 6.	Petrus Freres, Y.M., and Annatie Dubois, Y.D.
Jan. 20.	Jacobus Roos, Jr., widower, and Mareya Dubois, Y.D.
Feb. 16.	John Camzon, Y.M., and Elsy McMullan, Y.D.
Feb. 17.	Petrus Johannes Schonmaker, Y.M., and Rachel Hasbroek, widow.
1773.	
Oct. 4.	Georg Wirtz, Y.M., and Esther Hasbroek, Y.D.
1780.	
Oct. 16.	Stephanus Goetschius and Elizabeth Dubois.
1781.	
Jan. 6.	Wilhelmus Ostrander, Y.M., and Ester Benks, Y.D.
Jan. 10.	Nathaniel Web, Jr., Y.M., and Margrietje Doio, Y.D.
1783.	
Nov. - -	John Lefever and Elizabeth Dubois.
Nov. 20.	Wessel Dubois and Catarina Lefever.
Dec. 10.	Jeremias Wesmiller and Syntje Stricland.
Dec. 11.	Cornelius Polhemus and Phebe Sherad.
Dec. 14.	Daniel Everett and Anne Penny.
Dec. 25.	Josia Elting, Jr., and Ester Broadhead.

1784.
March 26. Dennis Coleman and Tjatje Roos.
June - - . Zacharias Hasbrouck and Rebecca Wering.
April - - . Martynus Frere and Maria Frere.
June 24.   Daniel Sluiter and Sara Bavier.
July 4.   Abram Elting, widower, and Dorothe Besmer, Y.D.
Oct. 3.   Jacobus Terwilger and Henna Burwell of New Hurly.
Oct. 31.   Jonathan Odle and Caty Terwilger at New Hurly.
Nov. 5.   Noach Lefever and Cornelia Bovier at New Hurly.
Nov. 6.   Hendrick Wesmiller, widower, and Anna Sluiter, widow, at New Paltz.
Nov. 11.   Moses Gee and Phebe Lane at New Paltz.
Nov. - -.   Ezechiel Frere and Elizabeth Sluiter.

1785.
March 10.   Abram P. (or D,) Doio and Anne Broadhead at New Paltz.
March 11.   Martynus Klaarwater and Lea Sluiter.
March 20.   James Ervin and Jannetje Van Keure, widow.
March 21.   Salomon Banker and Debora Numan.
March 23.   William A. Dewitt and Lea Dubois.

1787.
Jan. 15.   Jacob Low and Rebecca Van Wagen, widow.
Jan. 9.   Jehu Low and Elizabeth Snyder.

1795.
Feb. 26.   Abram Crispel, widower, and Jackemyntje Blonshan, widow.

REGISTER OF MARRIAGES BY JOHN H. MEIER, V.D.M., NEW PALTZ AND NEW HURLEY.

1799.
Nov. 19.   Cornelius Bruyn Dubois and Rebecca Dubois.
Dec. 8.   Dr. Garrit Hoornbeek and Lena Bennet.
Dec. 15.   Abraham Cherry and Elizabeth Ostrander.
Dec. 19.   Jacob I. Hasbrook and Ann Dubois.
1800.
Jan. 2.   Philip Cooper and Rebecca Dubois.
Jan. 29.   Joseph Seaman and Elizabeth Irwin.
Feb. 6.   Abraham Scutt (?) and Margaret Myer.
March 5.   Henry Dubois and Elizabeth Dejo.
March 20.   John Rose and Hannah Palmiteer.

April 24.	Archa P. Van Wagenen and Mary Freer.
June 29.	Jonas Freer and Wyntie Hasbrook.
Same date.	William McDonald and Mary Dubois.
July 10.	Walter Dubois, Jr., and Hannah Bodine.
July 11.	Jacob Hardenbergh and Jane Dubois.
Aug. 6.	Daniel Lowe and Elizabeth Gerow.
Aug. 20.	Stephen Terwilliger and Wyntie Freer.
Aug. 24.	John Jinkins and Mary Brodhead.
Sept. 7.	Solomon Eltinge, widower, and Treyntie Lowe, widow of Wilhelmus Schoonmaker.
Sept. 18.	John Swart and Lydia Pettey (?)
Oct. 12.	Moses Lefever and Margaret Vernoy.
Oct. 16.	Benjamin Terwilliger and Sarah Saxon.
Oct. 30.	Henry Alsdorf and Eve MacCollum.
Oct. 30.	Abraham Van Aken and Caty Teerpenning.
Nov. 6.	Isaac I. Lowe and Antje York.
Dec. 24.	William Brown and Jane Vandermerk.
Dec. 31.	Roelef Eltinge and Dinah Elting.
1801.	
Jan. 7.	Daniel Wilkeloo and Sally Palmitier.
Jan. 14.	James Scott and Hannah Keyser.
Jan. 29.	Mathuselah Dubois and Maria Lowe.
Feb. 5.	Jacob Wirtz and Treyntie Dubois.
Feb. 12.	Benjamin Constable and Mary Dunn.
April 5.	Benjamin A. Dojo and Sarah Freer.
April 12.	Robert Hood and Martha Wakman.
May 7.	Petrus P. Schoonmaker and Else Terwilliger.
June 24.	James Requa and Lena Dojo.
June 28.	Andrew Vernoy and Eliza Masten.
June 28.	Alexander Coe and Elizabeth Dubois.
July 2.	Evert Sluyter and Sarah Wakman.
July 4.	Jonathan Sluyter and Elizabeth York.
July 5.	Jacob Blanshou and Hannah Haynes.
Aug. 2.	Abraham Harris and Maria Waldron.
Aug. 27.	Michael Shearman and Abby Patty.
Sept. 5.	Cornelius Delamater and Lena Ostrander.
Oct. 17.	Peter York, Jr., and Sarah Freer, widow of Hugo (?) Sluyter.
Oct. 25.	Peleg Stevens and Hannah Moore.
Nov. 1.	Lodewyk Weller and Nancy Michaels.
Nov. 8.	Ebbert Dewitt and Wyntie Davis, widow of Richard Loundsbury.
Nov. 8.	Johannes I. Lefevre and Jane Lowe.
Nov. 12.	William Traphagen and Maria Alsdorf.

Dec. 1.	Isaac Squire and Sally Bishop.
Dec. 3.	Uriah Pride and Jane Van Buntschooter, widow of Abraham (?) McCollum.
Dec. 17.	David Teerpenning and Sally Van Steenberghen.
Dec. 27.	Thomas Hunter and Deborah Davenport.
Dec. 31.	Jacob Quick and Sally Forman.
1802.	
Jan. 7.	Uriah Gee and Lena Swart.
Jan 14.	Benjamin Schoonmaker and Maria Van Bommel.
Feb. 4.	Peter R. Johnson and Jane Dojo.
Feb. 7.	Henry Broune and Sarah Collier.
Feb. 16.	Joseph Dunn and Caty Bodine.
Feb. 18.	Benjamin Hasbrook and Rachel Hasbrook.
Feb. 18.	John Johnson and Jane Cosselin (?) (Corichin?) (Conclin?)
Feb. 24.	Eliphas Smith and Elizabeth York.
Feb. 25.	Richard Youngs and Rachel Dunn.
March 11.	Peter Een and Maria Freer.
March 24.	David Terwilliger and Maria Vandermark.
April 1.	Thomas Tompkins and Caty Vansile (?) widow.
April 18.	Abraham Jansen and Maritje Hardenburgh, widow.
June 13.	John Dinghee and —— Niffins.
July 18.	Andrew I. Lefever and Maria Bovier.
Aug. 1.	James Mitchell and Christina Cameron.
Aug. 15.	Charles Vernoy and Sarah Dubois.
Aug 26.	John Nees and Mercy Johnson.
Aug. 29.	Wm. Jenkins and Salome Goetchius.
Sept. 2.	Edward Parleman and Eve Windfield.
Sept. 5.	Jonathan Johnson and Gertrude Terwilliger.
Sept. 19.	Simon Rost and Ruth Terwilliger.
Oct. 2.	Isaac Van Wagenen and Maria Smits.
Oct. 8.	James S. Bruyn, Jr., and Anne Graham.
Nov. 28.	Josiah Doyo and Hannah Merrit.
Dec. 2.	Isaac Bevier and Maria York.
Dec. 2.	Christian Freer and Anne Freer.
Dec. 2.	Jacob Wiept or Wiesst and Elizabeth Crowes.
Dec. 29.	Lewis Hasbrook and Caty Banks.
Dec. 30.	Joshua Freer and Rachel Schoonmaker.
1803.	
March 18.	Herman M. Hardenbergh and Else Hasbrook.
March 20.	Elias Freer and Caty Teerpenning.
March 21.	Dennis Ostrander and Maria Klaarwater.
April 10.	Marinus Wiest and Catharina Sluyter.

A REGISTER OF MARRIAGES PERFORMED BY PETER D. FREELIGH, WHILE MINISTER OF THE CONGREGATIONS OF NEW PALTZ AND NEW HURLEY.

1808.
May 26.   John Warner and Maria Ostrander.
May 29.   James McCullogh and Catharine Louw.
June 2.   Daniel Slott and Betsy Stevans.
June 16.   Ezzekiel Sparks and Deborah York.
June 23.   Henry Ostrander and Ann Russel.
June 30.   Dr. John Bogardus and Gitty Lefever.
July 27.   Mathew Johnson and Hetty Laroy.
Aug. 7.   Peter York and Esther Simmons.
Aug. 21.   John Hogg and Betsy Le Munyer.
Sept. 11. Nathaniel Kniffins and Maria Freer.
Sept. 24. Augustine Dickensen and Elizabeth Pardee.
Oct. 10.   Jacobus Eltinge and Jane Rosa.
Oct. 21.   Jacob Halstead and Charity Van Aker.
Oct. 24.   Josiah Hasbrook and Elizabeth Viele.
Nov. 25.   Joseph Dubois and Maria Beesemere.
Dec. 18.   Charles Snyder and Elizabeth Decker.
Dec. 29.   John Shearman and Lea Ostrander.
1809.
Jan. 25.   Cornelius Ostrander and Elenor Everett.
Feb. 2.   John Snyder and Elizabeth Wilson.
Feb. 12.   John Pagh and Hannah Degroof.
Feb. 15.   William Hasbrook and Rachel Hasbrook.
Feb. 15.   William Stratton (?) and Tyny Traphagen.
Feb. 16.   Henry Hunt and Anny Snyder.
Feb. 16.   Noah Tearpenning and Polly Slotte.
Feb. 23.   Simon Rose and Elizabeth Hasbrook.
Feb. 26.   Simon Masten and Maria Tank (or Yank).
March 12. Jacobus Van Ostrant and Rachel Hill.
March 12. Solomon P. Hasbrook and Magdaline Lefever.
March 16. Solomon Lauw and Anny Dunn.
April 12. Jacob Terwilliger and Betsy Saxon.
April 30. Cornelius Rank and Mary, widow of George Kimbergh.
April 30. Thomas R. Hardenbergh and Rachel Bovier.
May 11.   William Irwin and Caty Forman.
June —.   Jonathan Freer and —— Auchmoedy.
June 30.   James N. Lefever and Elizabeth Johnson.
July 2.   Abraham Seaman and Lany Wintfield.
July 27.   Thomas Lemunyen and Phabe Lockwood.

July 29.	Richard Chambers and Elizabeth Beesemere.
Aug. 3.	Benjamin Constable and Hannah Traphagen.
Aug. 13.	Abraham Lefever and Sarah Lefever.
Sept. 21.	Meyndert Redmin and Fanny Maybee.
Oct. 19.	Joseph Hasbrook and Jane Hasbrook.
Oct. 28.	Thomas Klaerwater and Eve Davis.
Oct. 29.	Robert Lawson and Nancy Klayton.
Nov. 4.	Cornelius Delemater and Anny Sluyter.
Nov. 4.	Robert Todd and Lydia Ostrander.
Nov. 9.	Philip Bunton and Lany Kidney.
Nov. 16.	Cornelius Schryver and Lucretia Hull.
Dec. 14.	Mathew McCollum and Caty Steenbergh.
1810.	
Jan. 4.	Zadok Thorn and Jane Redmin, N. H.
Jan. 7.	Jacob Vandemerk and Susan Kimbergh, N. H.
Jan. 21.	Jonathan Clayton and Rebeccah Johnson, N. P.
Jan. 28.	James Sammons and Clara Brewster, N. P.
Jan. 30.	Philip Hasbrouk and Hetty Bovier, N. P.
Jan. 30.	Benjamin Deyoo and Sarah Dewitt, N. P.
Jan. 30.	David Deyoo and Catherine Freer.
Feb. 1.	John Billigee and Sally Rank, N. H.
Feb. 14.	Reverend Jacob R. H. Hasbrouk and Caty Davis, N.P.
Feb. 15.	Solomon Danelson and Jane Polhemus, N. P.
Feb. 25.	Oliver Smith and Patty Ferguson.
March 1.	Abraham Traphagen and Caty Dubois, N. P.
March 15.	John Slott and Rebeccah Sluyter, N. P.
March 22.	Ezzekiel Bovier and Nelly Van Bomelle.
March 29.	Abraham Hasbrouk and Mary Blenchan.
April 15.	Henry Tearpenning and Sally Byram.
April 20.	Christian Bovier and Magdalina Freer.
May 12.	James Kreig? and Anny Freer.
May 17.	James Titus and Anny Dubois.
May 24.	Daniel Terwilliger and Jane Vandemark.
June 3.	Henry Jones and Catherine Sparks.
July 7.	—— Barley and Betsy Freer.
July 26.	John I. Deyoo and Caty Wirtz.
Sept. 2.	Stephan Masten and Widow —— Archbald.
Sept. 13.	John Brown and Mary VandeMark.
Sept. 20.	Abraham Constable and Sarah Terwiliger.
Oct. 22.	Edward Claerwater and Elizabeth Freer.
Oct. 26.	Henry Deyoo Eltinge and Rebeccah Miller.
Oct. 26.	Benjamin Van Wagener and Sarah Ean.
Oct. 26.	George Dunn and Rebeccah Dubois.

Dec. 12.	Zachariah Hoyt and Mynje Kimbergh.
Dec. 22.	Soloman Cornwell and Eunice Ellis.
Dec. 29.	Jacob Sammons and Mary Crom.
Dec. 30.	Joseph Eltinge and Sarah Hardenburgh.
1811.	
Jan. 2.	William Vreedenburgh and Sally Terwiliger.
Jan. 13.	Peter Hasbrouck and Anny Freer.
Feb. 1.	Thomas Sammons and Maria Freer.
Feb. 14.	Henry Van Wyen and Elchie Freer.
Fec. 14.	Samuel Hasbrouck and Lydia Crispel.
March 17.	Jonathan Bovier and Judith Louw.
March 21.	Daniel Archer and Elizabeth Snyder.
March 31.	Reuben C. Kraig and Katherin Delemerter.
April 11.	Joseph Dubois, widower, and Maria Hardenbergh, widow of Simon Deyoo.
April 14.	John Campbell and Polly Raymond.
May 2.	Joseph Lemungen and Lany Danelson.
May 16.	Reuben Decker and Mary Snyder.
May 30.	William W. Deyoo and Sarah Hasbrouk.
May 30.	Jonathan Lefever Jr. and Dinah Hasbrouk.
June 23.	Simon Mullen and Lany Bovier.
June 29.	Abraham Relyea and Widow Rachel Deyoo.
June 30.	Richard Hardenberg and Maria Crispel.
July 4.	John B. Deyoo, widower, and Widow Deborah Tearpenning.
July 7.	David Tank and Jane Tank, (or Rank.)
Aug. 10.	Peter Dubois and Anny Blanchan.
Aug. 15.	Peter Stryker and Anny Dunn, widow of ―― Louw.
Aug. 24.	Art Freer and Maria Smith.
Sept. 8.	John Irwin and Betsy Hoffman.
Oct. 6.	Peter Redmen and Sally Bodine.
Oct. 31.	James Hais and Jane Saxton.
Dec. 1.	John Halstead and Maria Terwilliger.
Dec. 9.	Uriah Lockwood and Charity Terwilliger.
Dec. 9.	William Terwilliger and Susan Hunt.
1812.	
Jan. 1.	Henry Snyder and Lea Shurager.
Jan. 2.	Henry Dunn and Elizabeth Terwilliger.
Jan. 4.	Jacob Hutchins and Rhoda Wood.
Jan. 8.	Johannes Lefever and Sarah Dubois.
Jan. 22.	John Saxon and Catharine York.
Feb. 14.	Evert Hoffman and Lea Alsdorf.
Feb. 21.	Joseph Myndard and Susannah Macky.

Feb. 29.	Simon Freer and Maria Agmoedy.
Feb. 29.	John Freer and Eve Agmoedy.
Feb. 29.	Charles Gray and Sarah Terwilliger.
March 11.	Jonathan Louw and Jane Yendell.
March 15.	John Schoonmaker and Maria Deyoo.
March 26.	Aaron Saxton and Polly Wilkelow.
March 30.	Charles Eltinge and Lany Bovier.
April 30.	Jeremiah Bovier and Wyntje Smith.
April 30.	Isaac Hood and Elizabeth Freer.
May 22.	Elijah Aliger and Hannah Decker.
May 26.	Joseph Deyoo and Jane Deyoo.
June 7.	Zechariah D. Bayard and Rachel Weller.
June 7.	Jacob Schoonmaker and Anny Bayard.
June 10.	Abraham Deyoo, Jr., and Margaret Deyoo.
July 12.	Peter Klaerwater and Hannah Terwilliger.
July 12.	Josiah Wintfield and Peggy Webb.
July 19.	Matthew Sammons and Betsy Deyoo.
Aug. 16.	John Underhill and Hannah Berchal.
Aug. 23.	Abraham I. Deyoo and Maria Deyoo.
Sept. 8.	Levi Decker and Polly Dickinson.
Sept. 18.	Myndert Kidney and Hannah Bunton.
Sept. 24.	Peter Alsdorf and Ann Ostrander.
Sept 26.	Robert Kidney and Altje Hasbrouck.
Oct. 15.	John Hood and Rachel Freer.
Nov. 8.	James Owen and Rachel Wilson.
Nov. 26.	John Bearns and Rachel Van Ostrant.
Dec. 5.	Abraham Parleman and Rachel Steenbergh.
Dec. 24.	Simon Dubois and Hannah Sahler.
Dec. 31.	Caleb Simens and Esther Seaman.
1813.	
Jan. 10.	Ira Munson and Catherine Bayard.
Jan. 10.	John Hornbeek and Gertrude Dubois.
Jan. 20.	Thomas Dunn and Catherine Seaman.
Jan. 28.	John Van Steenbergh and —— Frere.
Feb. 17.	Abel Smith and —— Ostrander.
Feb. 18.	John Rank and —— Smith.
Feb. 20.	William Forsyth and Sarah Keesler.
Feb. 25.	Garrit Freer and Maria Waldron.
March 7.	Cornelius Brodhead and Dinah Eltinge.
March 16.	John Acker and Laura Hull.
April 7.	Henry Lockwood and Amy Selks.
April 22.	Daniel Louw and Huldah Elmore.
April 22.	Ezekiel Van Steenbergh and Joanna Terwilliger.
May 7.	—— Cosens and Jane Freeligh.

May 20.	Christopher Deyoo and Anny Freer, widow of Benjamin Dubois.
May 20.	Obadiah Terwilliger and Sally Ostrander.
May 27.	Jacob Freer and Anny or Amy Smith.
June 25.	Andrew Brown and Elsy Deyoo.
July 4.	Christian Deyoo and Nelly Hardenbergh.
July 8.	William Silkworth and Sally Palmatier.
Aug. 12.	Robert McCord and Jane Anderson.
Sept. 2.	Jeremiah Freer, Jr. and —— Vandemark.
Oct. 22.	Albert Jenkins and Maria Roosekrans.
Oct. 22.	—— Freer and —— Roose.
Nov. 7.	Townsend Bross and Rachel Van Natten.
Nov. 13.	Ephraim Stokes and Eliza Countryman.
Nov. 13.	William H. Ackert and Sophia Tearpenning.
Nov. 25.	Abraham Schoonmaker and Maria Sammons.
Dec. 2.	Nathaniel Dubois and Jacemyntje Blenchan.
Dec. 2.	Rolif S. Eltinge and Catherina Lefever.
Dec 26.	James Masten and Maria Whelpley.
1814.	
Jan 13.	Silvester Ostrander and Rebeccah Ostrander.
Jan. 15.	Samuel Raiment and —— Pardee.
Jan. 16.	Dennis Relyea and Catherine Smith.
Jan. 23.	Abraham Baxter and Cornelia Rank.
Jan. 23.	Jacob Jansen and Sophia Upregt.
Feb. 3.	Matthew Lefever and Sarah Lefever,
Feb. 17.	Abraham Lefever and Margaret Johnson.
Feb. 17.	John Burger and Sally Van Vliet.
Feb. 20.	John Claerwater and Hannah Crouse.
Feb. 20.	Martinus Davis and Wyntje Krom.
Feb. 24.	Abraham Vandelyn and ——
March 3.	William Tremper and Catherine Redmin, widow.
March 24.	Cornelius B. Van Wagenen and Sarah Sluyter.
April 5.	William Bearns and Widow Atkins.
April 14.	Lewis Schoonmaker and Jane Van Wagenen.
May 3.	Cornelius Carman and Gitty Wackman.
May 22.	James Quemby and Caty Davenport.
May 22.	Abraham Wooly and —— Dusenbury.
May 28.	Henry Deyo and Elizabeth Bovier.
June 21.	John Troup and Nelly Stokes.
July 11.	Henry Freer and Magdaline Smith.
July 17.	Nathaniel Deyoo and Catherine Hardenbergh.
May 29.	—— Degraff and —— Wesmiller.
Aug. 6.	—— S. North and Elizabeth Rosekrans.
Aug. 14.	John Deyoo and Ann Beesimere.

Sept. 22.	Simon H. Deyoo and Lea Lattin.
Oct. 6.	Jeremiah Masten and Mary Paulis.
Oct. 12.	William A. Weast and Rachel Leminger.
Oct. 12.	Noah Hasbrouck and Polly Branin.
Oct. 27.	Benjamin Upright and Ida Masten.
Oct. 27.	John Baylree and Jane Terwilliger.
Nov. 3.	Justus Sexton and Rebeccah Simmons.
Dec. 13.	Daniel Woolsy and Elizabeth Deyoo.
Dec. 29.	Gerrit Newkirk and Maria Bovier.
1815.	
Jan. 6.	Henry Dickinson Gue and Phoebe Smith.
Jan. 7.	Abraham Dubois and Halen (?) Jenkins.
Jan. 14.	Reuben Ostrander and Tyny Traphagen.
Jan. 15.	David Alsdorf and Hannah Jenkins.
Jan. 16.	Benjamin Hasbrouck, widower, and Mary Terwilliger, widow.
Jan. 26.	Jesse Lounsberry and Elizabeth Sinsapagh.
Jan. 28.	James De Hart and Margaret Sinsapagh.
Feb. 2.	Smith Rensem and Maria Lefever.
Feb. 19.	—— Sinsapagh and Tempy Alsdorf.
March 11.	John I. Hogteling and Gitty Louw.
March 25.	Daniel Roose and Widow Jane Sexton.
April 4.	—— Miller and —— Wackman.
May 22.	Lefever Dubois and Rebeccah Johnson, widow.
May 25.	John Halsted and Mary Wells.
June 1.	Philip Rank and Polly Dunn.
June 8.	Christopher Lefever and —— Deyoo.
June 11.	—— Vandemark and Mary Weller.
June 18.	Philip Dubois and Hetty Freer.
Sept. 14.	Daniel Riqua (?) and ——Merrit (?).
Oct. 12.	George D. L. Montanye and Margaret Burger.
Oct. 12.	Cornelius Reediker and Sally Teers.
Oct. 19.	Miles Wells and Jane Green.

BAPTISMS.

From Vol. II. of the New Paltz Reformed Dutch Church Book which are in Dutch with an occasional French entry.

1729, Aug. 10. Sara, child of Evert and Sara Ter Wellinge. Witnesses: This Feure, Jannetie Freure.

1730, June 28. Elzie, child of Yzaak and Maria Frere. Witnesses: Daniel and Maria DuBoy.

Maria, child of Anthony and Aaltie Westbroeck. Witnesses: Johannes, Jr., and Maria Hardenbergh.

1731, March 21. Loys, child of Johannes and Mary Hardenbergh.
Witnesses : Nathaniel and Catharina DuBoys.

Lena, child of Jeames and Geessie Spenieneck.
Witnesses : Jeames Achmudi, Lena Deckers.

Ariaantje, child of Petrus and Margaretha Terwillingh.
Witnesses : Abram and Wyntje Dejo.

May 30. Salomon, child of Sammuell and Maghdalena Bevier.
Witnesses: Simeon and Elizabeth LeFever.

Aug. 15. Johanna, child of Edward and Sara Whieler.
Witnesses : Nicolaas and Sara Roos.

1732, June 18. Christiaan, child of Mozes and Claartje Dejo.
Witnesses : Abraham Bevier, Maria Stockeraat.

Oct. 1. Daniel, child of Salomon and Sara Haasbroek.
Witnesses : Daniel and Marie DuBoy.

1733, Jan. 7. Charels, child of Johannes and Maria Hardenbergh.
Witnesses : Chareles and Maretie Broadhead.

Feb. 11. Hendrik, child of Willem and Eva Smith.
Witnesses : Zymon Helm, Elizabeth Hefer.

Sept. 16. Sara, child of Hendrik and Marghriet DeJoy.
Witnesses : Salomon and Sara Haasbroek.

Feb. 11. Samuel, Abraham, Mary, children of Thomas and Elizabeth Smith.
Witnesses : Nicolaas and Sara Roos, Jacob and Hester Haasbroek, Sammuel and Lena Beuvier.

May 20. Martynus, child of Jonas and Catharina Freer.
Witnesses : Simon Le Fever, Rebecka Freer.

Elizabeth, child of Thos. and Elizabeth Smith.
Witnesses : Abraham and Elzie Haasbroeck.

Nicholaas, child of Richard and Elizabeth Davids.
Witnesses : Nicholaas and Sara Roosa.

Luiis, child of Jonathan and Elizabeth DuBoy.
Witnesses : Luiis DuBoy, Catharina DuBois.

1734, March 24. Margaretha, child of John and Catharine Wilzon.
Witnesses : Jacob Watch, Lena Raillie.

Annatje, child of Willem and Marghriet Sluyter.
Witnesses : Dirck Ceyzer, Lea Van der Schuyven.

Maria, child of Mozes and Klaartie De Joy.
Witnesses : Jan and Maria Yn.

Yzaak, child of Yzaak Freere, and Maria De Joy.
Witnesses : Abraham De Joy, Elizabeth De Boy.

Abraham and Sarah, children of Zymon and Anna Helm.
Witnesses : Nicolaas and Sarah Roos, Gerrit and Anna Neuwkerk.

June 23. James, child of Andries and Beelletie Graham.
Witnesses : Nicholaas and Sara Roos.

Oct. 6. Meyls, child of Meyls and Catharine Couwle.
Witnesses : Edward and Susanna Brouwn.

1735, March 9, born January 9. Marie, child of Daniel and Wyntie Haasbroeck.
Witnesses : Salomon and Sara Haasbroeck.

May 16. Marghriet, child of Mozes and Claartje Do Yoo.
Witnesses : Benjamin Du Boy, Marghriet Do Yoo.

Jonas, child of Daniel and Wyntje Haasbroek.
Witnesses : Abraham and Elizabeth Doyoo.

Sara, child of Simon and Petronella Le Fever.
Witnesses : Abraham and Sara Haasbroek.

Joseph, child of Yzaak and Maria Frere.
Witnesses : Yzaak and Elzie Haasbroek.

1736, May 23. Thomus, child of Richard and Elizabeth Davids.
Witnesses : Jacobus and Tryntje Bruyn.

The following 3 entries are in French, the baptisms having been performed by Rev. J. J. Moulinars.

1739, April 29. Josaphat, child of Jacob and Ester Hasbroek.
Witnesses : Daniel and Jacob Hasbrouck.

Catherine, child of Philippus and Catherine Smith.
Witnesses : Laurens and Maria Alsdorf.

May 6, bo. April 2. Martin, child of Jean and Caterine Griffens.
Witnesses : Daniel Hasbrouck, Vuyne (?) D'Oyo.

1740, June 8. David, child of Daniel and Waantea (sic) Harsbrook.
Witnesses : Isaac and Mary Frere.

Youncha, child of Johannes and Rebecca Low.
Witnesses : Isaac and Marieka Lefever.

Margareta, child of Lowrance and Maria Alsdraugh.
Witnesses : Honnes Urien, Claurah Rhauk.

Ury, child of Jacob and Annah Nice (?)
Witnesses : Ury Moues, Magdalenah Mauses.

The baptisms dated June 8, 1740, were performed by Rev. Isaac Chelker and written in English.
Those dated Sept. 14, are also written in English by the same minister.

Sept. 14. Lawrance, child of Johans Ury and Clarah Rong.
Witnesses : Lawrance Alsstorf, Maria Alsstorff.

Daniel, child of Abraham and Elisabeth Doeau.
Witnesses : Benjamin and Ester Debaen.

Andrew, child of Simon and Petronella Lefever.
Witnesses : Mathew and Margaret Lefever.

1749. June 4. By Rev. J. H. Goetschius, Zacharias, child of Daniel Hasbroek and Wyntje Du Yo.
Witnesses : Jacob Hasbroek, Jr., and wife Mary.

1750, April 22. Catharina, child of Benjamin Smedes and Rachel Janse.
Witnesses : Benjamin Smedes, Jr., Elsje Dekker.

Evert, child of Sacharyas Hoffman and Maria Terwillige.
Witnesses : Jan De Wit, Anna Preskit.

Pieter, child of Pieter Du Jo and Elizabeth Helm.
Witnesses : Daniel Hasbrouk, Wyntje Du Jo.

Margriet, child of Jurri Twies (?) and Elizabeth Smith.
Witnesses : Abram Du Jo, Elizabeth de Booy.

Jacob Rutse, child of Adriaan Nieuwkerk and Marretje Rutsen.
Witnesses : Abram Rooza, Elizabeth Rutsen.

Aug. 30. By Rev. J. C. Fryenmoet, aged 29 years. Antje, child of Johannis Louw and Rebecca Freer.
Witnesses : Salomon and Jannetje Louw.

Cornelia, child of Johannes Bevieer and Magdalena Le Fever.
Witnesses : Mattheus Le Fever, Margriet Bevieer.

Oct. 19. Amelyna, child of Jacob Sluyter and Lydia Keyser.
Witnesses: Zacharias and Annatje Sluyter.

Cataryntje, child of Abram Bevier and Margriet Elten.
Witnesses: Johannes Bevier, Madlena Le Fever.

Daniel, child of Simon DuBois and Catharina Le Fever.
Witnesses: Nathaniel and Marytje Le Fever.

Oct. 21. Jannetje, child of Ari Terwilliger and Grietje Vinnik.
Witnesses: Petrus and Marritje Cool.

Mari, child of Sacharias Klaarwater and Sara Terwilligen.
Witnesses: Hugo and Mari Terwilligen.

1741, June 8. By Rev. Isaäc Chalker, in English: Catharina, child of John and Mary Hardenbergh.
Witnesses: Abraham Hardenbergh and wife Mary.

Magdalene, child of Isaac and Mary Freyer.
Witnesses: Joshua Elting and wife Magdelene.

Margaret, child of Johannes and Mary Celden.
Witness: Margaret Snese.

Nov. 8. Cornelia, child of Jonathan Du Bois and Elizabeth Fever.
Witnesses: Simon Le Fever, Peternella Hasbrouck.

Dec. 11. By Isaac Chalker, in English: a daughter (no name), child of Henrick Van Waigan.
Witnesses: Cornelius and Elizabeth Schoonmaker.

1742, April 4. By Isaac Chalker, in English, Celia, child of John Griffing.
Witness: Margaret Knees.

July 4. By I. Chalker, in English: Elsha, child of Daniel and Wencha Hasbrouck.
Witnesses: Isaac and Rachel Hasbrouck.

Madalena, child of Abraham and Margaret Deven. (?)
Witnesses: Josias Elting and wife Magdalena.

1750-51, Jan. 30. By Rev. Theodorus Frelinghuysen, preacher at Albany, Jannitje, child of Willem Schut and Elizabeth Freer.
Witnesses: Hugo Terwilligen, Jannetje De Freer.

Anna, child of Benjamin Du Bois and Maria Bovie.
Witnesses: Simon Du Bois, Catarina Lefever.

Geertje, child of William Robinson and Maria Sluyter.
Witnesses: Jacob and Cornelia Sluyter.

Jannetie, child of Barent Kool and Sara Spineks.
Witnesses: Evert Terwillige, Lena Spineks.

April 21. By J. H. Goetschius: Isaac, child of Abraham Rosa and Elisabet Rutse.
Witnesses: Isaac Rosa and wife Neeltje Crispel.

Dec. 1. Evert, child of Benjamin Terwilligen and Elsje Freer.
Witnesses: Jan Terwilligen, Maria Freer.

Dec. 8. Johannis, child of Jurian Troies (?) and Elizabeth Smit.
Witnesses: Johannis Matthew Louw, Rebecca Freer.

Maria, child of Hugo Freer, Jr., and Hester Dejoo.
Witnesses: Marynis Van Aken, Margrit Dejoo.

Saerah, child of William Haarloo and Marretje Fenicks (?).
Witnesses: Zachary Hofman, Mary Terwille.

1752, Jan. 28. By Rev. J. C. Frymoet: Simon, child of Pieter Dejoo and Elizabeth Helm.
Witnesses: Abram and Johanna Helm.

Lea, child of Jan Wintfiel and Elizabeth Smit.
Witnesses: Hendrick and Lea Smit.

Cornelis, child of Abram Cool and Sara Sluyter.
Witnesses: Cornelis Cool, Sytje Kuykendal.

Jonathan, child of Johannis Bevier and Magdalena Le Fever.
Witnesses: Abraham Lefever, Maria Bevier.

Simion, child of Jacobus Bevier and Antje Freer.
Witnesses: Abraham Bevier, Margriet Elte.

Jonas, child of Gerrit and Maria Freer.
Witnesses: Jonas Freer, Catrina Stokkerat.

Helena, child of Theunis Van Steenberge and Lena Crispel.
Witnesses: Jan and Maria Van Steenbergen.

May 17. By Dom. Goetschius: Margritje, child of Abraham Lefebre and Maria Beviere.
Witnesses: Abraham Bevie and wife Margrietie Elten.

May 18. Ester, child of Jacob Hasbroek, Jr., and Janatje Du Bois.
Witnesses: Isaac Hasbroek, Jr., and wife Maria Breun.

Maria, child of Zacharias Hoffman and Maria Terwilligen.
Witnesses : Evert Terwilgen and wife Sara Freer.

Sept. 2. By Do. Meynema : Philip, child of Abraham De Joo and Lizabeth Du Bois.
Witnesses : Isaak, Jr. and Mary Freer.

Edwart, child of Edwart Woodt, Jr., and Catrina Van de Merker.
Witnesses : Edwart Woodt, Susanna Seat.

Daniel, child of Arberam Van de Merke.
Witnesses : Freer Van de Merke, Geertje Tak.

1753, July 8. By Dom. I. H. Goetschius : John, child of Jan Terwilge and Jacomyntje V. de Merke.
Witnesses : Barent Kool and wife Sara Pennik.

Elisabeth, child of Cornelius Terwilge and Catrina V. Netta.
Witnesses : Abraham Terwilge, Lisabeth Van Nette.

Oct. (?) 7 (?). Johann, child of Johan George Niec (?) and Elizabeth Smitt.
Witnesses : Johan George and Claatje Ranck.

Oct. 7. By Do. B. Vrooman : Abraham, child of Thomas Quick and Maria Terwilligen.
Witnesses : Abraham Terwilligen, Catrina Van der Merk.

Eva, child of Benjamin Hasebrouck and Elidia Schoonmaker.
Witnesses : Phillip Dubois, Hester Schoonmaker.

Nov. 4. Wouter, child of Eduwaard Sluyter and Lea Van Schuyve.
Witnesses : Hendrick ———, Lea Smith.

Geertruy, child of Andreas Lefever and Rachel Dubois.
Witnesses : Nataniel and Geertruy Dubois.

Abraham, child of Matheus Allen and Margrita Donalson.
Witnesses : Benjamin and Maria Dubois.

* Nov. 25. Magdalena, child of Johannes Bevier and Magdalena Lefever.
Witnesses : Matheus and Margareta Lefever.

---

* These baptisms were entered in such a manner in the original that it is impossible to say positively who were parents and who were witnesses. Mr. B. Fernow who semanuscript translation is in the Library of the Genealogical and Biographical Society reverses the names of these parents and witnesses, *i. e.* he records as the names of parents what our translator understands to be witnesses, and *vice versa*.

*Jannetje, child of Johan Jurrie Ranck and Clara Steenbrinck.
Witnesses: Jacob and Jannetje Hasbroeck.
Nov. 2. By Do. C. J. Fryenmoet, preacher at Menissink: Isak and And ies, children of Simon Du Bois and Catryntje Le Fever.
Witnesses: Coenraet Vernooy and wife Margriet Le Fever, Johannes Bevier, Jr., Rachel Le Fever.
Maria, child of Jacobus Bruyn and Jane Grame.
Witnesses: Abram Hasbrouk and wife Cathrina Bruyn.
Johannes, child of Petrus Vreligh and Maria Wood.
Witnesses: Edward Wood and wife Susanna Scott.
Lena, child of Isak Dio and Echje Frere.
Witnesses: Johannes Dio, Lena Achmoetie.
1753, Feb. 23. By Dom. Theodorus Frielinghuysen: Anna, child of Jacob Helm and Margarita Smit.
Witnesses: Simon and Anna Helm.
May 16. By Benjamin Meynema: Nikolaas, child of Abraham Hardenberg and Maria Hasebroek.
Witnesses: Isaak Haasebroek, Petronella Hasebroek.
Roelf Elting, child of Abraham Bevier and Margriet Eltinge.
Witnesses: Roelof Eltinge, Hester Bevier.
Elias, child of Jacobus Bevier and Antje Freer.
Witnesses: Benjamin Du Bois, Marie Bevier.
Maria, child of Jacob Teerpenning and Marietje Beem.
Witnesses: Louwerens Alstorf, Maria Tomas.
Kornelis, child of Johannes and Johanna Sluiter.
Witnesses: Johannes and Margrieta Sluiter.
Isaak, child of Johannes Le Vewer and Sara Ver Nooi.
Witnesses: Petrus Le Vewer, Lizabet Fernooi.
Annaatje, child of Moses Jork and Maria Freer.
Witnesses: Poetrik York, Mesjel Van Leuwen.
*1754, Jan. 1. Catharina, child of Gerrit and Maria Freer.
Witnesses: Johannes and Agetta Freer.
*Jan. 20. John, child of Richard Hennisce and Rebecca Griffin.
Witnesses: Joseph and Margarita Griffin.
*March 3. Benjamin, child of Hugo Freer, Jr., and Hester Dojo.
Witnesses: Benjamin Freer, Mally Ecmoedy.

*See note at foot of page 99.

* Abraham, child of John Coader and Lea Van de Keyk (?).
Witnesses : Jacob Helm, Margriet Smit.

* March 24. Annetje, child of Edward Wood and Catharina Van de Merken.
Witnesses : Abraham and Jaquemeytie Van de Merken.

* Cornelia, child of Willem Robbertson and Maria Sluyter.
Witnesses : Aldert Ploeg, Cornelia Sluyter.

* April 14. Elizabeth, child of Daniel Lefever and Catharina Conteyn.
Witnesses : Pieter and Cornelia Conteyn.

* June 2. Maria, child of Willem Sluyter and Maria Keyser.
Witnesses : Jacob and Maria Teerpenning.

* Aug. 11. Jonathan, child of Jacob and Sarah Freer.
Witnesses : Jacobus and Antje Bevier.

* Hendericus, child of John and Maria Etkins.
Witnesses : Hendericus and Lea Smit.

* Oct. 13. Elias, child of Abraham Hardenbergh and Maria Hasbrouk.
Witnesses : Johannes and Antje Jansen.

* Lidea, child of Teunis Van Steenbergen and Lena Chrispel.
Witnesses : Themotheus and Rachel V. Steenbergen.

Oct. 20. Benjamin, child of John Windfeald and Elizabeth Smitt.
Witnesses : Jacob and Maria Teerpenning.

* Oct. 29. Noach, child of Abraham Le Fever and Maria Bevier.
Witnesses : Johannes and Magdalena Bevier.

* Jannetje, child of Johannes Sluyter and Maria Weynant.
Witnesses : Jurry and Jannetje Weynant.

1755, Jan. 1. Maria, child of Adrian Nieuwkerk and Marytje Rutse.
Witnesses : Abraham and Maria Hardenberg.

Jan. 5. Simeon, child of Petrus Oostrander and Debora De Joo.
Witnesses : Frederick and Debora Fort.

March 18 (born March 5). Josea, child of Jacob Hasebroucq, Jr., and Jannitje Dubois.
Witnesses : Wilhelmus and Rachel Dubois.

* See note at foot of page 99.

Catarina, child of Jan Teerpenning and Elisabeth Aarsdalen.
Witnesses : Philip and Catarina Aarsdalen.

Maria, child of Abraham Bevier and Margarita Elton.
Witnesses : Abraham and Maria Lefever.

Nicholaes, child of Joseph Griffin and Margarita Wieler.
Witnesses : Nicholaes Keyser and Anna Wieler.

Alexander, child of George Forgenson and Elisabeth Davis.

Rebecca, child of Abraham Rosa and Elisabeth Rutse.
Witnesses : Pieter Dejou, Elisabet Helm.

Annetje, child of Johan Adam Hofman and Rosina Rally
Witnesses : Johan Jurrie Rang, Clara Steenbrinck.

Evert, child of Johannis and Anna Sluiter.
Witnesses : Evert and Lea Sluiter.

June 15. Johannes, child of Benjamin Dojo and Jenneke Van Vliet.
Witnesses : Johannes and Agetta Freer.

Maria, child of Benjamin Smedes and Rachel Jansen.
Witnesses : Mattheus and Rachel Smedes.

Aug. 10. Johanna, child of Jacob Witfield and Catryna Helm.
Witnesses : Abraham and Johanna Helm.

Aug. 24. Georgius Wilhelmius, child of Hermanus Oostrander and Barbara Terwilgen.
Witnesses : Georgius Wilhelm Terwilgen and Lena Oostrander.

Ezechiel, child of Jan Terwilgen and Jakomyntje Vander Merke.
Witnesses : Johannes and Maria Terwilge.

Jacob, child of Gideon Louw and Rachael Sammons.
Witnesses : The parents.

Marretje, child of Johannes Klyn and Lisabeth Kyser.
Witnesses : William Robbersen and wife, Maria Sluyter.

Margretha, child of Cornelius Kerner and Janetje Keeter.
Witnesses : Cornelius Kyser and Katrina Keeter.

Sara, child of Jacobus Bevier and Antje Freer.
Witnesses : Johannes Bevier and wife Madlena.

1756, Jan. 27. Eva, child of Jacob Helm and Maragrietje Smith.
Witnesses : Johannes and Annatje Smit.

Abraham, child of Abraham Kool and Sara Sluyter.
Witnesses: Wouter and Maragrieta Sluyter.

Jermia and Willem, children of William Roberson and Maria Sluyter.
Witnesses: Wouter Sluyter, Anganietje Keyser, Willem Sluyter, and Maria Kyser.

Simeon, child of Petrus Oostrander and Debora Dojoo.
Witnesses: Simon and Marytje Freere.

Hannah, child of Mathew Allen and Margret Dannelson.
Witnesses: Abraham Dannelson and Elizabeth Ecmoedy.

Willem, child of Willem Sluyter and Maria Kyser.
Witnesses: Willem Robbertson and Maria Sluyter.

April 17. Maria, child of Andries and Rachel Lefever.
Witnesses: Leuwies and Ester de Boey.

Rachel, child of Simon de Boes and Catrina Lefever.
Witnesses: Benjamin de Boes and Mareytje Bovie.

Jerimia, child of Johannes Louw and Rebecka Freer.
Witnesses: Johannes and Maria Louw.

Margrita, child of Pieter Dejoo and Elizabeth Helm.
Witnesses: Christophel Dejoo and Debora Van Vliet.

Lena, child of Jurrie Hees (or Nees) and Elizabeth Smith.
Witnesses: Abraham Bovie and Margrita Eltinge.

Cornelia, child of Jacob Sluyter and Liedia Keyser.
Witnesses: Albert Ploegh and Cornelia Sluyter.

No date. Nathaniel, child of Johannis Bevier and Madalena Lafever.
Witnesses: Nathaneel and Maria Lafever.

Antje, child of Johannis and Annatje Sluiter.
Witnesses: Dirk and Neeltje Sluiter.

Arie, child of Cornelius Terwilligen and Catrina Van Nette.
Witnesses: Cornelius Cool and Sytje Cuikendal.

Ezechiel, child of Gerrit ? and Maria Freer.
Witnesses: Martinus Freer and Rachel Terwilligen.

No date. Petrus, child of Edward Wood, Jr., and Catrina Vandermerken.
Witnesses: Petrus Vandermerken and Helena Woodt.

Nov. 7. Lea, child of Johannes Krispell and Anatje Ritzen.
Witnesses: Antoni and Catrina Krispell.

Joseph, child of Joseph Coddington and Catrina Vander Merken.
Witnesses: Abraham De Yoo and wife Elisabeth.

Jeremia, child of Hugo Vreer and Hester De Joo.
Witnesses: Benjamin De Joo and wife Janetje.

Janetje, child of Benjamin Terwilge and Elsje Vreer.
Witnesses: Joseph and Wyntje Vreer.

1757, Jan. 16. Catarina, child of Richard Hannyson and Rebecca Griffin.
Witnesses: Louwerents and Anna Griffin.

Marritje, child of Abraham Hardenbergh and Maria Hasbrouk.
Witnesses: Johannes, Jr., and Maria Hardenberg.

Noach, child of Cornelius Kalleheyn and Margariet Johnson.
Witness: Matthew Steel.

Alida, child of Thomas Etkins and Maria Dekker.
Witnesses: Joseph Etkins and Alida Dekker.

Maria, child of Abraham Danielson and Elizabeth Eckmoedy.
Witnesses: Jacobus and Dievertje Hasbrouk.

Feb. 13. Anatje, child of Hermanus Oostrander and Barbara Terwilgen.
Witnesses: Johannes Terwilge and wife Antje.

April 27. Nathan, child of Abraham Lefever and Maria Bovier.
Witnesses: Jacobus Bovier and Antje Freer.

May 1. Elizabeth, child of Jacob Windfield and Catrina Helm.
Witnesses: Pieter and Elizabeth De Joe.

Margrita, child of Joseph Griffin and Margrita Wieler.
Witnesses: Jacob Hasebroek and Jannitje De Boeys.

Aug. 21. Hugoo, child of Willem Schut and Elizabeth Freer.
Witnesses: Moses York and Maria Freer.

Geertje, child of Johannes De Joo and Sara Van Wagenen.
Witnesses: Abraham Van Wagenen and Hillegont Crappel.

Jacob, child of Jacob Teerpenning and Mareytje Beem.
Witnesses: Boudeweyn and Elizabeth Teerpenning.

Louwrens, child of Simon Aelsdorf and Maria Teerpenning.
Witnesses: Jan Teerpenning and Elizabeth Aelsdorf.

Jazaph, child of Benjamen De Boey and Maria Bovier.
Witnesses: Jacob Bovier and Annaetje Vernoej.

Lidias, child of Isack De Joo and Eghje Freer.
Witnesses; Petrus and Lidia Freer.

Maria and Louwra, children of Jacob Rutsen Hardenbergh and Dina Van Bergh.
Witnesses: Johannes and Maria Hardenbergh, Frederick Van Berk and Louwra De Vroom.

Nov. 20. Sherk, child of Sherk Van Keuren and Mari Vreer.
Witnesses: Benjamin Van Keuren and wife Malle Bunschooten.

Lena, child of John Klyn and Lisabeth Keiser.
Witnesses: Dirk and Lena Sluuter.

Nov. 25. Rosina Barbara, child of Jacob and Anna Maria Hubsch.
Witnesses: The parents.

Nov. 27. Catrina, child of Edward Wood, Jr., and Catrina Van der Merken.
Witnesses: Daniel Wood and Lea Van der Merken.

1758, Feb. 5. Maria, child of Isaac Hasebrouck, Jr., and Maria Bruyn.
Witnesses: Jacob and Maria Hasebrouck.

Maria, child of Jacobus Bevier and Antje Freer.

Hester, child of Michael Sax and Johanna Bovie.
Witnesses: Isaac and Elisabeth Bevie.

Levi, child of Pieter Dojou and Elisabeth Hellen.
Witnesses: Abraham and Elisabeth Dojou.

Feb. 19. David, child of Stophel De Jo and Debora Van Vliet.
Witnesses: Benjamin De Jo and wife Janetje.

Rachel, child of Jan Teerpenning and Lisabeth Alsdorf.
Witnesses: Jan Wildfield and wife Lisabeth.

July 26. Margrita, child of Willem Sluyter and Maria Keyser.
Witnesses: Petrus Burger and Margrita Sluyter.

Abraham, child of Benjamen Dojo and Janneca Van Vliet.
Witnesses: Christophel Dojo and Debora Van Vliet.

Jonas, child of Johannes Bovie and Lena Fever.
Witnesses : Jacobus Bevie and Antje Freer.

Lowies, child of Jacob Hasebroek and Jannitje De Boey.
Witnesses : Lowies Bovie and Ester De Boey.

July 23. Maragrieta, child of Abraham Kool and Sarah Sluyter.
Witnesses : Thomas and Maragrieta Farrington.

Aug. 20. Cattryntje, child of Nathaniel and Marytje Lefever.
Witnesses : Simon Dubois and wife Cattryntje.

Elizabeth, child of Jacob Helm and Margrieta Smit.
Witnesses : Pieter Doyo and wife Elizabeth.

Catharina, child of Andries Lefever and Rachel Dubois.
Witnesses : Abraham Lefever and wife Maria.

Sara, child of Joseph Coddington and Catharina Vandemerke.
Witnesses : Jacob Hasbrouck, Jr., and wife Jannetje.

Rachel, child of Abraham Hardenbergh and Maria Hasbrouck.

Sept 3, Benjamin, child of Benjamin Terwilger and Elsje Freer.
Witnesses : Benjamin Freer, Jr., and wife Elizabeth.

Oct. 29. Ezechiel, child of Johannis M. Louw and Rebecca Freer.
Witnesses : Johannis Teerpenningh and wife Jannetje Freer.

Abraham, child of Abraham Bevier and Margrietje Eltinge.

William, child of Abraham Donaldson and Elizabeth Auchmoetie.
Witnesses : Jonathan Louw and wife Magdalena.

1759, March 3. Sara, child of Jacobus Hasebroek and Divertje Van Wagenen.
Witnesses : Habraham Hasebroek, Jr., and Rachel Sleght.

Maria, child of Gerrit, Jr., and Maria Freer.
Witnesses : Huwe Freer, Jr., and Hester De Joo.

Petrus, child of Daniel Levever and Catrina Conteyn.
Witnesses : Petrus Levever and Maria Louw.

June 13. Rachel, child of Abraham Lefever and Maria Bovie.

Solomon, child of Johannes Dojo and Sarah Van Wagene.
Witnesses : Johannes Freer and wife Agetta.

Sept. 6. Rakel, child of Bodewyn and Elizabeth Teerpenning.
Witnesses : Jan Teerpenning and Elizabeth Alsdorpt.

Maria, child of Jacob Fenkenkar and Maria L. Repinbergh.
Witnesses : Michael Sax and Johanna Bevier.

Sept. 9. Maria, child of Hans Jacob Stips? and Maria Granigje.
Witnesses : Joh. and Maria Grootsch and Philip Beker.

Oct. 16. Johannes Bevier, child of Michael Sax, and Johanna Bevier.
Witnesses : Isaac and Elisabeth Bevier.

Everdt, child of John Terwilligen and Maria Van Wagenen
Witnesses : Johannes and Rachel Blanjohn.

Benjamin, child of Joseph Griffin and Margrith Wiler.
Witnesses : Benjamin and Elsie Terwilligen.

Nov. 10. Marcus, child of Marcus Wekman and Martha Litz.
Witnesses : Willem and Hilletje Litz.

Jonathan, child of Andreas DuBois and Sara Lefeber.
Witnesses : Lewis DuBoi and wife Catryna.

Lea, child of Edward Wood, Jr., and Catrina Vander Merken.
Witnesses : William and Hanna Wood.

Sara, child of Philip Bovier and Treyntje Louw.
Witnesses : Petrus Van Wagenen and Sara Louw.

Wessel, child of Lewis Dubois and Catharina Broedhead.
Witnesses : Wessel and Catharina Broedhead.

Edwerd, child of Roeluf Litz and Saertje Sluyter.
Witnesses : Johannes and Merya Kroos.

1760, Jan. 17. Bregje, child of Jacob, Jr., and Sara Freer.
Witnesses : Benjamin, Jr., and Elizabeth Freer.

Jacob, child of Johannes and Elizabeth Kleyn.
Witnesses : Jacob and Margrita Helm.

April 15. Annitje, child of Petrus Vander Merken and Helena Wood.
Witnesses : Abraham and Jaccomyntje Vandemerke.

Aug. 24. Annatie, child of Jacob Helm and Margritt Schmit.
Witnesses : Jacob and Catrina Wembfield.

Jacob, child of Joseph Coddington and Catrina Vandemerke.

Angenittie, child of Jacob Tinkenau and Marieliss Reydenberger.
Witnesses : Jacob Beeker and Maria Dorothe.

Johon, child of Willem Schutt and Elisabeth Freres.
Witnesses : John and Maria Terwillige.

Johannes, child of Petrus Ostrander and Cristina Ranck.
Witnesses : Hanjoory and Saartie Rank.

Sept. 7. Lous, child of Johannes Hardenberg and Maria Lefever.
Witnesses : Johannes, Sr., and Maria Hardenberg.

Oct. 26. Elisabeth, child of Joh. Heinerich Wesmuller and Anna Maria Reppichhausen.
Witness : The mother.

Sartie, child of Hannes and Johanna Sluyter.
Witnesses : Abraham Kool and wife Sara.

Jacob, child of Petrus Lefever and Elisabeth Vernoy.
Witnesses : Daniel Lefever and wife Cathrina.

Nov. 9. Judica, child of Henery Harp and Lidia Wood.
Witnesses : Williem Wood and Cornelia Tapper.

Dec. 21. Thomas, child of Isaak Freres and Hester Jansen.
Witnesses : Zachary and Anna Jansen.

1761, Jan. 4. Willem, child of Benjamin Dioo and Jannetie Van Vliet.
Witnesses : Jan and Sary Van Vliet.

Jan. 18. Zacharias, child of Hieronimus Burger and Lena Sluyter.
Wittnesses : Zacharias and Neeltie Sluyter.

Joannes, child of Andres Lefever and Rachel Dubois.
Witnesses : The parents.

Feb. 1. Jannetie, child of Jacobus Bevier and Antie Freres.
Witnesses : The parents.

Jonas, child of Johannes Freres, Jr., and Sarah Bever.
Witnesses : Jonas Freres and wife Catrina.

Mar. 29. Antie, child of Abraham Kool and Sarah Sluyter.
Witnesses : Hannes and Annatie Sluyter.

April 12. Lisabeth, child of George Forgeson and Lisabeth Davis.
Witnesses: The parents.

May 10. James, child of Abraham Danielson and Elisabeth Achmudy.
Witnesses: David and Hester Achmudy.

Aug. 30. Margritt, child of Daniel York and Maria V. Aake.
Witnesses: Jan and Grittie V. Aake.

Sept. 13. Anna, child of Hanyorg Lucker and Lisabet Wind.
Witnesses: Philip Alsdorf and Anna Rang.

Petrus, child of Abraham Klaarwaater and Lisabeth Burger.
Witnesses: Jacob Sax and wife Mareytie.

Nov. 3. Lea, child of Rulof Litz and Sarah Sluyter.
Witnesses: Evert Sluyter and wife Lea.

Dec. 20. Sarah, child of Pitter Dojo and Elisabeth Helm.
Witnesses: Isaak Van Wagene, Jr., and wife Sarah.

Elisabeth, child of John Terwilliger and Maria Van Wagene.
Witnesses: Johannes Louw, Jr., and Rachel Van Wagene.

Dec. 24. Cathrina, child of Petrus Vander Merke and Elena Wood.
Witnesses: Edwerd Wood and wife Cathrina.

Dec. 25. Grittie, child of Petrus Oostrander and Christiana Rang.
Witnesses: Lourentz and Grittie Rang.

1762, Jan. 3. Maria, child of Pitter Burger and Margritt Sluyter.
Witnesses: Henerik Ses and Maria Sluyter.

Jan. 31. Elias, child of Aldert Ploeg and Cornelia Sluyter.
Witnesses: Jacob Berger and wife Sarah.

Feb. 14. Catrin, child of Joseph Griffin and Margritt Willer.
Witnesses: Henerik and Maria Wesemiller.

Simon, child of Jacob Winfield and Cathrina Helm.
Witnesses: Jacob and Margritt Helm.

Feb. 28. Brechie, child of Gerret and Maria Freres.
Witnesses: Jonas Frere and Grittie Louw.

Simon, child of Abraham Helm and Cathrina Smedes.
Witnesses : Pitter Dojo and wife Elisabeth.

June 6. Joseph, child of Joseph Coddington and Cathrina Vander Merken.
Witnesses : The parents.

June 20. Mari, child of Jonathan Terwilliger and Maria Freres.
Witnesses : Daniel and Mareytie Freres.

Aug. 15. Derk, child of Bodewyn and Elisabeth Teerpenning.
Witnesses : Simon Alsdorff and wife Maria.

Sept. 26. Maria, child of John Etkens and Margrith Sluyter.
Witnesses David Etkens and Neeltie Sluyter.

Oct. 17. Petrus, child of Johannes Hardenberg, Jr., and Maria Lefefer.
Witnesses : Petrus Lefefer and wife Elisabeth.

Nov. 21. Samuel, child of Benjamin Dubois and Maria Beviers.
Witnesses : Andres and Sarah Beviers.

Jannetie, child of Isaak Dojou and Echie Freres.
Witnesses : The parents.

Marteynes, child of Johannes Freres and Sarah Beever.
Witnesses : The parents.

Dec. 19. Wouter, child of Jacob Berger and Sarah Schneyder.
Witnesses : Wouter and Anganitta Schneyder.

Philip, child of Abraham Lefefer and Maria Bevier.
Witnesses : Corneles Brink and wife Hester.

1763, Feb. 13. Abraham, child of Daniel Dojou and Margritt Lefefer.
Witnesses : Abraham Dojou and wife Elisabeth.

March 27. Joseph, child of Simon Dubois and Cathrina Lefefer.
Witnesses : The parents.

Mareytie, child of Isaak Freres and Hester Jansen.
Witnesses : Petrus Van Wagenen and wife Saartie.

Sarah, child of Derk Keiser and Sarah De Lang.
Witnesses : Jacob and Mareya Sluyter.

April 17. Elisa, child of Jacobus Bevirs and Antie Freres.
Witnesses : The parents.

May 1. Daniel, child of Williem Litz and Deborah Smit.
Witnesses : Johannes Smit and Helletie Litz.

Josia, child of Christian Dojou, Jr., and Alida Terwilliger.
Witnesses : Moses Dojou and wife Claartie.

Jannetje, child of Johannes Kleyn and Elisabeth Keyser.
Witnesses : Pitter and Helegond Muller.

Johannes, child of Antoney Lepold Friderich Wilkenlow and An Marie Glaserin.
Witnesses : The parents.

June 5. Sarah, child of Petrus Lefefer and Elisabeth Vernoy.
Witnesses : Johannes Lefefer and Maria Vernoy.

June 19. Koenrad, child of Hyeronymus Burger and Lena Sluyter.
Witnesses : Koenerad and Cathrin Burger.

July 17. Benjamin, child of Jacobus Hasbroek and Divertie Van Wagenen.
Witnesses : Benjamin and Elisabeth Van Wagenen.

July 31. Elias, child of Hannes Dojou and Sarah Van Wagenen.
Witnesses : The parents.

Sept. 11. Debora, child of Petrus Ostrander and Christina Rang.
Witnesses : Jonathan Ostrander and Deborah Borehans.

Nov. 6. Johannes, child of Jan Teerpenning and Elisabeth Alsdorf.
Witnesses : Han Yorey Rang and wife Claartie.

Jeremias, child of Henerich and Maria Wesmuller.
Witnesses : The parents.

Dec. 4. Jonathan, child of Jonathan Terwilliger and Marie Freres.
Witnesses : Joseph Freres and sister Wyntie.

1764, Jan. 1. Augustynus, child of Petrus Vander Merke and Helena Wood.
Witnesses : Benjamin Isak Freres and Lea Vander Merken.

Feb. 12. Lucas, child of Pitter Dojou and Elisabeth Helm.
Witnesses : Jan Terwilliger and wife Maria.

April 8. Elisabeth, child of Andres Lefefer and Rachel Dubois.
Witnesses : The parents.

Benjamin, child of Bodewyn and Elisabeth Teerpenning.
Witnesses : Benjamin Freres and wife Elisabeth.

Elsjie, child of Gerret and Maria Freres.
Witnesses : Elisa Freres and Elsie Haasbroek.

May 13. Sarah, child of Benjamin Hasbroek and Lidya Schonmaker.
Witnesses : Willem Osterhout and wife Sarah.

Maria, child of Joseph Coddington and Cathrina Vander Merken.
Witnesses : The parents.

May 31. Lucas, child of Jan Terwilligen and Maria Van Wagenen.
Witnesses : Johannes Hardenbergh, Jr., and wife Maria.

June 3. Henerik, child of David Ekkert and Maretie Ploeg.
Witnesses: Emerich Schreyfer and wife Elisabeth.

July 8. Maria, child of Henery Green and Maria Dojou.
Witnesses : Matheus Lefefer and wife Margritt.

Daniel, child of Zacharias Sluyter and Breghie York.
Witnesses : Daniel and Weyntie Freres.

Rachel, child of Joseph Griffin and Margritta Wieler.
Witnesses : John Griffin and Rachel Smith.

Johannes, child of Denie Relie and Mareytie Van Vliet.
Witnesses: Nathanael Lefefer and wife Mareytie.

Sept. 9. John, child of John Windfiel and Elisabeth Schmith.
Witnesses : Isaak Windfiel, young man, and Maria Windfiel, young woman.

Sept. 23. David, child of Roelof Lits and Sarah Sluyter.
Witnesses : Benjamin and Maria Sluyter, young man and young woman.

Jerzok, child of Christoffel Dojou and Debora Van Vliet.
Witnesses : Salomon Louw and wife Judik.

Moses, child of Daniel York and Maria Van Aken.
Witnesses : Moses York and wife Maria.

Madlena, child of Daniel Lefefer and Cathrina Cantyn.
Witnesses : Petrus Cantyn and wife Magdalena.

Oct. 21. Jonathan, child of Loys I. Dubois and Cathrina Broded.
Witnesses: Charols W. and Geertruyd Broded, young man and young woman.

Nov. 4. Sarah, child of Jacob Sluyter and Lidia Keyser.
Witnesses : Evert Sluyter and wife Lea.

Dec. 2. Salomon, child of Jan Hasbroek and Rachel Van Wagenen.
Witnesses : Jacobus Hasbroek and wife Dievertie.

1765, Feb. 24. Elisabeth, child of Andres Dubois and Sarah Lefefer.
Witnesses : Nathanael and Cornelia Dubois, young man and young woman.

Mareytie, child of Daniel Dojou and Margritt Lefefer.
Witnesses : Nathanael Lefefer and wife Mareytie.

Apr. 14. Laura, child of Petrus Ostrander and Cristina Rang.
Witnesses: Helmus and Lena Ostrander, young man and young woman.

Isaak, child of Isaak Freres and Hester Janson.
Witnesses : Jonathan Terwilliger and wife Maria.

Apr. 28. Cathrina, child of Han York Luker and Elisabeth Wagener.

May 26. Jacob, child of Friderich Wilkelow and Ana Marie Glaserin.
Witnesses : the parents.

The following baptisms have been copied from a book marked 4. The heading of this record is in Dutch, the translation of which is as follows : " Baptismal register of the new Congregation founded at the New Paltz, on August 29 and 30, 1767."

Aug. 30, Do. Rysdyk has baptized :

1767, Aug. 30. Rachel, child of Philippus DuBoys and Anna Heuwe.
Witnesses : Rachel DuBoys and David Low.

Marytje, child of Gerrit Aartse Van Wagenen and Annatje Bosch.
Witnesses : James Van Wagenen and wife Margriet Middag.

Henricus, child of Teunis Oosterhoud and Johanna Helm.
Witnesses: Petrus Cool and Annatje Dewit, his wife.

1768, Jan. 25. Sarah, child of Rulof Elting and Maria Low.
Witnesses: Dirk Dirksen Wynkoop and wife Sarah Elting.

Catharyntien, child of Salomon Low and Judic Van Vliet.
Witnesses: Jan Lamater and wife Catharina Van Vliet.

May 25; born May 6. Catharina, child of Petrus Van Wagena and Sara Low.
Witnesses: Abraham Een and wife Catharina Van Wagena.

Born March 9. Catharina, child of Cornelis Low and Elizabeth Schoonmaker.
Witnesses: Adriaan Wynkoop and wife Catharina Low.

Mattheus, child of Abraham Hes and Catharina Sparreks.

Nov. 8; born Oct. 18. Elias, child of Abraham Een and Catharina Van Wagena.
Witnesses: Aart Hansz and Rebecca Van Wagena.

1769, Aug. 22; born July 4. Geertje, child of Dirk D. Wynkoop and Sara Eltinge.
Witnesses: Dirk Wynkoop and Geertje Cool, his wife.

Born May 31. Catryntje, child of Roelof Josiasz Eltinge and Maria Louw.
Witnesses: Salomon and Catryntje Eltinge.

1770, Jan. 29; born Dec. 15, 1769. Salomon, child of Salomon Louw and Judick Van Vliet.

Born Dec. 8, 1769. Magdalena, child of Abraham Elting and Dina Duboys.
Witnesses: Josia Elting and wife Magdalena Duboys.

May 26; born Feb. 26. Philippus, child of Henrikus Dubois, Jr., and Rebecka Van Wagenen.

Aug. 10; born June 14. Lucas, child of Petrus Van Wagenen and Sarah Louw.

Oct. 29. Johannes, child of Abraham Hess and Catharina Sparrecks.

1771, May 26; born Feb. 17. Rachel, child of Abraham Een and Cathrina Van Wagena.
Witnesses: Rachel Van Wagena and Petrus Schoonmaker.

Born Feb. 21. Nancy, child of Daniel Wood and Margaretha Torner.

Born April 26. Abraham, child of Jacob Chiedly and Hester Klaarwater.
Witnesses: Eva and Abraham Klaarwater.

Born Jan. 4. Abraham, child of Cornelis Louw and Elizabeth Schoonmaker.
Witnesses: Cornelis Cool and wife Maria Schoonmaker.

Born Jan. 27. Jannetje, child of Roelof Jo. Eltinge and Maria Louw.

Born March 27. Samuel and Lea, twins of Abraham Smedes and Geertje Zwart.
Witnesses: Josua Smedes, Beletje Smedes, and Aldert Rosa.

Oct. 14; born Aug. 12. Cornelia, child of D. Dirck Wynkoop and Sarah Elting.
Witnesses: Mattheus Ten Eyck and wife Cornelia Wynkoop.

Born June 22. Daniel, child of Isac Louw and Francisca Everit.
Witnesses: Petrus Van Wagenen and wife Sarah Louw.

1772, May 21; born Feb. 26. Maria, child of Henricus DuBoys, Jr. and Rebecca Van Wagena.
Witnesses: Gerrit Van Wagena and wife Marytje Frair.

1773, Feb. 24; born Oct. 30, 1772. Cornelia, child of Dirck D. Wynkoop and Sarah Elting.
Witnesses: Mattheus Ten Eyck and wife Cornelia Wynkoop.

Born Sept. 18, 1772. Maria, child of Petrus V. Wagenen and Sarah Louw.
Witnesses: Rulof Elting and wife Maria Louw.

Born Dec. 10. Esther, child of Isac Louw and Francisca Beverit.

May 10; born March 24; Johannes, child of Roelef J. Eltinge and Maria Low.
Witnesses: Jacob Low and Antje Low.

1774, Feb. 2. Gerrat, child of Hendrik DuBoys, Jr., and Rebecca V. Wagenen.
Witnesses: Jan V. Wagenen and wife Gritjen Louw.

Nov. 13; born July 26. Roeleph, child of Roeleph J. Eltinge and Maria Low.

Born Aug. 20. Isaak, child of Isaak Low and Fransciska Evert.

Born Aug. 1. Henry, child of Methusalem Dubois and Geertruyd Bruyn.
Witnesses: Henry Dubois, Jr., and Rebecca Van Wagenen.

Dec. 11; born Nov. 21. Jacobus, child of Cornelius Dubois, Jr., and Geertruyd Bruyn.
Witnesses: Jacobus, Sr., and Maria Bruyn.

1775, Feb. 5; born Dec. 5, 1774. Ann, child of Gerardus Hardenbergh and Ann Ryerson.

March 5; born Dec. 22, 1774. Jamyme, child of David Wilson and Hannah Comfort.

Born Dec. 7, 1774. Sartye, child of Garret Dekker and Margrita Cok.

Oct. 29. Aert, child of Petrus Van Wagenen and Sarah Low.
Witnesses: Aert Van Wagenen and Rebecca Frair.

Maria, child of Roeleph Elting and Maria Low.

Dec. 3. Johannis, child of Matthew McAvey and Yannetje Tapper.

1776, April 14; born March 28. Elizabeth, child of David Low and Rachel Delemetre.
Witnesses: Salomon Low and Sarah Bosch.

May 12; born April 23. Yannetje, child of Hendricus Dubois, Jr., and Rebecca Van Wagenen.
Witness: Margret Hue.

June 16; born April 12. Margreta, child of Gerardus Hardenbergh and Nancy Ryerson.

July 7; born June 17. Cornelius Bruyn, child of Methusalem Dubois and Geertruyde Bruyn.
Witnesses: Cornelius Dubois, Jr., and wife Geertruyde Bruyn.

Born June 11. Abraham, child of Johannes Pattel Volk and Lena Rose.
Witnesses: Abraham Rose and Maria Denport.

Born June 30. Lydia, child of Johannes Sluyter and Elizabeth Keyser.

Nov. 10; born Sept. 4. Yannetye, child of Simeon Ralyea and Magdelena Deyoe.

Dec. 15; born Nov. 19. Jacobus, child of Cornelius Dubois, Jr., and Geertruyde Bruyn.

1777, Feb. 2 ; born Dec. 29, 1776. Yannetje, child of Isaac Low and Francisca Everit.

March 9 ; born Jan. 31. Jonathan, child of Wilhelmus Schoonmaker and Cathrina Low.

1778, Feb. 1 ; born Dec. 22, 1777. Tryntye, child of Methusalem Dubois and Geertruyde Bruyn.

April 26 ; born April 24. Catelyna, child of David Low and Rachel Delemetre.
Witnesses : Benjamin and Elizabeth Delemetre.

Born April 22. Wilhelmus, child of Cornelius Elting and Blandina Almendorf.
Witnesses : Coenraet W. Almendorf and Yanneke Low, wid. of Wilhelmus Almendorf.

May 24 ; born May 14. Jane, child of Cornelius Dubois, Jr., and Geertruy Bruyn.

July 5 ; born May 17. Sara, child of Petrus Van Wagenen and Sara Low.
Witnesses : Petrus Bevier and Sarah Low.

Born May 14. Sarah, child of David Soper and Jean Boyd.

Dec. 25 ; born Nov. 15. Methusalem, child of Henuricus Dubois, Jr., and Rebecca Van Wagenen.
Witnesses : Methusalem Dubois and Geertruy Bruyn.

1779, March 21 ; born Feb. 17. Johannis, child of Johannis Suert and Rachel Garretson.

May 16 ; born May 8. Gideon, child of Petrus Low and Cathrina Hess.

June 27 ; born June 13. William, child of Wilhelmus Rosekrans and Yanneke Van Keure.

Baptisms copied from Vol. III. of the New Paltz R. D. Church Books :

1765, June 9. Cathrina, child of Abraham Helm and Cathrina Smedes.
Witnesses : The parents.

Elisabeth, child of Marcus Ostrander and Elisabeth De Graaf.
Witnesses : Henrik Ostrander and wife Elisabeth.

June 23. Lea, child of Hannes and Annatie Sluyter.
Witnesses : Evert Sluyter and wife Lea.

Lea, child of Hieronymus Burger and Lena Sluyter.
Witnesses : Evert Sluyter and wife Lea.

July 7. Weyntie, child of Abraham Claarwater and Elisabeth Schoonmaker.
Witnesses : Frederik and Mareytie Claarwater, young man and young daughter.

John, child of Williem Hood and Anna Griffin.
Witnesses : George and Cathrina Huber.

Janeke, child of Petrus Lefefer and Elisabeth Vernoi.
Witnesses : Andris DeWit and wife Janeke.

July 21. Margritt, child of Johannes Freres, Jr., and Sarah Bever.
Witnesses : Simon Freres, young man, and Sarah Bevirs, young woman.

Oct. 27. David, child of Isaak Dojou and Eggie Freres.
Witnesses : The parents.

Nov. 9. Rebecka, child of Edwerd Wood and Cathrina Vandermerk.
Witnesses : Aardt Van Wagene and wife Rebecca.

1766, Jan. 19. Maria, child of Bodowyn and Elisabat Taerpenning.
Witnesses : Petrus Ostrander and wife Cristina.

Eva, child of Hans Bartel Volk and Lena Roos.
Witnesses : Gysabert and Maria Roos, young man and young woman.

Feb. 2. David, child of Joseph Coddington and Cathrina Vandermerke.
Witnesses : The parents.

Jonathan, child of Christian Dojou and Alida Terwilliger.
Witnesses : Johannes and Margritt Dojou, young man and young woman.

Margritta, child of Nicolaas Sluyter and Neeltie Willer.
Witnesses : Corneles and Margritt Sluyter, young man and young woman.

Feb. 23. Maria, child of Jacob Berger and Sarah Sluyter.
Witnesses : Abraham Crom and wife Maria.

March 16. Maria, child of Joseph Terwilliger and Annatie Weller.
Witnesses Willem Weller and wife Maria.

March 30. Edward, child of Petrus Vander Merke and Lena Woed.
Witnesses : The parents.

April 13. Maria, child of Zacharias Sluyter and Brechie York.
Witnesses : Moses York and wife Maria.

Annatie, child of Johannes Klyn and Elisabeth Keyser.
Witnesses : Johannes Sluyter and wife Annatie.

Elisabeth, child of John Teerpenning and Elisabeth Alsdorf.
Witnesses : Denie Relie and wife Mareytie.

April 27. Isaak Freres, child of Jonathan Terwilliger and Marie Freres.
Witnesses ; Abraham Dojou and wife Bettie.

May 25. Simon Lefefer, child of Abraham Dojou, Jr., and Elsje Lefefer.
Witnesses : Andres Lefefer, Jr., young man, and mother Petronella.

June 15. Margritta, child of Johannes Smidt and Roseyntje Van Aake.
Witnesses : Henrick Smidt and wife, Sarah Shmidt. (sic)

June 29. Simon, child of Henry Green and Maria Dojou.
Witnesses : Simon Dubois and wife Catreyntie.

July 13. Daniel, child of David Eckert and Maritie Ploeg.
Witnesses : Daniel York and wife Maria.

July 27. Sarah, child of Jan Terwilliger and Maria Van Wagene.
Witnesses : Kobus Hasbroek and wife Divertie.

Aug. 10. Cornelia, child of Andres Lefefer and Rachel Dubois.
Witnesses : The parents.

Aug. 24. Jacobus, child of Marcus Ostrander and Elisabeth DeGraaf.
Witnesses : Jacobus DeGraaf, young man ; Jannetie DeGraaf, young woman.

Sept. 7. Ariantie, child of Willem Elsworth and Jannetie Deen.
Witnesses : Jorsy Deen and Ariantie his wife.

Oct. 26. Roelef, child of Petrus Hasbroek and Sarah Bevirs.
Witnesses : Abraham Bevirs and wife Margritt.

Cathrina, child of Pitter Dojou and Lisabeth Helm.
Witnesses : J. M. Goetschius and wife Cathrina.

Nov. 23. Maria, child of Johannes Dojou and Sarah Van Wagenen.
Witnesses : Abraham Van Wagene, Jr., young man ; Maria Van Wagene, young woman.

Geesje, child of Johannes Walran and Elisabeth Ein.
Witness : Margritt Ein, young woman.

Lydia, child of Cristoffel Dojou and Debora Van Vliet.
Witnesses : Jan Freres and wife Lydia.

Dec. 26. Maria, child of Joseph Griffin and Margritt Whiler.
Witnesses : The parents.

1767, Jan. 1. Elisabeth, child of Daniel Freres, Jr., and Annatie Dojou.
Witnesses : Pitter Dojou and wife Elisabeth.

Feb. 15. Debora, child of Denie Rellie and Maria Van Vliet.
Witnesses : Christoffel Dojou and wife Debora.

Levi, child of Petrus Ostrander and Christina Rang.
Witnesses : Stoffel Ostrander and wife Aaltie.

March 1. Johannes, child of Jan Hasbroek and Rachel Van Wagene.
Witnesses : Aardt Joh. and Annatie Van Wagene, young man and young woman.

Elsjie, child of Daniel Dojou and Margritt Lefefer.
Witnesses : Abraham Dojou, Jr., and Maria Dojou, young woman.

April 13. Charels, child of Loys I. Dubois and Cathrina Broadhet.
Witnesses : The parents.

Annatie, child of Petrus Borehans and Debora Ostrander.
Witnesses : Johannes Fort and wife Rebecca.

Born Feb. 15, 1766, Charity, child of Martynus Griffin and Rachel Sopus.
Witnesses : Joseph Terwilliger and wife Annatje.

April 26. Isaak, child of Petrus Lefefer and Elisabeth Vernoy.
Witnesses : Corncles I. Vernoy and wife Maria.

May 10. Simon, child of Andres Dubois and Sarah Lefefer.
Witnesses: Simon Dubois and wife Cathryntie.

Martynus, child of Gerret and Maria Freres.
Witnesses: Jacobus Bevirs and wife Antie.

May 31. Sarah, child of Hermanus Ostrander and Barbara Terwilliger.
Witnesses: Andres Dubois and wife Sarah.

Johannes, child of Petrus Ancton and Margritta Dojou.
Witnesses: Christian Dojou and wife Alida.

July 12. Maria, child of Johannes Hardenberg, Jr., and Maria Lefefer.
Witnesses: Daniel Lefefer and wife Cathrina.

Aug. 23. Elsjie, child of Joseph Freres and Sartie Terwilliger.
Witnesses: Benjamin Freres, young man, and Elsjie Terwilliger, young woman.

Elisabeth, child of Johannes Smidt and Roseyntie Van Aake.
Witnesses: Jan Windfiel and wife Elisabeth.

Cathryntie, child of Josaphat Hasbroek and Cornelia Dubois.
Witnesses: Simon Dubois and wife Catreyntie.

Levi, child of Johannes Freres Jr. and Sara Bever.
Witnesses: Jonas Freres Jr., young man, and Fenny Everit, young woman.

Sept. 6. Maria, child of Heronumus Burger and Lena Sluyter.
Witnesses: Jacob Sax and wite Maria.

Oct. 25; born Oct. 20; Jacob, child of Jacob Hasbroek and Jennetie Dubois.
Witnesses: Loejs Bevirs and wife Hester.

Hugo, child of Daniel Freres and Maria Helm.
Witnesses: Hugo Freres and wife Hester.

Lena, child of Johannes Bartel Vol and Lena Roos.
Witnesses: John Parker and wife Lena.

Nov. 22. Jannetie, child of Johannes and Anna Sluyter.
Witnesses: The parents.

Benjamin, child of Jonathan Terwilliger and Marie Freres.
Witnesses: Benjamin Isaak Frerers, young man, and Maria Dojou, young woman.

Dec. 6. Benjamin, child of Benjamin Dojou and Jenneke Van Vliet.
Witnesses: The parents.

Johannes, child of Matheus Decker and Magdalena Bevirs.
Witnesses: Johannes Decker, young man, and Jaccomyntie Bevirs, young woman.

Annatie, child of Matheus Maste and Margritt Weller.
Witnesses: Joseph Terwilliger and wife Annatie.

Dec. 31. Maria, child of Daniel Freres, Jr., and Annatie Dojou.
Witnesses: Jonathan Terwilliger and wife Maria.

1768, March 20; born Oct. 26, 1767; Lourenz, child of Marteynus Griffin and Rachel Soper.
Witnesses: Isaak Freres and wife Hester.

May 8. Jacob, child of Henery Green and Maria Dojoux.
Witnesses: The parents.

May 22. Elisabeth, child of Daniel Dojou and Margritt Lefever.
Witnesses: The parents.

June 5. Benjamin, child of Joseph Caddington and Cathrina Vandermerk.
Witnesses: The parents.

Moses, child of Christian Dojou Jr., and Alida Terwilliger.
Witnesses: The parents.

July 3. Nathan, child of Pitter Dojou and Elisabeth Helm.
Witnesses: Abraham Jr., and Maria Dojou, young woman.

July 17. Elisabeth, child of Jacobus Hasbroek and Divertie Van Wagenen.
Witnesses: The parents.

Petrus, child of Henerich Wesemuller and Maria Rippighausen.
Witnesses: The parents.

Aug. 23. Marya, child of Daniel Dubois and Cathrina Lefever.
Witnesses: Abraham Lefever and wife Maria.

September 25. Anna, child of Petrus Ostrander and Christina Ranck.
Witnesses: Denie Rellie Jr., young man, and Anna Rank, young woman.

Oct. 9. Ardt, child of John Terwilliger and Maria Van Wagene.
Witnesses: Ardt Jr., and Elisabeth Van Wagene, young man and young woman.

Simon, child of Petrus Hasbroek and Sarah Bevirs.
Witnesses: Jacobus Hasbroek and wife Dievertie.

Nov. 6. Mareya, child of Marcus Ostrander and Elisabeth Degraff.
Witnesses: Jonathan Ostrander and wife Lydia.

Nov. 20. Elisabeth, child of Abraham Bevirs, Jr., and Maria Dubois.
Witnesses: Cornelius Vernoy and wife Cornelia.

1769, Jan. 22. Johannes, child of Johannes and Elisabeth Kleyn.
Witnesses: Nicolaas Albartus and wife Cornelia.

Feb. 5. Lydia, child of Sem Sammons and Rachel Schonmaker.
Witnesses: Benjamin Hasbroek and wife Lydia.

David, Child of Moses Freres and Judik Van Aake.
Witnesses: Benjamin Freres and wife Elisabeth.

March 5. Sarah, child of Andres Lefefer and Rachel Dubois.
Witnesses: The parents.

March 14. Zacharias, child of Isaak Freres and Hester Jansen.
Witnesses: Zacharia Jansen young man, and sister Rachel, young woman.

Maria, child of John Teerpenning and Elisabeth Alsdorpf.
Witnesses: Simon Alsdorff and wife Maria.

Johannes and Kobus, children of Willem Whiller and Margritt Killy.

March 19. Johannes, child of Johannes Bartel Volk and Lena Roos.
Witnesses: Abraham Klaarwater and sister Eva.

April 30. Johannes, child of Petrus Vandermerke and Helena Woedt.
Witnesses: The parents.

June 11. Mareya, child of David Ostrander and Engeltie Kouwenover.
Witnesses: Hans Kouwenover and wife Cathrina.

Maria, child of Henerik Dojou and Jannetie Schut.
Witnesses: Jan Terwilliger and wife Maria.

June 25. Abraham, child of Petrus Lefever and Lisabeth Vernoy.
Witnesses: Jacob Bevirs and wife Annatie.

Corneles, child of Johannis Freres, Jr., and Sarah Beaver.
Witnesses: The parents.

July 6. Johannes, child of Jacob Berger and Sarah Sluyter.
Witnesses: Johannes Blaynjohn and wife Rochelle.

July 7. Anna Cathrina, child of Frederick Heyms and Seletie Griffin.
Witnesses: Johan Frederick Heyms and wife Rosina Barbara.

July 23. Abraham, child of Denie and Maria Kelie (or Relie?)
Witnesses: Abraham Lefever and wife Maria.

Aug. 6. Weyntie, child of Josaphat Hasbrouque and Cornelia Dubois.
Witnesses: David Hasbrouque, Young Man and Weyntie Hasbrouque, widow.

Sept. 3. Andres, child of Nathanael Lefever and Maria Dojou.
Witnesses: Andres Lefever and wife Rachel—child's grandparents.

Oct. 15. Johannes, child of Henricus Rosekrantz and Maria Hardenberg.
Witnesses: John Hasbroek, Young Man, and Tryntie Van Wagene, Young Woman.

Oct. 29. Margritt, child of Daniel Freres and Maria Helm.
Witnesses: Jacob Helm and wife Margritt.

Nov. 26. Johannes, child of Johannes Walderon and Elisabeth Enn.
Witnesses: The parents.

1770, Jan. 21. Edward, child of Hieronymus Burger and Lena Sluyter.
Witnesses: Everd Sluyter and wife Lea.

Simon, child of Elisa Freres and Martha Everit.
Witnesses: Gerret Freres and wife Marya.

Feb. 4. Johanna, child of Petrus Ostrander and Cristina Rang.
Witnesses: Gideon Ostrander and Anna Rang, Young Woman.

March 4. Nathanael, child of Daniel Dojou and Margritt Lefever.
Witnesses : The parents.

March 18. Elisabeth, child of Joseph Coddington and Cathrina Vandermerken.
Witnesses : The parents.

Loura, child of Joseph Terwilliger and Annatie Weller.
Witnesses : Evert Hoffman, Young Man, and Marya Weller, Young Woman.

April 24. Maria, child of Christiaan Doyo, Jr., and Alida Terwilger.
Witnesses : The parents.

Albartus, child of Abraham Kool and Sara Sluyter.
Witnesses : Albartus and Annaatje Sluyter.

Apr. 29. Leentje, child of Jacob Windfield and Cathrina Helm.
Witnesses : Jimmy Keen and wife Leentje Windfield.

Christoffel, child of Henry Green and Maria Dejo.
Witnesses : The parents.

May 6. Daniel, child of Petris Smedes, Jr., and Elsje Hasebroek.
Witnesses : David and Weyntje Hasebroek.

May 27. Sarah, child of Jacob Jacobse Freres and Margriet Een.
Witnesses : Jacob Freres, Jr., and wife Sarah.

Isaak, child of Zacharias Sluyter and Brechie York.
Witnesses : Isaak Freres and wife Hester.

July 1. Petrus, child of Benjamin Sluyter and Margritt Bernert.
Witnesses : Wilhelmus Sluyter, Young Man, and Catrin Bernet, Young Woman.

July 13. Gerret, child of Gerret, Jr., and Maria Freer.
Witnesses : The parents.

July 15 ; born June 20. Johnny, child of Marteynus Griffin and Rachel Sopus.
Witnesses : Petrus Schoonmaker and wife Rachel.

Maria, child of Johannes Hardenberg, Jr., and Maria Lefefer.
Witnesses : Daniel Lefefer and wife Cathrina.

Jannetie, child of Jonas Frers, Jr., and Magdalena Bevirs.
Witnesses : Jacobus Bevirs and wife Antie.

Aug. 26. Jonas, child of Loejs Jonath. Dubois and Catrina Broadhet.
Witnesses : The parents.

Loura, child of Jacob Frers, Jr., and Sarah Freres.
Witnesses : The parents.

Sept. 9. Sarah, child of Abraham Bevirs, Jr., and Maria Dubois.
Witnesses : The parents.

Oct. 21. Adam, child of Derk Keyser and Sara Delang.
Witnesses : Adam Hofman and Elisabeth Van Wagenen.

Nov. 5. Philippus, child of Petrus I. Schonmaker and Rachel Van Wagenen.
Witnesses : Jan Terwilliger and wife Maria.

1771, March 17. Maria, child of Joseph Freer and Sara Terwilger.
Witnesses : Jonathan and Maria Terwilger.

Benjamin, child of Frederick Heyms and Seelitje Griffin.
Witnesses : Benjamin and Maria Dubois.

June 16. Abraham, child of Hendrik Wesemiller and Maria Rippighausen.
Witnesses : Abraham Le Fevre and wife Maria Bevier.

Sept. 12. Jerimia, child of Petrus Haasbrouk and Sara Bevier.

Jesaja, child of Wuoter Sluyter and Margriet Bartin.

Abram, child of Nathaniel Lafaver and Maria De Yoo.
Witnesses : Abram De Yoo and Elizabeth DeBois.

Sept. 29. Moses, child of Paulus Freer and Lisabeth Van Wagenen.
Witnesses : Hugo Freer and wife Hester.

Nelly, child of Jeremias Lindebecker and Nelly DeLang.

David, child of Johannes Vreer and Sarah Bever.

Oct. 3. John, child of Joh. Griffin and Margriet Wieler.

Oct. 6. Nelly, child of Frans De Lange and Grietje Hellebeeker.

Dec. 29. Catharina, child of Jonas Freer, Jr., and Magdalena Bevier.
Witnesses: Johannes Freer, Jr., and wife Sarah Bevier.

Catharina, child of Stephanus Eckert and Maria Dekker.

Daniel, child of Josaphat Haasbrouck and Cornelia Du Bois.

David, child of Jonathan Terwilliger and Maria Freer.
Witnesses: Benjamin Terwilliger and wife Elsje Freer.

1772, Feb. 16; born, Jan. 27. David, child of Martynus Griffen and Ragel Sope.
Witnesses: David Sope, Nelly Griffen.

Born Jan. 1. Abraham, child of Henry Green and Maria De Joo.

Absalom, child of Matheus Maesten and Margriet Weller.
Witnesses: Cornelius Maasten and wife Dina Ellen.

Born Jan. 15. Rochelle, child of Petrus Fiele and Maria Romyn.

July 8. Elias, child of Jacob J. Freer and Margariet Ein.

Maria, child of Daniel York and Maria Van Aaken.
Witnesses: Petrus and Maria York.

Esther, child of Joseph Coddington and Catharina Van de Merken.

Oct. 30. Claartje, child of Christiaan De Jo and Alida Terwillige.

Daniel, child of Daniel Freer and Maria Helm.

Elisa, child of Wilhelmus Oostrander and Saratje Rallie.
Witnesses: Denier Rallie and Maria Van Vliet.

Nov. 1. Samuel, child of John Terwilligen and Maria Van Wagenen.

William, child of Hendrick Dejo and Jannetje Schut.
Witnesses: Simeon Ralje, Jr., and Lena Dujo.

Johannes, child of Frederick Heymes and Sealy Griffen.
Witnesses: Martin and Maria Root.

Nov. 22. Hugo, child of Zacharias Sluyter and Breche York.
Witnesses: Petrus and Maria York.

1773, May 9. Margarita, child of Cornelius DeBoys, Jr., and Geertruy Bruyn.
Witnesses : Cornelius DeBoys and Margarita Van Hoogteelink.

Jonathan, child of Daniel De Yoo and Maragriet LaFever.

Born December 27, 1772. Abram, child of Petrus Van De Merken and Helena Wood.

Born Feb. 13, 1773. Abram, child of Petrus J. Schoonmaker and Rachel Van Wagenen.
Witnesses : Abram Een and Catharina Van Wagenen.

Esther, child of Daniel Freer, Jr., and Annatje Deyoo.
Witnesses : Isaac Freer and Esther Jansen.

Moses, child of Matheus and Elizabeth La Fever.
Witnesses : Daniel La Fever and Catharina Cantinne.

Petrus Edmundus, child of Petrus Smedes, Jr., and Elsje Hasbrouk.
Witnesses : Jacob Smedes and Maria Dekker.

Elisa, child of Henrikus Teerpenning and Maria Van Aaken.
Witnesses : Eliza and Sophia Van Aaken.

Mary, child of Robert Masters and Mary Parker.

Jenneke, child of Tuenis Van Vliet and Lammertje Romeyn.

Aug 12 ; born Aug. 2. Ammelena, child of Benjamin Sluyter and Maragrieta Berner.
Witnesses : Wilhelmus and Jannetje Sluyter.

Born July 28. Maragriet, child of Gerret and Maria Freer.

Oct. 3. Benjamin, child of Gerhardus Hardenberg and Nancy Reyersen.

Oct. 10. Wyntje, child of Josaphat Haasbroek and Cornelia De Boi.

Luwis, child of Nathaniel Leffeber and Maria De Jo.

Hester, child of Simeon Lenjee, Jr., and Magdelena De Jo.

Robert, child of Willem Hoed and Anaetje Sluyter.

Nov. 20. Abraham, child of Joseph Hasbrouk and Elizabeth Bevier.
Witnesses : Abraham Hasbrouk and Catharina Bruyn.

Lidia, child of David Oostrander and Engeltje Cowenover.

Nov. 21. Eva, child of Johannes Smith and Jesyntje Van Aken.
Witnesses : Johannes and Eva Ekker.

Elizabeth, child of Ephraim Keyser and Lena Kleyn.
Witnesses : Johannes and Elizabeth Kleyn.

1774, Jan. 19. Joseph, child of Benjamin Haasbrouck and Elidia Schoonmaker.

Mattheus, child of Jan and Maria Le Fevre.
Witnesses : Mattheus Le Fevre and Maria Bevier.

Sarah, child of Jacob Windvield and Cathrina Helm.

Cathrina, child of Frederick Wilkelo and Anna Maria Glaesing.

Lydia, child of Cornelis Canneway and Annatje Sluyter.

Jonathan, child of Albertus Sluyter and Maria Weyt.

Jacob, child of Joost Koens and Cathrina Woester.

April 18. Louis Brodhead, child of Louis J. DuBois and Catharina Brodhead.
Witness : Louis Brodhead.

Rachel, child of Daniel DuBois and Catharina Lefever.
Witnesses : Benjamin Du Bois and Maria Bevier.

Echje, child of Henry Green and Maria De Joo.

Isaac, child of Joseph Freer and Saartje Terwilleger.
Witnesses : Isaac Terwilleger and Rebecka Spinnik.

June 26. Jacob, child of Georgius Wirtz and Esther Hasbrouk.
Witnesses : Jacob Hasbrouk, Jr., and Jannetje DuBois.

Sarah, child of Johannes Waldron and Elizabeth Een.
Witness : Sarah Een.

Born April 28. Leah, child of Martynus Griffin and Rachel Sooper.
Witnesses : Johannes Dejoo and Lea Vandemerken.

Abram, child of Jeronimus Burger and Lena Sluyter.
Witnesses : Abram Sluyter and Elizabeth Davis.

Ellenor, child of Pieter La Roy and Rachel Mabee.
Witnesses : Jacobus Filkins and Ellenor Phillips.

Sarah, child of Petrus Hasbrouk and Sarah Bevier.
Witnesses : Elias Hasbrouk and Elizabeth Sleght.

Rachel, child of Jonas Freer, Jr., and Magdalena Bevier.
Witnesses : Jonas Freer and Catharina Stokraad.

Abram Salomon, child of Salomon Bevier and Nellie Griffin.
Witness : Margariet Eltinge.

Edward, child of Johannes Parleman and Catharina Van Stienbergh.
Witnesses : Abram and Lidia Van Stienberg.

July 10. David, child of Petris and Maria Viele.

Sept. 15. Agatta, child of Zacharias Sluyter and Bregje York.

Annatje, child of Daniel York and Maria Aaken.
Witnesses : Jacob Freer and Annatje Van Aaken.

Abram, child of Johannes Kleyn and Elizabeth Keyser.
Witnesses : Abram Sluyter and Elizabeth Davies.

Dennis, child of Mathew McCavy and Jannetje Tapper.

Ann, child of Joseph Coddington and Catharina Vander Merken.

Margariet, child of Frederick Heems and Seletje Griffin.
Witness : Margariet Griffin.

Dec. 7. Elizabeth, child of Benjamen Wintfield and Annatje York.

Maria, child of Samuel Bevier and Rachel Achmody.
Witnesses : Jacob Bevier and Maria York.

1775, March 12. Jacob, child of Simon Dujoo and Antje Low.
Witnesses : Jacob Low and Rebecca Elting.

John, child of Daniel Dyver and Maragrieta Snies.

Altje, child of Teunus Van Vliet and Lammetje Romeyn.

Jonathen, child of John De Graaf and Annatje Smith.

Benjamin, child of Abraham Sluyter and Elizabeth Davids.

John, child of Roberd Masters and Mary Parker.

May 14. Benjamin, child of Petrus Schoonmaker and Rachel Van Wagenen.
Witnesses : Benjamin and Sarah Van Wagenen.

Daniel, child of Petrus Smedes, Jr., and Elsje Hasbrouck.
Witnesses : Jesaias and Weintje Hasbrouck.

Tomas (or Jonas?) and Jesaias, children of Jacob Keter and Amelena Sluyter.
Witnesses: Dirk Keter, Sarah Delange, Abraham Keter, and Rachel Keter.

Syme, child of Simeon Rallje, Jr., and Lena Dejo.

July 2. Maria, child of Jan Davids and Eva Helm.

Maria, child of Jacob and Maria Bevier.
Witnesses: Moses and Maria Jork.

Maria, child of Matthewis and Elizabeth Lefever.
Witnesses: Jan and Maria Lefever.

Aug. 10. Catharina, child of Simon Freer and Annatje Blanjan.
Witnesses: Gerret, Jr., and Maria Freer.

Abraham, child of William Hood and Annatje Sluyter.

1776, Jan. 21. William child of David Haasbrook and Maria Hoogland.

Johannis, child of Petrus Lefaver and Elizabeth Van Noy.
Witnesses: Nathan Van Noy and Yannetye Hoornbeck.

Elizabeth, child of Daniel Frear, Jr., and Annatye Deyoe.

Isaac, child of Frederick Wilkeloe and Anna Maria Gleserin.

Elizabeth, child of Nathaniel Feaver and Maria Deyoe.

Cathrina, child of Lowrans Hendrikson and Hanna Winfield.
Wittnesses: Jacob and Cathrina Winfield.

Roeleph, child of Salomon Bevier and Nelly Griffin.
Wittnesses: Roeleph J. Eltinge and Maria Low.

Elizabeth, child of Paulus Freer and Elizabeth Van Wagenen.
Witnesses: Abram Lea and Cathrina Van Wagenen.

Nancy, child of James McClaghley and Catey Duseney.

Bowdewine, child of Samuel Teerpenning and Maria Alsdorf.

May 28. Simon, child of Josavat Hasbrouck and Cornelia Dubois.

Archer, child of Henry Green and Maria Dojo.

Elisa, child of Elisa Freer and Marta Evered.
Witnesses: Jonas Freer and Maddelena Bevier.

Sept. 8. Maria, child of Johannis Smith and Roseyntye Van Aaken.

Born July 15; Andrias, child of Martinus Griffen and Rachel Soper.
Witnesses: Andrias and Lena Lefever.

Jacobus, child of Samuel Bevier and Rachel Achtmude.

Maria, child of Abram Dubois and Magdelena Bevier.
Witnesses: Benjamin Dubois and Maria Bevier.

Maria, child of Wouter Sluyter and Margreta Barten.

Oct. 29; born Sept. 29. Jacob, child of Georgius Wirtzs and Hester Hasbrouck.
Witnesses: Jacob and Jannetje Hasbrouck.

Wauter, child of Wilhelmus and Jannetje Sluiter.

Maria, child of Johannes Waldran and Elisabeth Een.

Maragrietje, child of Petrus Hasbrouck and Sara Bavier.
Witnesses: Abraham and Maria Bavier.

Abraham, child of Johannes, Jr., and Maria Lefever.
Witnesses: Abraham and Maria Lefever.

1777, Jan. 5. Annatje, child of Jacob I. Frere and Margrietje Ein.

Elsje, child of Robert Poor and Mary Serjent.

Elisabeth, child of Frederik Hyms and Sieltje Griffen.
Witnesses: Benjamen and Elisabeth Frere.

Maria, child of Petrus Smedes, Jr., and Elsje Hasbrouck.

Matheus, child of Christian Doiau and Alida Terwilliger.

Betsy, child of Mathew McAvie? and Jane Tappen.

Joseph, child of Simeon Doio and Antje Low.

Maria, child of Jacob Bevier and Maria York.
Witnesses: Moses and Maria York.

Gerret, child of Teunus Van Vliet and Lammetje Romein.

March 12. Josua, child of Jonas Frere and Magdalena Bevier.
Witnesses: Petrus Freer and Annatje Dubois.

May 25. James, child of David Soper and Jane Boyd.

Margriet, child of James Dunn and Anne Lane.

June 15. John, child of Salomon Bavier and Elanor Griffin.
Witnesses : John and Ellanor Griffin.

Hester, child of Hugo and Maria Frere.
Witnesses : Hugo Frere and Hester Doiau.

Aug. 24. John, child of Elias and Cornelia Hardenberg.
Witnesses : John, Jr., and Peggy Hardenberg.

Aug. 31. Ann, child of Lowis Dubois and Catarina Broadhead.
Witnesses : The parents.

Oct. 5. Andreas, child of Isack and Maria Lefever.
Witnesses : Andreas and Rachel Lefever.

Oct. 26. Rachel, child of Petrus I. Schoonmaker and Raghel Van Wagene.
Witnesses : The parents.

Janes (or James), child of Hendric Tice and Catarina Van Tessel.
Witnesses : The parents.

Nov. 9. Annatje, child of Simon Frere and Annatje Blonjan.
Witnesses : Stoffel and Debora Doiou.

Evert, child of Abraham Sluiter and Elisabeth Davisse.
Witnesses : The parents.

— 7 ; born — ember 14. Samuel, child of Matheus and Jacomyncha Bavier.
Witnesses : The parents.

Born Nov. — . Jacob, child of Daniel Frere and Maria Helm.
Witnesses : The parents.

Dec. 21 ; born Dec. 6. Ezechiel, child of Simeon Low and Christina McMollin.
Witnesses : The parents.

Born Dec. 6. Catarina, child of Abraham Ein and Catarina Van Wagene.
Witnesses : The parents.

1778, Jan. 1 ; born Dec. 6, 1777. Maria, child of Mattheus and Elisabeth Lefever.
Witnesses : John and Maria Lefever.

Born Dec. 9, 1777. Maria, child of David Hasbrouck and Maria Hoogland.
Witnesses : The parents.

Feb. 1 ; born Dec. 10, 1777. Maria, child of Daniel Diver and Margrietje Nies.
Witnesses : The parents.

Feb. 22 ; born Feb. 20. Ester, child of Paulus Frere and Elizabeth Van Wagene.
Witnesses : Jonathan and Maria Terwilliger,* Samuel Schoonmaker, and Annatje Van Wagene.

Jacob, child of Cornelius Keizer and Elsje Etkins.
Witnesses : Jacob Keizer and wife.

April 22 ; born March 12. Maritje, child of Simon Ralyea and Magdalena Doyo.
Witnesses : The parents.

May 10 ; born April 23. Cornelius, child of Petrus Lefever and Elizabeth Vernoy.
Witnesses : Isack and Maria Lefever.

May 24 ; born April 23. Agetta, child of Saccharias Sluiter and Bregje Jork.
Witnesses : The parents.

Born April 26. Elizabeth, child of Thomas Lamonjon and Catharina Johnson.
Witness : Mother.

Born July 16. Elizabeth, child of Isack Johnson and Hannah Lemonjon.
Witnesses : The parents.

June 21 ; born May 25. Sartje, child of Matthew McKaby and Jannetje Tappen.
Witnesses : The parents.

Born May 24. Rachel, child of Nathaneel Lefever and Maria Doiou.
Witnesses : The parents.

Born Feb. 27. Thomas, child of Gerardus Hardenberg and Ann Ryerse.
Witnesses : The parents.

* From the way in which they have been entered in the original it is impossible to say whether the Terwilligers were witnesses for Diver or Frere.

Born May 13. John, child of Elisa Frere and Martha Everet.
Witnesses : Johannes Frere and Sarah Bever.

July 5 ; born June 5. Elisabeth, child of Johannes Kleyn and Elizabeth Keyser.
Witnesses : The parents.

July 19 ; born July 10. Moses Depui, child of Ruben DeWitt and Elizabeth Depuy.
Witnesses : Moses Depuy and Elizabeth Klaarwater.

Born June 30. Jacobus, child of Jacob Bevier and Maria York.
Witness : Johannes York.

Aug. 23 ; born Aug. 11. Antje, child of Samuel Bavier and Rachel Agmoedy.
Witnesses : The parents.

Sept. 20 ; born Aug. 11. Rachel, child of Daniel York and Maria Van Aken.
Witnesses : The parents.

Born March 5. Isack, child of Benjamin Frere and Anna Parker.
Witness : Benjamin Frere.

Born Aug. 22. Maria, child of Daniel Dubois and Catarina Lefever.
Witnesses : The parents.

Oct. 4 ; born Aug. 26. Maria, child of Wilhelmus and Jannetje Sluiter.
Witnesses : The parents.

Nov. 22 ; born Oct. 31. Jannetje, child of Benjamin Doiou and Jenneke Van Vliedt.
Witnesses : The parents.

Born Sept. 1 ; Petrus, child of Petrus York and Margriet Van Leuwe.
Witnesses : Petrus Van Leuwe and Regina Velten.

Born Oct. 29 ; Elisbeth, child of Jacob Shely and Ester Klaarwater.
Witnesses : The parents.

Nov. 29 ; born Sept. 27. Jackemyntje, child of Jacobus Personius and Rachel Keyser.
Witnesses : The parents.

Dec. 27; born Nov. 29. Jesaias, child of John Terwilliger and Maria Van Wagene.
Witnesses: The parents.

Dec. 30; born Nov. 7. Martynus, child of Martynus Griffin and Rachel Soper.
Witnesses: David Sopier and Jenne Boid.

1779, Jan. 31; born Dec. 28, 1778. Elisabeth, child of Daniel Doio and Margriet Lefever.
Witnesses: The parents.

Born Dec. 6, 1778. John, child of Teunis Van Vliet and Lambertje Romyn.
Witnesses: The parents.

Born June 18, 1778? Rachel, child of Josaphat Hasbrouck and Cornelia Dubois.
Witnesses: The parents.

Born Jan. 8, at 2 P.M. Margrietje, child of Salomon Bavier and Nella Griffin.
Witness: Margrietje Bavier.

Feb. 21; born Feb. 2. Agetta, child of Frederick Hyms and Seltje Griffin.
Witnesses: The parents.

March 14; born Dec. 4, 1778. Eva, child of Henery Green and Maria Doio.
Witnesses: Christoffel Doio and Eva Douo.

March 14; born Dec. 18, 1778. Beletje, child of Wauterus Sluiter and Margrietje Berton.
Witnesses: The parents.

April 11. Maria, child of Daniel Van Leuwe and Elizabeth Etkins.
Witnesses: Petrus Van Leuwe and Regina Velte.

Elisabeth, child of Frederik Keyzer and Cornelia Sluiter.
Witnesses: The parents.

April 18; born March 24. Samuel, child of Petrus Hasbrouck and Sara Bavier.
Witnesses: Mattheus and Jackemyntje Bavier.

May 16; born Dec. 5,. 1778. Abraham, child of Isack Herres and Jannetje Frere.
Witnesses: The parents.

Born Apr. 14, 1779. Elias, child of Jonas Frere and Magdalena Bavier.
Witnesses: Elias and Jannetje Bavier.

May 30; born Jan. 11. Jeny, child of Robin Poor and Polly Serjent.
Witnesses: The parents.

Born May 15. Margrietje, child of Andries Bavier and Jakemyntje Dubois.
Witnesses: The parents.

June 6; born April 5. Nathan, child of Johannes Hoornbeek and Maria Vernoy.
Witnesses: The parents.

June 20; born May 4. David, child of Joseph Hasbrouck and Elisabeth Bavier.
Witnesses: David Bevier and Mary Hasbrouck.

Born May ———. Mary, child of Benjamin Alliger and Sarah Rosekrans.
Witnesses: Frederick Rosekrans and Ann Moul.

Born May 14. Robert, child of Robert Masters and Mary Parker.
Witnesses: The parents.

Born Aug. 12, 1778? Robert, child of Michael Ophrel (?) and Margriet Hennessey.
Witnesses: The parents.

Born March 16. Jannetje, child of Joseph Frere and Sarah Terwilliger.
Witnesses: Evert and Maria Terwilliger.

July 4; born June 4. Margrietje, child of John Jr. and Maria Lefevour.
Witnesses: Jonathan Vernoy and Margrietje Lefevour.

Born June 25. Jannetje, child of Georgius Wertz and Ester Hasbrouck.
Witnesses: The parents.

Born May 31. Magdalena, child of Petrus Smedes, Jr., and Elsje Hasbrouck.
Witnesses: Petrus B. and Elizabeth Smedes.

July 18; born June 20. Petrus, child of Isack and Maria Lefevour.
Witnesses: Petrus Lefevour and Elizabeth Vernoy.

Born June 17. Petrus, child of Lourence Hendricks and Johanna Windtfield.
Witnesses : Daniel and Tryntje Windtfield.

Aug. 8 ; born Aug. 3. Sarah, child of John A. Dewitt and Rachel Bavier.
Witnesses : Salomon and Sarah Low.

Born June 27. Elias, child of Elias and Cornelia Hardenberg.
Witnesses : The parents.

Born June 19. Petrus, child of Dirk Janson and Margrietje Van Steenberg.
Witnesses : Antonie and Jannetje Frere.

Aug. 29 ; born Aug. 7. Dirk, child of Matheus McCaby and Jannetje Tappan.
Witnesses : The parents.

Sept. 5 ; born Aug. 15. Abraham, child of Simon Doio and Antje Low.
Witnesses : Capt. Abraham and Elizabeth Doio.

Sept. 19 ; born Aug. 31. Margrietje, child of Daniel Wood and Margrietje Tornar.
Witnesses : The parents.

Born Sept. 2. Isack, child of Abraham Janson and Catryntje Bavier.
Witnesses : The parents.

Oct. 3 ; born Sept. 23. Cornelius, child of Tjerck Dewitt and Elsje Depui.
Witnesses : Cornelius Depui and Maria Vernoy.

Born Sept. 24. Daniel, child of Simeon Low and Christina McMollen.
Witnesses : The parents.

Oct. 31 ; born Sept. 23. Joseph, child of Andries Dubois and Maria Doio.
Witnesses : The parents.

Nov. 21 ; born Oct. 17. Elizabeth, child of Bodewin and Elizabeth Teerpenning.
Witnesses : The parents.

Rachel, child of David and Maria Hasbrouck.
Witnesses : The parents.

Born Oct. 17. Agetha, child of Jonathan Frere and Margrietje Doio.
Witnesses: Johannes Frere and Agetha Doio.

Dec. 5; born Nov. 1. Margrietje, child of Cornelius Duand, Jr., and Geertruy Bruyn.
Witnesses: The parents.

1780, Jan. 30. Jonathan, child of Benjamin Sluiter and Margriet Berner.
Witnesses: The parents.

Feb. 6; born Jan. 9. Paulus, child of Jeremias Frere and Sara Van Wagenen.
Witnesses: Paulus Frere and Elizabeth Van Wagenen.

Born Nov. 21, 1779. George, child of Edward Wood and Ann Westluck.
Witnesses: Edward Wood and Catarina Van der Merken.

Feb. 20; born Dec. 28, 1779. Maria, child of Benjamin I. Frere and Anna Perkens.
Witnesses: Jonathan and Maria Terwilliger.

March 5; born Feb. 21. Rebecca, child of Jeremias Low and Wyntje Weler.
Witnesses: The parents.

March 26; born Feb. 6. Cornelia, child of Samuel Bavier and Rachel Achmoedy.
Witnesses: The parents.

April 23; born March 20. Timotheus, child of David Sopier and Jane Boid.
Witnesses: The parents.

Born Feb. 16. Petrus, child of Petrus Schoonmaker and Rachel Van Wagene.
Witnesses: Petrus Van Wagene and Sara Low.

Born March 27. Isack, child of Jacob Bavier and Maria York.
Witnesses: The parents.

April 26; born Feb. 3. Sara, child of Ephraim Kyser and Lena Klyn.
Witnesses: Johannes Kyser and Jacob Klyn.

June 4; born May 13. Margriet, child of Jacob Kyser, Jr., and Ammalyna Sluiter.
Witnesses: The parents.

June 18; born Aug. 28, 1780 (*sic.*). John, child of William Donnolson and Magdalena Nies.
Witnesses: Daniel and Margriet Diver.

Born May 24. Jacob, child of Johannes A. (?) Hardenberg and Rachel Dubois.
Witnesses: The parents.

Born March 15. Johannes, child of Isack Jonson and Hannah L. Monjon.
Witnesses: The parents.

Born April 8. Abraham, child of Abraham Palmatier and Elizabeth Lane.
Witnesses: The parents.

Magdalena, child of Johannes Lits and Leentje Emson.
Witnesses: The parents.

July 2; born Feb. 19. Elizabeth, child of Jury Nies and Tryntje Van Keure.
Witnesses: The parents.

Born Jan. 27. Isack, child of Jordan Perhemes and Lidia Doio.
Witnesses: The parents.

July 30; born June 20. Jonas, child of Jesaias Hasbrouck and Maria Bavier.
Witnesses: Jonas and Catarina Hasbrouck.

Born July 15. Margriet, child of Wauterus Sluiter and Margriet Barton.
Witnesses: The parents.

Born July 3. Antje, child of Johannes York and Jannetje Bavier.
Witnesses: Jonas and Madlena Frere.

Born July 13. Margrietje, child of Mattheus and Jackemyntje Bavier.
Witnesses: Abraham Bavier and Margrietje Elting.

Aug. 6; born July 27. Nathaneel, child of Mattheus and Elizabeth Lefevour.
Witness: Marytje Lefever.

Aug. 27; born Aug. 3. Gerret Amos, child of Hugo Frere and Annatje Dewitt.
Witnesses: Gerret and Maria Frere.

Born Aug. 17. Caty, child of Salomon Bavier and Nellie Griffin.
Witnesses : The parents.

Born July 29. Margriet, child of David Low and Rachel Lemerter.
Witnesses : John and Margriet Van Wagene.

Sept. 10 ; born Aug. 29. Magdalena, child of Cornelius Elinge and Blandina Elmondorph.
Witnesses : The parents.

Born Aug. 15. Magdalena, child of Cornelius Kyser and Elsje Etkins.
Witnesses : Andries and Maria Kyser.

Sept. 24 ; born July 30. Wilhelmus, child of Abraham Sluyter and Elizabeth Davis.
Witnesses : The parents.

Born Aug. 31. Lena, child of Wilhelmus and Jannetje Sluyter.
Witnesses : Hieronimus Burger and Lena Sluyter.

Born Aug. 23. David, child of David Etkins and Margriet Sluyter.
Witnesses : The parents.

Born Aug. 20. Petrus, child of Zacharias Sluyter and Bregje Jork.
Witnesses : The parents.

Oct. 8 ; born Sept. 16. Catarina, child of Daniel I. Frere and Annatje Doio.
Witnesses : Levi Doio and Catarina Terbos.

Oct. 22 ; born Sept. 22. Catarina, child of Simon Frere and Annatje Blonjan.
Witnesses : Christian Doio and Alida Terwilliger.

Born Sept. 17. Isack, child of Gilbert Saxton and Tjatje Bever.
Witnesses : The parents.

Nov. 5 ; born Oct. 9. Maria, child of Daniel Frere and Maria Helm.
Witnesses : The parents.

Dec. 17 : born Nov. 3. Tryntje, child of Gideon Hornbeek and Abigael Davis.
Witnesses : The parents.

1781, Jan. 1 ; born Nov. 21, 1780. Stephanus, child of Isack Harres and Jannetje Frere.
Witnesses : The parents.

Born Dec. 6, 1780. Catarina, child of Jonathan Doio and Maria Lefever.
Witnesses : Daniel Lefever and Catarina Cantine.

Feb. 18 ; born Dec. 1, 1780. Polly, child of Mathew McCaby and Jannitje Tappen.
Witnesses : The parents.

Born Jan. 24. Rebecca, child of Antony Frere and Jannitje Low.
Witnesses : Jacob Low and Lena Elting.

Born Oct. 24, 1780. John, child of Charles Brodhead and Mary Oliver.
Witnesses : John and Mary Broadhead.

Born Feb. 2. Maria, child of Paulus Frere and Elizabeth Van Wagene.
Witnesses : John and Maria Terwilger.

Born Oct. 9, 1780. Eliza, child of Eliza Frere and Martha Everet.
Witnesses : The parents.

Born Jan. 12. Abraham, child of Johannes Suert and Rachel Gerritze.
Witnesses : The parents.

Feb. 25 ; born Feb. 1. Caty, child of Martin Griffin and Rachel Sopier.
Witnesses : The parents.

Born Jan. 19. Catrientje, child of Petrus Veley and Gerretje Frere.
Witnesses : The parents.

Born Jan. 14. Abraham, child of William Donaldson and Magdalin Nies.
Witnesses : The parents.

Born Jan. 21. Jannetje, child of Dirk Janson and Margrietje Steenberg.
Witnesses : The parents.

April 16 ; born March 16. Catarina, child of Andries Dubois and Maria Doio.
Witnesses : The parents.

May 13 ; born Feb. 10. Daniel, child of John Barret and Seletje Parmetier.
Witnesses : The parents.

June 10 ; born May 25. Joseph, child of Joseph Hasbrouck and Elizabeth Bavier.
Witnesses : Joseph and Elizabeth Hasbrouck.

Born April 29. Abraham, child of Daniel Dubois and Catarina Lefever.
Witnesses : Benjamin Dubois and Maria Bavier.

Born Aug. 20, 1778. Isack, child of Hendricus Bos and Wyntje Frere.
Witnesses : Isack (?) and Marytje Frere.

Born Dec. 29, 1779. Johannes, probably the same parents as above.
Witnesses : Johannes Boss and Jannetje Dubois.

June 26, Moses, born July 7, 1777 ; John, born July 14, 1780, children of William Elsworth and Jane Dean.
Witnesses : The parents.

Born Feb. 14. Jurry, child of Lourence Nies and Annatje Degraef.
Witnesses : The parents.

Daniel St. John, born Jan. 20, 1779 ; Mary, born Aug. 26, 1780, children of Joseph Elsworth.
Witnesses : William Elsworth and Mary Bos.

July 8 ; born June 3. Maria, child of Jonas Frere and Magdalen Bavier.
Witnesses : The parents.

Born May 29. Johannes, child of Petrus Smedes and Elsje Hasbrouck.
Witnesses : David Hasbrouck and Maria Hogland.

Aug. 26 ; born Aug. 10. Josia, child of Jesaias Hasbrouck and Maria Bavier.
Witness : Margrietje Elting.

Born July 15. Frederick, child of Teunis Van Viet and Lambertje Romyn.
Witnesses : Frederick Van Vliet and Catarina Waters.

Sept. 9 ; born July 26. Lea, child of Benjamin Windfield and Annatje York.
Witnesses : The parents.

Born Aug. 3. Elizabeth, child of Daniel York and Maria Van Ake.
Witness : Elizabeth Van Wagene.

Born Aug. 16. Wilhelmus, child of Hieronimus Burger and Lena Sluiter.
Witnesses : Wilhelmus and Jannetje Sluyter.

Born Aug. 22. Jacob, child of Frederick Keiser and Cornelia Sluyter.
Witnesses : Jacob and Elizabeth Keyzer.

Born Aug. 22. Martynus, child of Petrus Klaarwater and Sarah Sluyter.
Witnesses : Martynus and Maria Klaarwater.

Born Aug. 11. Rebecca, child of Simon Doio and Antje Low.
Witnesses : Isack Dubois and Rebecca Doio.

Born July 27. Abraham, child of Nathanel Lefevour and Maria Doio.
Witnesses : Abraham Doio and Elizabeth Dubois.

Born July 8. Joseph, child of Josia Terwilger and Margriet Griffin.
Witnesses : Joseph, Jr., and Catarina Coddington.

Sept. 13 ; born Feb. 31. (Sic.) Zacharias, child of Josaphat Hasbrouck and Cornelia Dubois.
Witness : Zacharias Hasbrouck.

Febe, Annie, and Elizabeth, children of Icabod Williams and Sibel Clark.

Rympe, Matheus, Rebecca, and John children of David Maccy and Lena Storm.
Witnesses: Alexander Maccy, Thankfull Tuttle, and Montgomery Ely.

Rachel and Peter, children of Peter Leroy and Rachel Maby.

Sept. 23 ; born Sept. 2. Catarina, child of Georgius Wirtz and Ester Hasbrouck.
Witnesses : Rynier Van Nes and Catarina Heger.

Oct. 7 ; born Sept. 6. Rachel, child of Isack and Maria Lefever.
Witnesses : The parents.

Oct. 21 ; born Sept. 22. Abraham, child of Methusalem Dubois and Catrientje Bavier.
Witnesses : Margariet and Abraham Bavier.

Nov. 25; born Oct. 5. John, child of Jordan Perhemus and Lidia Doio.
Witnesses: The parents.

Born Nov. 4. Isack, child of Isack Low and Francisca Everet.
Witnesses: The parents.

Born Oct. 2. Cornelia and Maria, children of Emanuel Consalis and Sarah Bevier.
Witnesses: The parents, and Conraed and Maria Bevier.

Dec. 28; born Oct. 29. Elizabeth, child of Gerardus Hardenberg and Nancy Ryerson.
Witnesses: The parents.

1782, Jan.—; born Nov. 24. 1781. Rachel, child of Philippus Doio and Gertruy Lefever.
Witnesses: Andries and Catarina Lefever.

Born Dec. 28, 1781. Petrus, child of Abraham Een and Catarina Van Wagenen.
Witnesses: Petrus Lefever and Elizabeth Vernoy.

Jan. 13; born Dec. 18, 1781. Josia, child of Cornelius Dubois and Gertruy Bruyn.
Witnesses: The parents.

Jan. 20; born Dec. 26, 1781. Christian, child of Jeremias Frere and Sara Van Wagene.
Witnesses: Hugo Frere and Hester Do . .

Born Dec. 10, 1781. Uria, child of Salomon and Arriantje Dubois.
Witnesses: Hendricus—and Rebecca Vanw.

Feb. 10; born Jan. 8. Methusalem, child of Petrus Hasbrouck and Sara Bavier.
Witnesses: Methusalem and Catarina Dubois?

Born Sept. 15, 1781. Maria, child of Simon Raljie and Magdalena Doio.
Witnesses: The parents.

Feb. 24, born Jan. 25, 1781. Catarina, child of Jacob Bavier and Maria York.
Witnesses: The parents.

Born Jan. 31. Charity, child of Salomon Bavier and Nella Griffin.
Witnesses: Charity Griffen.

Born Jan. 19. Elizabeth, child of Isack Dubois and Rebecca Doio.
Witnesses : Hendrick and Elizabeth Doio.

March 3 ; born Feb. 22. Jannetje, child of Simeon Low and Christina McMullen.
Witnesses : The parents.

May 7. Annatje, child of John Terwilger and Maria Van Wagene.
Witnesses : The parents.

June 2 ; born April 10. Jannetje, child of Wilhelmus and Jannetje Sluiter.
Witnesses : The parents.

June 16 ; born March 29. David, child of David Sopier and Jane Boid.
Witnesses : The parents.

Born Feb. 14. Abraham, child of Jacob Kyser Jr., and Ammalena Sluiter.
Witnesses : The parents.

Born May 10. William, child of Mathew Mc Caby and Jannetje Tappen.
Witnesses : The parents.

Born May 20. Elias, child of Johannes York, and Jannetje Bavier.
Witnesses : Elias and Maria Bavier.

Born May 13. Catarina, child of Edwerd Wood, Jr., and Enne Wesley.
Witnesses : George Wessey, Jr., and Catarina Wood.

Date of baptism, torn ; born June 23. Maria, child of Gideon Hornbeek and Abigael Davis.
Witnesses : The parents.

Born—14. Jenie, child of Abraham Goetschius and Jenie Camble.
Witnesses : The parents.

Born June 20. Samuel, child of John and Maria Lefever.
Witnesses : The parents.

Aug. 4 ; born July 12. Jasia, child of Samuel Bavier and Rachal Achmody.
Witnesses : The parents.

Born June 29. Ezechiel, child of Nathaneel Wheb and Margrietje Doio.
Witnesses : The parents.

Sept. 1 ; born Aug. 16. Jacob, child of Coenraedt Burger and Elizabeth Terwilger.
Witnesses : The parents.

Sept. 15 ; born Aug. 4. Jonas, child of Nathaneel Lefever and Maria Doio.
Witnesses : The parents.

Oct. 13 ; born Aug. 29. Judic, child of Johannes Smit and Resyntje Van Ake.
Witnesses : Isack and Judic Van Ake.

Elizabeth, child of Petrus York and Margriet Van Leuwe.
Witnesses : The parents.

Born Aug. 7. Michael, child of Simon Viele and Neltje Parmetier.
Witnesses : Isack Parmetier and Rachel Yurry.

Oct. 27 ; born Oct. 13. Jacob, child of Jeremias Low and Wyntje Weeler.
Witnesses : The parents.

Nov. 10. Rachel, child of James Scott and Catrina Janson.
Witnesses : The parents.

Born Oct. 17. Elizabeth, child of Simeon Frere and Annatje Blonjan.
Witnesses : Benjamin and Elizabeth Frere.

Born Oct. 8. Catarina, child of David Low and Rachel Lamerter.
Witnesses : Jan and Catarina Lamerter.

Dec. 28 ; born Nov. 17. Maria, child of Elias and Cornelia Hardenberg.
Witnesses : The parents.

1783, Jan. 12 ; born Dec. 26, 1782. Jenneke, child of Cornelius Eltinge and Blandina Elmondorph.
Witnesses : The parents.

Jan. 19 ; born Dec. 12, 1782. Johannes Frere, child of Zacharias Sluyter and Bregje York.
Witnesses : The parents.

Feb. 21 ; born Dec. 12, 1782. Isack Bovier, child of Abraham Janson and Catryntje Bovier.
Witness : Magdalena Bovier.

Born Jan. 11. Simon, child of Mathew and Elizabeth Lefever.
Witnesses: The parents.

Feb. 23; born Jan. 13. Elizabeth, child of Jonathan Doio and Maria Lefever.
Witnesses: Abraham and Elizabeth Doio.

Born Feb. 23. Abram, child of Philippus Doio and Geertruy Lefever.
Witnesses: Abram and Elizabeth Doio.

March 2. Cetje, child of Frederik Kittle and Sarah Burger.
Witnesses: The parents.

April 6; born March 8. Abigael, child of Josia Ferris and Alida Van Alst.
Witness: Jane Farres.

Born Jan. 19. Simon, child of Richard Janson and Grietje Van Steenberg.
Witnesses: The parents.

Born Feb. 9. Martha, child of Eliza Frere and Martha Everet.
Witnesses: Daniel Everet and Margriet Frere.

Born Feb. 13. Abraham, child of Isack Harres and Jannetje Frere.
Witnesses: The parents.

Born Feb. 4. Joseph, child of Peter Wells and Annatje Osseltje Scryver.
Witnesses: Joseph and Maria Wells.

April 13; born Feb. 7. Eliza, child of Johannes Suart and Rachel Gerretze.
Witnesses: The parents.

May 4; born March 17. Elizabeth, child of Andries Dubois and Maria Doio.
Witnesses: The parents.

May 18; born March 28. Jannetje, child of Martyn Griffin and Rachel Sopier.
Witnesses: The parents.

Born March 25. Charles, child of Petrus Smedes and Elsje Hasbrouk.
Witnesses: The parents.

Born April 11. Elizabeth, child of Wauter Sluiter and Margriet Barton.
Witnesses: The parents.

May 25. Maria, child of Jacob Klein and Lidia Valkenburg.
Witnesses: Johannes Klein and Elizabeth Kyser.

Jonathan, child of Efraim Kyzer and Lena Klyn.
Witnesses: Evert Sluiter and Annatje Klein.

Born April 29. Abraham, child of Thomas Klaerwater and Lea Wood.
Witnesses: Henry Harp and Eva Klaerwater.

Born May 10. Evert, child of David Etkins and Margrita Sluiter.
Witnesses: The parents.

June 8; born May 24. Elsje, child of Jesaias Hasbrouck and Maria Bavier.
Witnesses: Petrus Smedes and Elsje Hasbrouck.

Born Feb. 19. Freelove, child of Guilbert Saxon and Sarah Armstrong.
Witnesses: The parents.

June 29; born May 26. Altje, child of David Hasbrouck and Maria Hogland.
Witnesses: The parents.

Aug. 5; born June 28. Sarah, child of Cornelius Keyser and Elsje Etkins.
Witnesses: Jacob and Sarah Frere.

Aug. 10; born April 20. Polly, child of John Barret and Seletje Parmetier.

Born Sept. 8, 1781. Maria, child of Robert Leroy and Dina Parmetier.
Witnesses: The parents.

Aug. 31, born Aug. 11. Cornelius Bruyn, child of Cornelius Dubois and Geertruy Bruyn.
Witnesses: The parents.

Sept. 14. Isack, child of Zebulon Roberson and Maria Barton.
Witnesses: Wauter Sluiter and Margriet Barton.

Born Aug. 3. David, child of Jordan Perhemes and Lidia Doio.
Witnesses: The parents.

Born Aug. 25. Wilhelmus, child of Methusalem Dubois and Catharina Bavier.
Witnesses: The parents.

Born Aug. 25. Rebecca, child of Hendricus Dubois and Rebecca Van Wagene.
Witnesses: Jacob Dubois and Rebecca Van Wagene.

Born July 22. James, child of Abraham Wood and Phebe Aswin.
Witnesses: The parents.

Born Aug. 4. Petrus, child of Samuel Carson and Elizabeth Nyberg.
Witnesses: The parents.

Oct. 5; born Sept. 2. Jenneke, child of Hugo Frere, Jr., and Anna Dewitt.
Witnesses: Andries Dewitt and Jenneke Vernoy.

Born Sept. 26. Ester, child of Jeremias Frere and Sara Van Wagene.
Witnesses: The parents.

Born Sept. 23. Jesaias, child of Daniel Frere and Maria Helm.
Witnesses: The parents.

Oct. 26; born Oct. 12. Bregje, child of Benjamin —— and Annatje York.
Witnesses: Zacharias Sluiter and Bregje York.

Nov. 9; born Oct. 22. Philip, child of Joseph Hasbrouck and Elizabeth Bavier.
Witnesses: Philip Bavier and Ann Dewitt.

Born Oct. 22 at 9 p.m. Lowis, child of Stephanus Goetschius and Elizabeth Dubois.
Witnesses: Lowis Dubois and Catarina Broadhead.

Born Oct. 6. Jacobus, child of Hugo Doio and Catarina Terbush.
Witnesses: The parents.

Dec. 7; born Nov. 6. Daniel, child of Isack and Maria Lefever.
Witnesses: The parents.

Dec. 29; born Nov. 16. Simeon, child of Jonas Frere and Magdalena Bavier.
Witnesses: The parents.

Born Sept. 3, 1782. Sara, child of William Weler and Margret Kelly.
Witnesses : The parents.

Born Dec. 4, 1783. Elsje, child of John, Jr., and Jannetje Terwilger.
Witnesses : Evert and Sara Terwilger.

1784, Jan. 4 ; born Nov. 27, 1783. Nelly, child of Salomon Bavier and Nelly Griffin.
Witnesses : The parents.

Born December 13, 1783. Benjamin, child of Abraham Doio, Jr., and Bregje Frere.
Witnesses : Benjamin and Jenneke Doio.

Feb. 8 ; born Nov. 18, 1783. Jannetje, child of Mathew McCaby and Jannetje Tappen.
Witnesses : The parents.

March 7 ; born Feb. 11. Sara, child of Jonathan Frere and Margrietje Doio.
Witnesses : Jacob and Sara Frere.

March 21 ; born Feb. 20. Salomon, child of Petrus Hasbrouck and Sarah Bavier.
Witnesses : The parents.

Born Feb. 15. Maria, child of Nathanel Web and Margrietje Doio.
Witnesses : The parents.

April 18 ; born Feb. 15. Joseph, child of Joseph Coddington, Jr., and Marybah Hardford.
Witnesses : Joseph Coddington and Catarina Vandemerk.

Born Oct. 27, 1783. Rachel, child of Petrus Klaarwater and Sarah Sluiter.
Witnesses : Samuel Bavier and Rachel Achmoedy.

April 25, born March 15. Zacharias, child of Johannes York and Jannetje Bavier.
Witnesses : Zacharias Sluiter and Bregje York.

May 9 ; born March 11. Annatje, child of Jacob Klein and Lidia Van Valkenburg.
Witnesses : Johannes and Annatje Kleyn.

May 30 ; born April 25. Maria, child of John L. Monjon and Elizabeth Wells.
Witnesses : The parents.

Born April 18. Catryntje, child of Isack Dubois and Rebecca Doio.
Witnesses : The parents.

Born Nov. 15, 1783. Ezechiel, child of Laurence Nees and Annatje Degraaf.
Witnesses : The parents.

June 20 ; born June 4. Maria, child of Simeon Low and Christina McMollin.
Witnesses : The parents.

July 4 ; born June 10 ; Maria, child of Willem Smitt and Madlena Achmody.
Witnesses : David Achmody and Maria Degraaf.

Born April 4. Susanna, child of James Dun and Anne Lane.
Witnesses : The parents.

July 11 ; born June 13 ; Amelyna, child of Jacob Keyzer and Amelyna Sluiter.
Witnesses : The parents.

Aug. 1 ; born June 5 ; William, child of William Hood (or Wood ?) and Sarah Coddington.
Witnesses : The parents.

Born July 11. Elizabeth, child of Edwerd Wood and Ann Wesly.
Witnesses : The parents.

Aug. 22 ; born July 23. Ezechiel, child of Jacob Bovier and Maria York.
Witnesses : The parents.

Sept. 5 ; born Aug. 5. Sara, child of Martynus and Maria Frere.
Witnesses : Jonas and Catarina Frere.

Oct. 3 ; born Sept. 15. Nathanel, child of John Lefever and Egje Zwart.
Witnesses : The parents.

Born Sept. 7. Jenneke, child of Egbert Dewitt, Jr., and Elizabeth Smitt.
Witnesses : Andries Dewitt and Jenneke Vernoy.

Born Aug. 25. Lidia, child of Samuel Bavier and Rachel Achmody.
Witnesses : The parents.

Oct. 17 ; born Sept 12. Lowis, child of Wessel Dubois and Catarina Lefever.
Witnesses : Lowis Dubois and Catarina Broadhead.

Born Sept. 30. Jenneke, child of Johannes Doio and Cataria Critsinger.
Witnesses : Benjamin and Jenneke Doio.

Nov. 14 ; born Oct. 19. Isack, child of Abraham Bovier and Marytje Frere.
Witnesses : Isack Frere and Hester Janson.

Nov. 28 ; born Oct. 27. Dina, child of Josia Elting and Hester Broadhead.
Witnesses : Abraham and Jannitje Elting.

Born Sept. 24. Rachel, child of Simon Vilie and Nele Parmetier.
Witnesses : Jacobus Vilie and Tryntje Palmetier.

Born Aug. 24. John, child of Guilbert Saxon and Sarah Armstrong.
Witnesses : The parents.

Dec. 19 ; born Nov. 19. Cornelius, child of Matheus Bovier and Jackemyntje Bovier.
Witnesses : Cornelius Vernoy and Maria Bovier.

1785, Jan. 1 ; born Dec. 1, 1784. Alexander, child of John A. Hardenberg and Rachel Dubois.
Witnesses : The parents.

Born Nov. 24, 1784. John Alsdorph, child of Daniel Frere, Jr., and Annatje Doio.
Witnesses : Johs. Alsdorph and Agetta Doio.

Jan. 23 ; born Dec. 6, 1784. Ezechiel, child of Jesaias Hasbrouck and Maria Bovier.
Witnesses : The parents.

Born July 5, 1784. Andries, child of Josaphat Hasbrouck and Cornelia Dubois.
Witnesses : The parents.

Born July 18, 1784. Michael Wyant, child of Israel Wering, Jr., and Jane Wyant.
Witnesses : The parents.

Jan. 25 ; born Oct. 28, 1784. Charla, child of Zacharias Hasbrouck and Rebecca Wering.
Witnesses : The parents.

Born Nov. 7, 1784. Sarah, child of Solomon Wering and Arriantje Snediker.
Witnesses : Lucas Thaller and Sarah Snediker.

Feb. 12 ; born Dec. 29. Mauritius, child of George Wertz and Ester Hasbrouck.
Witnesses : Mauritius Wirtz and Catarina Heger.

Feb. 13 ; born Jan. 12. Johannes, child of Paulus Frere and Elizabeth Van Wagene.
Witnesses : Johannes A. and Rebecca Van Wagene.

Born Jan. 29. Neeltje, child of Isack Herres and Jannetje Frere.
Witnesses : The parents.

May 1 ; born March 19. Eva child of Petrus Davis and Betje Helm.
Witnesses : John and Eva Davis.

May 22 ; born April 11. Hanna, child of Isack Kyser and Betty Stawbridge.
Witnesses : The parents.

June 12 ; born April 25. Noach, child of Salomon Bovier and Ellenor Criffin.
Witnesses : The parents.

Born May 14. Christoffel, child of William Davis and Catarina Smitt.
Witnesses : William Davis and Lena Achmoedy.

Born May 26. Catarina, child of Jonathan Doio and Maria Lefever.
Witnesses : Daniel Lefever and Catarina Cantine.

June 16 ; born May 28. Benjamin, child of Petrus York and Margriet Van Leuve.
Witnesses : The parents.

June 19 ; born June 4. Maria, child of Cornelius Dubois and Gertruy Bruin.

July 24 ; born July 5. Ezechiel, child of Ezechiel Frere and Elizabeth Sluiter.
Witnesses : Martynus and Maria Frere.

Born June 5. Salomon, child of Johannes I. Frere, Jr., and Margrietje Bennet.
Witnesses : Salomon and Jannetje Frere.

July 31 ; born July 8. Mararita, child of David Low and Rachel Lemerter.
Witnesses : Jeremia Hoogteling and Margrita Lemerter.

Aug. 11 ; born June 26. Joseph, child of Hendricus Doio and Phebe Wolsy.
Witnesses : The parents.

Aug. 28 ; born July 27. Elizabeth, child of David Hasbrouck and Maria Hoogland.
Witnesses : The parents.

Sept. 25 ; born Aug. 5. Johannes, child of Simeon Frere and Annatje Blonjan.
Witnesses : The parents.

Oct. 2 ; born Aug. 7. Abram, child of Nathaneel Lefever and Maria Doio.
Witnesses : The parents.

Born Sept. 27. Elizabeth, child of Philip Doio and Gertruy Lefever.
Witnesses : Elizabeth Dubois and Abraham Doio.

Oct. 9 ; born Aug. 11. Catryntje, child of Petrus and Cornelia Bovier.
Witnesses : The parents.

Oct. 16 ; born Aug. 21. Rachel, child of Eliza Frere and Martha Everet.
Witnesses : The parents.

Oct. 23 ; born Sept. 9. David, child of Joseph Coddington and Moribah Hartford.

Born July 3. Daniel, child of Hugo Doio and Catarina Bosh.

Nov. 20 ; born July 16. Daniel, child of Jordan Perhemus and Lidia Doio.
Witnesses : The parents.

Born Oct. 29. Catarina, child of Matheus and Elizabeth Lefever.
Witnesses : Daniel Lefever and Catarina Cantine.

Born July 3. Jannetje, child of Petrus Vilie and Gerretje Frere.
Witnesses : Johannes Van Kleek and Jannetje Vilie.

Born Oct. 26. Sara, child of Jeremias Frere and Sara Van Wagene.
Witnesses : The parents.

Born Sept. 10. Annatje, child of Wouter Sluiter and Margriet Barton.
Witnesses : The parents.

1786, Jan. 14 ; born Nov. 29, 1785. Rachel, child of Andries Dubois and Maria Doio.
Witnesses : The parents.

Born Dec. 10, 1785. Philip, child of Methusalem Dubois and Catryntje Bovier (?).
Witnesses : The parents.

Born Dec. 27, 1785. Maria, child of Jacob Wilkelo and Elizabeth Hood.
Witnesses : The parents.

Born Oct. 3, 1785. Levi Paling, child of Levi Doio and Margrietje Paling.
Witnesses : The parents.

1786, Jan. 1 ; born Dec. 12, 1785. Maria, child of Abram D. Doio and Anne Broadhead.
Witnesses : Charls Broadhead and Maria Oliver.

Born Dec. 19, 1785. Matheus, child of Teunis Sammens and Rachel Terwilger.
Witnesses : The parents.

Feb. 5 ; born Oct. 3, 1785. Jacob, child of Martyn Griffin and Rachel Sopier.
Witnesses : The parents.

Born Dec. 26, 1785. Gerret Frere, child of Salomon Doio and Bregje Frere.
Witnesses : Gerret and Maria Frere.

Born Dec. 18, 1785. Debora, child of Jacob Lefever and Lidia Doio.
Witnesses : Christoffel Doio and Debory Van Vliet.

Born Dec. 28, 1785. Rolof Elting, child of Abram A. Bovier and Maytje Frere.
Witnesses : Rolof Hasbrouck and Margrietje Elting.

Feb. 19 ; born Sept. 15, 1785. Annatje, child of Mathew McCaby and Jannetje Tappen.
Witnesses : The parents.

Feb. 23 ; born Dec. 29, 1785. Abram, child of Noach Elting and Annatje Doio.
Witnesses : The parents.

Feb. 26 ; born Sept. 27. Jacobus, child of Abram Elting and Dorothea Besmer.
Witnesses : The parents.

Jan. 1 ; Elizabeth, born Oct. 31, 1785. Hendrick, born Oct. 30, 1777. Children of Johannes Shuart and Rachel Gerretze. Note on margin of original : " His baptismal day forgotten, and registry neglected."
Witnesses : The parents.

Born May 31, 1784. Maria, child of William Elsworth and Jane Dean.

Born Oct. 25, 1784. John, child of Thomas Jones and Mary Lemonjon.

Born Oct. 20, 1785. Johannes, child of Peter Wells and Osseltje Schryver.
Witnesses : Johannes Emerik Schryver and Elizabeth Burger.

Born March 23, 1785. Sally, child of Enos Bussy and Betsy Wever.
Witnesses : Isack Palmetier and Sally Wever.

Born Oct. 11, 1785. Jenetta, child of David Weaver and Catarina Wilsy.

Born Dec. 28, 1785. Hendrik, child of Johannes Nees and Sarah Palmetier.

Born Feb. 3, 1785. Abraham, child of James Danelson and Hulda Roberson.

Born June (?) 23, 1785. Mary, child of William Danelson and Magdalen Nees.

Born Feb. 9, 1785. Elizabeth, child of John Barret and Selitje Palmetier.

March 13 ; born Feb. 6. Abram, child of Abram Hess or Ness and Paggy Hert.
Witnesses : The parents.

April 23 ; born Feb. 13. Elizabeth, child of Josia Hasbrouck and Sarah Dekker.
Witnesses : The parents.

May 21 ; born Feb. 24. Maria, child of Johannes York and Jannetje Bovier.
Witnesses : The parents.

May 25 ; born April 9. Elizabeth, child of Martynus Klaarwater and Lea Sluiter.

Born March 9. Johannes, child of Petrus Smedes and Elsje Hasbrouck.
Witnesses : The parents.

June 5 ; born April 21. Catarina, child of Hendric Wakman and Lidia Hert.
Witnesses : Methusalem Dubois and Catarina Bovier.

Born April 23. John, child of Abram Hog and Jannetje Doio.
Witnesses : The parents.

May 14 ; born April 21. James, child of Joseph Hasbrouck and Elizabeth Bevier.
Witnesses : The parents.

June 10 ; born March 21. Benjamin, child of Daniel Dubois and Catrina Lefever.
Witnesses : Benjamin Dubois and Maria Bovier.

June 4 ; born May 16. Sara, child of John and Jannetje Terwilger.
Witnesses : Lucas and Sara Terwilger.

June 20 ; born April 30. Catrina, child of Zacharias Sluiter and Bregje York.
Witnesses : The parents.

Born May 9. Benjamin, child of John Bever and Catrina Wood.
Witnesses : The parents.

July 2 ; born June 9. Eva, child of Benjamin Windfield and Annatje York.

Selly, child of Rolof Litz and Sara Sluiter.

Born May 22. Petrus Lefever, child of Elias Bavier and Sara Lefever.
Witnesses : Petrus Lefever and Elizabeth Vernoy.

Born May 15. Syntje, child of Hendric Raljie and Elizabeth Wesmiller.

Born May 19. Daniel Frere, child of Evert Terwilger and Maria Frere.
Witnesses : Daniel Frere and Annatje Doio.

Born March 28. Daniel, child of Israel Wering and Jenny Wygant.
Witnesses : The parents.

July 23 ; born Jan. 27. Hannah, child of Numan Waring and Pally Caddington.
Witnesses : The parents.

Born June 4 Elizabeth. child of Thomas Jones and Mary Lemonjon.
Witnesses : The parents.

Aug. 20 : born May 27. Joseph, child of William Hood and Sara Caddington.
Witnesses : The parents.

Born July 23. Andries Lefever, child of Wessel Dubois and Catarina Lefever.
Witnesses : Andries and Elizabeth Lefever.

Born July 14. Johannes, child of Johannes Rosekrans and Magdalena Brink.
Witnesses : The parents.

Sept. 4 ; born Aug. 14. John, child of Charles Demsy and Elizabeth Pennic.

Oct. 1. Jacob, child of Simeon Low and Christina McMollen.

Born Sept. 11. Jacobus, child of Frederic and Eva Schonmaker.
Witnesses : The parents.

Oct. 8 ; born Aug. 15. Jonathan, child of Jacob Bovier and Maria York.

Born July 30. Jonathan, child of Jonas Frere and Magdalena Bovier.

Oct. 15 ; born Sept. 14. Maria, child of Josia Doio and Catarina Blonjan.

Oct. 29 ; born Aug. 18. Catrien, child of Petrus Keter and Geertje Roos.

Nov. 5. Nathanel, child of Johannes Lefever and Elizabeth Dubois.
Witnesses : Nathanel Lefever and Maria Doio.

Born Aug. 1. John, child of Zacharias Hasbrouck and Rebecca Wering.

Born Sept. 11. Gerret Frere, child of Isack Van Wagenen and Elsje Frere.
Witnesses : Hugo Frere. Jr., and Annatje Dewitt.

Born Oct. 25. Rachel, child of Stephanus Goetschius and Elizabeth Dubois.
Witness: Rachel Goetschius.

Nov. 26; born Sept 1. Christian, child of Samuel Bovier and Rachel Achmody.

Dec. 31; born Oct. 22. Elizabeth, child of Petrus Dewitt and Rachel Vanleuwe.
Witnesses: Timothy and Anne Wood.

Born Oct. 14. Peter Tappen, child of James Dun and Anne Lane.

George, child of Joseph Dun and Mary Wickam.

Born Nov. 18. Isack Heegman, child of Simon Vilie and Neltje Palmetier.
Witnesses: Isack and Neltje Hegeman.

Born Nov. 12. Elizabeth, child of Simon Raljie and Lena Doio.

Born Nov. 18. Debora, child of David Low and Rachel Lemerter.
Witnesses: Christoffel Snyder and Debora Low.

1787, Jan. 1; born Dec. 4, 1786. Maria, child of Isack Dubois and Rebecca Doio.

Jan. 6; born Nov. 25, 1786. Catarina, child of Jesaias Hasbrouck and Maria Bovier.
Witness: Catarina Smedes.

Jan. 21; born Nov. 16, 1786. Catrina, child of Hermanus Osterhout and Catrina Vroom.

Born Nov. 10, 1786. Martynus, child of Gerret Devenport and Catrina Osterhout.

Feb. 25; born Jan. 18. John, child of John McNeel and Anne Carman.

Elizabeth, child of Hendric Snyder and Maria Terwilger.
Witnesses: Benjamin Frere and Elizabeth Terwilger.

Feb. 11; born Feb. 17 (sic). Philip, child of Adam Jeple and Arriantje Hendriks.

Born Jan. 24. Francis, child of Isack Herres and Anatje Frere.

April 15; born Feb. 22. Thomas, child of Thomas Klaarwater and Lea Wood.

Born March 5. Hendrick, child of Jonathan Frere and Margriet Doio.
Witnesses : Hendric Doio and Elizabeth Beem.

Born Nov. 5, 1783. Anne, child of John Stevens and Susanna Avry.
Witness : Dorkas Achmody.

Born Feb. 3, 1787. Jemes, child of John Stevens and Susanna Avry.
Witness : Dorkas Achmody.

May 6 ; born April 16. Fredric, child of Joseph Klaarwater and Lidia Wood.

Born April 9. Asaph, child of Samuel Dubois and Jenneke Lefever.
Witnesses : Benjamin Dubois and Maria Bovier.

Born April 13. Abram, child of Abraham Bovier and Maytje Frere.

June 10 ; born April 29. Clasine, child of Hendrick Doio, Jr., and Phebe Wolsy.

Born May 19. Petrus, child of Petrus Hasbrouck and Sara Bovier.

Born May 18. Elias, child of John I. Frere, Jr., and Margrietje Bennet.

June 17. Polly, child of John Kritzinger and Lea Litz.
Witnesses : Daniel Litz and Polly Kritzinger.

Born May 1. Mauris, child of Eliphas Jerom and Experience Buling (or Risling ?)

June 21 ; born June 4. Methusalem, child of Isack Schonmaker and Sara Dubois.

July 8 ; born March 7. Hosea, child of Jordan Purhemus and Lidia Doio.

Born June 20. Sushanna, child of John Barret and Selettje Palmetier.

July 22 ; born June 15. Sarah, child of Isack and Maria Lefever.

Born June 25. Cornelia, child of Jonatha ⸱ Doio and Maria Lefever.

Born June 22. Thomas, child of John ⸱⸱ monjon and Elizabeth Wells.

July 29; born May 27. Simon, child of Johannes I. Frere and Laura Terwilger.

Aug. 12; born July 10. Abram Frere, child of Abram Simmons and Molly Gee.
Witnesses: Edward Simmons and Hannah Frere.

Sept. 2; born July 31. Teunis, child of Jan Lefever and Egje Zwart.

Born July 21. Abram and Charles, children of Josia Elting and Hester Broadhead.

Born May 13. Gilbert, child of Mathew McCaby and Jannetje Tappen.

Born Aug. 6. Maria, child of John C. Hardenberg and Jenneke Dewitt.

Sept. 23; born Aug. 14. Hugo, child of Benjamin H. Frere and Elizabeth Windfield.
Witnesses: Hugo Frere and Ester Doio.

Born Aug. 28. Sarah, child of William Smitt and Magdalena Achmody.
Witnesses: Hendric Smitt and Sarah Van Wagene.

Nov. 11; born Oct. 20. Maria, child of Salomon Bovier and Ellenor Griffin.
Witnesses: Jesaias Hasbrouck and Maria Bovier.

Born Sept. 11. John, child of Henery Harp and Catrien Devenport.

Born Sept. 28. Edword Weslyk, child of Edward Wood and Enne Weslyk.

Born Oct. 10. Elizabeth, child of Elias Davis and Molly Klarwater.

Born Oct. 9. Levi Dewitt, child of Lauwrence Hendrics and Johanna Windield.
Witnesses: Levi Dewitt and Wyntje Schoonmaker.

Dec. 1. Wyntje, child of David Hasbrouck and Maria Hoogland.

Born Oct. 31. Philippus, child of Petrus and Cornelia Bovier.

Dec. 2; born Nov. 5. Gertruy, child of Methusalem Dubois and Catrientje Bovier.

Born Nov. 16. Daniel, child of Samuel Broadhead and Dina Dubois.
Witnesses : Daniel Broadhead and Blandina Elmondorph.

Johannes, child of Marcus Wekman and Jennie Cool.

Born Sept. 22. Robert, child of Joseph Coddington and Meriba Hardford.

Dec. 9 ; born Nov. 16. Sarah, child of Benjamin Wood and Eva Smitt.
Witnesses : James Achmod, Jr., and Sarah Smitt.

Born Nov. 19. Sarah, child of Daniel Van Wagene and Caty Law.

1788, Jan. 1 ; born Nov. 22, 1787. Elizabeth, child of David Van Husen and Anna Catrina Hyns.
Witnesses : Benjamin Hyns and Sile (?) Griffen.

Jan. 6 ; born Dec. 16, 1787. Jannetje, child of Cornelius C. Brink and Maria Raljie.

Born Aug. 22, 1787. Hanna, child of Nathanel Web and Margrietje Doio.

Born Dec. 15, 1787. Benjamin, child of Zacharias Hofman and Maria Terwilger.

Born Nov. 30, 1787. Laura, child of Casparus Van Ostrant and Eva Vrelinghuisen.

Feb. 10 ; born Nov. 24, 1787. Jacob, child of Peter Wood and Wyntje Klarwater.

Born Dec. 23, 1787. John, child of Petrus Jork and Margriet Van Leuwe.
Witness : John Van Leuwe.

Born Jan. 22, 1788. Bregje, child of Daniel Sluiter and Sara Bovier.

Born Dec. 17, 1787. Art, child of Jeremias Frere and Sara Van Wagene.
Witnesses : Abram Een and Catrina Van Wagene.

Born Jan. 16, 1788. Elizabeth child of Elias Bovier and Sara Lefever.

March 2 ; born Jan. 23, 1788. Jacob Snyder, child of Jehu Low and Elizabeth Snyder.
Witnesses : Jacob and Elizabeth Snyder.

Born Feb. 6. John, child of Charles Broadhead and Sara Hardenberg.

Born Feb. 3. Jacemyntje, child of Noach Elting and Annatje Doio.

Born Oct. 14, 1787. Daniel Everet, child of Elisa Frere and Martha Everet.

Born Feb. 6, 1788. Jonathan, child of John Hofman and Lena Bovier.

Born Dec. 15, 1787. Abram, child of Frederic Hopensted and Margriet Richard.

Born Nov. 30, 1787. Jacob, child of Isack Dubois and Debora Raljie
Witnesses: Jacob Dubois and Rebecca Van Wagenen.

March 10, 1788; born Feb. 18. David, child of Benjamin Doio, Jr., and Susanna Kritzinger.
Witnesses: Johs. B. Doio and Catrina Kritzinger.

Born Jan. 31. Petrus, child of Jacob Lefever and Lidia Doio.
Witnesses: Petrus Lefever and Elizabeth Vernoy.

March 24; born Feb. 19. Dina, child of Ezechiel and Magdalena Elting.

April 13; born March 2. Salomon, child of Noach Lefever and Cornelia Bovier.
Witnesses: Salomon and Rachel Lefever.

Born March 9. Catrien, child of Wessel Dubois and Catrien Lefever.

Born Jan. 1. Silvanus, child of Numan Waring and Maria Coddington.

Born Feb 9 Rebecca, child of Wauter Sluiter and Margriet Barton.

Born March . aniel, child of Abram P. (or D.) Doio and Anne Broadh ..!.
Witnesses: ni l Doio and Margriet Lefever.

Born Marc . Annatje, child of Josia Doio and Catrina Blonjan.
Witnesses: . Frere and Annatje Blonjan.

Born Feb. L.:na, child of Henry Green and Maria Doio.

Born Dec. 7, 1787. Maria, child of Isack Rynes and Elizabeth Bakker.

Baptismal dates torn, born April? 3, 1788. John, child of Zacharias Hasbrouck and Rebecca Wering.

Born Jan. 18. Selly, child of Hendrick Wekman and Lidia Hert.

Born May 7. Simon, child of Isack Dubois and Rebecca Doio.

Born May 15. Uria, child of William Weeler and Margriet Celly.

Born Feb. 20. George Graham, child of Isack Hardenberg and Rachel Graham.

Born May 19. Hanna, child of Cornelius Dubois (rest torn). Witnesses: Dirk Wynkoop and Hanna Elting.
(Lower part of leaf in original torn off).

Born July 6. Margrita, child of John Stoks? and Susanna Kerner.
Witnesses: Cornelis T. and Margrita Kerner.

Born July 8. Geertje child of Matheus and Elizabeth Lefever.
Witnesses: Petrus Lefever and Geertje Wynkoop.

Aug. 17; born July —. Annatje, child of Jacob Wilkelo and Elizabeth Hood.

Aug. 24; born July 21. Jeremias, child of Hendrick Raljie and Elizabeth Wesmiller.

Born July 30. Maria, child of Willem Doio and Sarah Elting.
Witnesses: Rolof Elting and Maria Low.

Aug. 7; born Aug. 6. Thimothy Brandel, child of Coenraad Burger and Sara Hart.
Witness: Thimothy Brandel.

Born June 28. Jacob, child of Daniel Klaarwater and Maria Silie.

— 7; born Aug. 21. Debora, child of Johannes York and Jannetje Bovier.

Aug. 4, born July 12. David, child of Wilhelmus and Jannetje Sluiter.

No date of baptism; born Aug. 7. Annatje, child of Martynus Klaarwater and Lea Sluiter.

Born Nov. 20, 1787. Ephraim, child of Ephraim Kyser and Lena Klyn.

Sept. 28; born Aug. 30. Johs. Hendricus, child of Johannes Berenhart and Sara Sluiter.
Witnesses: Hendric W.... and Anna Sl....

Born Aug. 28. Jonathan, child of Johannes Lefever and Elizabeth Dubois. (Lower part of leaf in original torn off.)

Nov. 2; born Sept. 25. Sarah, child of Elias Ein and Elizabeth Hasbrouck.
Witnesses: Jacobus Hasbrouck and Divertje Van Wagene.

Nov. 29; born Oct. 15. Maria, child of Hugo Frere and Anna Dewitt.
Witnesses: Isack Van Wagene and Elsje Frere.

Dec. 14; born Nov. 11. Magdalena, child of Jonas Frere and Magdalena Bovier.

Willem, child of Jonathan Traphagen and Maria Terwilger.
Witnesses: Willem Traphagen and Martyntje Westervelt.

Dec. 21; born Nov. 13. Noagh, child of Jesaias Hasbrouck and Maria Bovier.

1789, Jan. 1; born Nov. 15, 1788. Thomas, child of Abram Bovier and Marytje Frere.
Witnesses: Thomas Frere and Hester Janson.

Jan. 8; born Nov. 18, 1788; Luther, child of Joseph Hasbrouck and Elizabeth Bovier.

Feb. 1; born Dec. 24. Syntje, child of Jemes Achmody and Elizabeth Smitt.
Witnesses: Johannes and Syntje Smitt.

Born Nov. 19, 1788. Jacob, child of John Sort and Lena Van Leuwe.
Witnesses: Jacob Van Leuwe and Antje Wood.

Born Dec. 28, 1788. Piter, child of Levi Doio and Margrietje Pawling.

Feb. 8; born Jan. 1. Jacobus, child of Nathanel —— and Maria Doio.

Born Dec. 24, 1788. Abram, child of Samuel Dubois and Jenneke Lefever.

Born Jan. 3, 1789. Maria, child of Samuel Bovier and Rachel Achmody.

Born Jan. 8. Rachel, child of Petrus and Cornelia Bovier.

Born Jan. 15. Judic, child of Ezechiel Low and Eva Stryker.
Witnesses : Salomon Low and Sara Boss.

Born Jan. 15. Antje, child of Matheus Contryman and Margriet Stoks.
Witness : Antje Stoks.

Born Jan. 24. Cherles Smedes, child of John Hardenberg and Jeneke Dewitt.

Feb. 19 ; born Sept. 27, 1788. Elizabeth, child of Daniel Diver and Margriet Nies.

Born Feb. 4. Elizabeth, child of Daniel Karney and Laura Kontryman.

March 1 ; born Feb. 4. Gerret, child of Ezechiel Frere and Elizabeth Sluiter.
Witnesses : Isack Van Wagene and Elsje Frere.

Born Sept. 20, 1788. Egje, child of Jordan Perhemus and Lidia Doio.

April 5 ; born March 9. Catrina, child of Stephanus Goetschius and Elizabeth Dubois.
Witness : Jonathan Dubois.

Born March 10. John Admundus, child of Johannes Hasbrouck and Caty McDonald.

May 3 ; born April 4. John, child of Hendric Doio, Jr., and Phebe Peek.

May 24 ; born April 8. Edward, child of Thomas Klarwater and Lea Wood.

Born May 16. Jacob, child of Jeremias Low and Wyntje Weeler.

Born April 23. Henery, child of Jacob Green and Rachel Sammons.

Born April 13. Benjamin, child of Petrus Davis and Elizabeth Helm.

Born April 9. John Parrain, child of Simon Helm and Maria Schonmaker.
Witnesses : John and Nella Parrain.

Born March 3. Elizabeth, child of Isack Harres and Jannetje Frere.

June 7 ; born April 6. Johannes, child of Simon Vilie and Nella Palmetier.
Witness : Johannes Vielie.

June 2, born April 11. Abram, child of William Litz and Elizabeth Palmatier.

June 7 ; born April 30. Jacob, child of Joseph Coddington and Meriba Hartford.

June 21 ; born June 7. Hester, child of Daniel Van Wagene and Tryntje Low.
Witnesses : Jonathan Van Wagene and Ester Johnson.

Born April 10. Johannes, child of Salomon Doio and Bregje Frere.
Witnesses : Jacob Doio and Catrina Frere.

Born May 11. Jeremias, child of Jacob Bovier and Maria York.

June 28 ; born March 1. Annie, child of Philip Lemonjon and Maria Wells.

Born Sept. 27, 1788. Elizabeth, child of Cornelius Swam and Ester Lemonjon.

Born May 25, 1789. Nancy, child of Thomas Jones and Maria Lemonjon.

Born May 1. John Davis, child of Abram Sluiter and Elizabeth Davis.

July 12 ; born June 20. Maria, child of Petrus Lefever, Jr., and Magdalena Elting.
Witnesses : Rolof Elting and Maria Low.

Born June 25. Maria, child of Philippus and Catryntje Elting.
Witnesses : Rolof Elting and Maria Low.

Aug. 9 ; born July 11. Abram, child of Petrus Hasbrouck and Sarah Bovier.

Born July 2. Gertruy, child of Isack and Maria Lefever.
Witnesses : Philip Doio and Geertry Lefever.

Aug. 22 ; born Aug. 3. Samuel, child of Simeon Low and Christina McMollen.

Born July 20. Sarah, child of Abram B. Doio and Bregje Frere.
Witnesses : Jacob and Sarah Frere.

Born June 8. Phanny, child of Francis Handmor and Phebe Gilbert.

Sept. 13 ; born Aug. 18. Levi, child of Hendricus Contryman and Maria Conneway.
Witnesses : Cornelius Coneway and Anna Sluiter.

Born Aug. 5. Walter, child of Wauterus Sluiter and Margriet Barton.

Born July 28. Edward, child of Peter Wood and Wyntje Klarwater.

Born Aug. 4. Dina, child of Rolof Hasbrouck and Jannetje Elting.

Born Aug. 14. Jacobus, child of Benjamin I. Hasbrouck and Elizabeth McCenly.
Witnesses : Jacobus Hasbrouck and Divertje Van Wagene.

Born Aug. 6. Johannes, child of Johannes B. Doio and Catrien Kretzinger.

Sept. 20 ; born Aug. 26. Jenny, child of Benjamin Windfield and Annatje York.
Witnesses : John Windfield and Jenny Van Ostrand.

Oct. 26 ; born Sept. 17. William, child of Levi P. McDonald and Nancy Wood.

Born Oct. 3. Rebecca, child of Daniel Sluiter and Sarah Bovier.

John, child of Robert Leroy and Deana Palmetier.

Nov. 8 ; born Sept. 26. Antje, child of Richard Stocks and Antje Carner.

Born Sept. 28. Maria, child of Isack and Francisca Low.

Nov. 22 ; born Oct. 31. Maria, child of Philip Doio and Gertruy Lefever.

Born Sept. 21. Hendricus Doio, child of Noach Elting and Annatje Doio.

Dec. 6 ; born —— 28. Annatje and Cornelius, children of Stephanus Scryver and Sartje Van Stenberg.
Witnesses : Peter Wells and Anna Oscela Scryver.

1790, Jan. 3 ; born Nov. 25, 1789. Catrina, child of William Smitt and Magdalena Achmody.
Witnesses : William Davis and Catrina Smitt.

Jan. 9 ; born Nov. 18, 1789. Lea, child of Petrus Keter and Gertruy Rosa.

Jan. 24 ; born Dec. 15, 1789. Antje, child of Elias Bevier and Sara Lefever.

Born Dec. 7, 1789. Johannes, child of Isack Hardenberg and Rachel Graham.

Born Oct. 23, 1789. Alida, child of Nathan Doio and Sarah Manny.

Feb. 14 ; born Jan. 29. Abram, child of Jonathan Doio and Maria Lefever.

Cornelius, child of Marcus Wecman and Jannatje Kool. Witnesses : Marcus Wecman and Martha Litz.

Born Dec. 24, 1789. Sara, child of Cornelius Dubois and Gertruy Bruin.

Feb. 23 ; born April 4, 1789. Maria, child of Johannes Wiest and Barbara Hoogteling.

Samuel, child of Elias Terpenning and Catrien Eccer.

Born July 25, 1789. William, child of William Danolson and Magdalen Neas.

Anne, child of John Bever and Catrien Wood.

Born Feb. 7. Martinus, child of Martynus Schryver and Greatje Terpenning.

Born July 18. Maria, child of David Goff and Johanna Devoe.

Cornelia, child of Piter Bever and Abigael Clerk.

March 7 ; born Jan. 26. Rachel, child of Isack Frere, Jr., and Sara Terwilger.
Witnesses : Zacharias Frere and Rachel Dubois.

Born Feb. 9. Christian, child of Josia Doio and Catrina Blonjan.
Witnesses : Christian Doio and Alida Terwilger.

Born Feb. 20. Joseph, child of John Ripple and Elizabeth Divine.

Born Jan. 18. Elihu, child of Methusalem Dubois and Catrientje Bovier.

May 9 ; born Feb. 12. Maria, child of Edward Wood, Jr., and Anny Weslye.
Witnesses : Owen and Mary Elles.

Born March 29. Elizabeth, child of Jehu Low and Elizabeth Snyder.
Witnesses : Jacob C. and Elizabeth Snyder.

Born March 15. Jacobus Van der Veer, child of Casparus Van Ostrant and Eva Frlinghuisen. (Sic.)

May 25. Joseph, child of John Lemonjon and Elizabeth Wells.

Born Feb. 20. John, child of Cornelius Degraaf and Annetje Van demerk.

Born April 10. Polly, child of Art Terwilger and Sara Saxon.

June 6 ; born May 18. Catrina, child of John I. Frere, Jr., and Margrita Bennet.
Witness : Catrina Frere.

Born April 29. Elisa, child of Simon Raljie and Lena Doio.

July 3 ; born June 14. Daniel, child of Moses York and Enne Petterson.
Witnesses : Daniel York and Maria Van Aken.

July 4. Sara, child of David Low and Rachel Lemerter.
Witnesses : Cornelus C. Lemerter and Sara Krom.

Born June 8. Benjamin, child of John, Jr. and Jannetje Terwilger.

Born Feb. 28. Wyntje, child of Efraim Deccer and Maria Terpening.
Witnesses : Daniel and Wyntje Hasbrouck.

Born Feb. 12. Annatje, child of Simeon Terpening and Peggy Smitt.

Born May 31. Marytje, child of Isack Dubois and Debory Raljie.
Witnesses : Denie Raljie and Marytje Van Vliet.

Born May 7. Benjamin, child of John Alliger and Catrina Low.

Born May 2. Annatje, child of Adam Jepol and Arriantje Hendricks.

Born May 9. Jonas, child of Elisa Frere and Martha Everet.

July 18 ; born May 14. Anne, child of John Dun and Sarah Lockwood.

Born May 26. Abraham, child of Daniel Klaerwater and Maria Siely.

Margriet, child of Elias and Cornelia Hardenberg.

July 25 ; born March 14. Enne, child of Efraim Kyser and Lena Klyn.

Aug. 30 ; born Sept. 20, 1786. Peter and Nency bo. Oct. 4, 1788, children of Thomas Burian and Maria Preslar.

Born May 31. John Tallor, child of Jacob Hornbec and Sally Thomson.

Sept. 5 ; born Aug. 5. Maria, child of Isack Dubois and Rebecca Doio.

Born Sept. 16. Jeremia, child of Jeremia Elles and Susanna Brown.

Sept. 19 ; born May 14. Nelle, child of William Wood and Sara Caddington.

Cornelius, child of Hendric Ralyie and Elizabeth Welmiller.

Sept. 26 ; born Sept. 4. Anatje, child of Jeremias Frere and Sara Van Wagenen.

Born Sept. 12. David, child of William Wood, Jr., and Cattrina Frere.

Born May 30. Charls, child of Hendricus Wecman and Lidia Hert.

Oct. 30 ; born Sept. 26. Sarah, child of Johannes Lefever and Elizabeth Dubois.

Born Sept. 24. Jonathan, child of Wessel Dubois and Catrien Lefever.
Witnesses : Jonathan Dubois and Rachel Goetschius.

Born Oct. 6. Cornelius Van Vliet, child of Denie Raljie, Jr., and Annatje Vanvliet.
Witnesses : Corns. Van Vliet and Lena Gerrison.

Born Sept. 7. Maria, child of John Windfield and Jenny Van Ostrant.

Born Sept. 11. Maria, child of Jonathan Traphagen and Maria Terwilger.

Daniel, child of Laurence Hendricks and Johanna Windfield.

Born Oct. 5. Catryntje, child of Ezechiel and Magdalena Elting.

Nov. 21 ; born Oct. 27. Maria, child of Gerret Van Bunschoten and Rebecca Totton.

Born Oct. 20. Willem, child of Willem Doio and Sara Elting.

Born Oct. 25. Elisabeth, child of Matheus Contryman and Margriet Stooks.

Born Oct. 12. Maria, child of Martynus and Maria Frere.

Nov. 28 ; born Nov. 11. Sarah, child of William Davis and Catrina Smitt.
Witnesses : Eliphas and Sarah Smitt.

Nov. 29 ; born Nov. 24. Annatje, child of Benjamin Doio, Jr., and Susanna Kritzinger.

Born Nov. 16. William, child of Johannes Hasbrouck and Caty McDonald.
Witnesses : William McDonald and Bridget Krom.

Born Oct. 15. Abram, child of Abram Hog and Jannetje Doio.

Dec. 26 ; born Nov. 29. Matheus, child of Petrus Bovier and Cornelia Bovier.
Witnesses : Matheus and Jackemyntje Bovier.

1791, Jan. 9 ; born Nov. 28, 1790. Jacob, child of Jonathan Frere and Margrietje Doio.
Witnesses : Jacob and Sara Frere.

Born Dec. 13, 1790. Anatje, child of Evert Sluiter and Grietje Kyser.
Witness : Anatje Kyser.

Jan. 11 ; born Oct. 13, 1790. John, child of Cornelius Smith and Ester Lemonjon.

Born Oct. 4, 1790. James, child of Thomas Jones and Mary Lemonjon.

Born Nov. 25, 1790. Betsy, child of Robert Leroy and Diana Palmetier.

Born Oct. 26, 1790. Margriet, child of Jeremia Devoe and Lena Danelson.

Jan. 16 ; born Nov. 9, 1790. William, child of Benjamin Wood and Eva Smitt.
Witnesses : Hendric Smitt and Lena Achmody.

Jan. 31 ; born Dec. 29, 1790. Thomas, child of Abram A. Bovier and Marytje Frere.
Witnesses : Thomas Frere and Hester Johnson.

Born Dec. 28, 1790. Annatje, child of Evert Terwilger and Maria Frere.
Witnesses : Peter Frere and Annatje Terwilger.

Feb. 5 ; born Nov. 25, 1790. Jesaias, child of Jesaias Hasbrouck and Maria Bevier.

Born Jan. 7. Petrus Low, child of Daniel Van Wagenen and Catryntje Low.

Feb. 20 ; born Oct. 25, 1790. Hendric and Hugo,* children of Jordan Polhemus and Lidia Doio.

March —; born Feb. 23. Richard, child of Lowis Hardenberg and Catrien Daly.

April 3; born Jan. 30. Abram, child of Timothy Branen and Maria York.

Born Feb. 7. Rolof, child of Salomon Elting and Cornelia Lefever.
Witnesses : Rolof Elting and Maria Low.

Born March ? Moses, child of Johannes Wilkelo and Jackemyntje Trowbridge.

Born Jan. 26. Christoffel, child of Jacob Lefever and Lidia Doio.
Witnesses : David Doio and Rachel Een.

April 10 ; born March 17. Jonathan, child of Isack Kyser and Elizabeth Trowbridge.

April 25 ; born Feb. 2. Jacob Rutze, child of Lowis and Polly Hardenberg.

Born Feb. 12. Levi, child of Salomon and Hester Low.

May 8 ; born April 5. Salomon, child of Ezechiel Low and Eva Stryker.
Witnesses : Solomon Low and Sara Bosch.

Born April 4. Catryntje, child of Isack Low and Francisca Everit.

May 15 ; born April 15. Elizabeth, child of Samuel Dubois and Jenneke Lefever.
Witnesses : Petrus Lefever and Elizabeth Vernoy.

* This item is rather indefinite in the original, and possibly may have been intended for one child, named Hendric Hugo.

June 5 ; born Feb. 2. Elisabeth, child of Philip Lemonjon and Mary Wells.

June 13. Nella, child of Matheus Hess and Martha Litz. Witness : Nella Shaw.

Maria, child of probably the same as above. Witness : Robert Hess.

June 26 ; born March 7. Margriet, child of Joseph Simmons and Annetje Myer.

Born May 26. Magdalena, child of Matheus and Elizabeth Lefever. Witnesses : Petrus Lefever, Jr., and Magdalena Elting.

July 9 ; born June 22. Elsje, child of Philip Doio and Gertruy Lefever.

Born May 30. Levi, child of Josia Hasbrouck and Sarah Dekker.

Born April 12. Clarissia, child of Francis Handmore and Phebe Gilbert.

July 10 ; born June 3. Evert, child of Jacob Green and Rachel Sammons.

Born April 26. Rachel, child of Daniel Sluiter and Sara Bovier.

July 29 ; born March 16. Polly, child of Thomas Rogers and Hennah Van Zyl.

Born July 7. Rebecca, child of Philip and Tryntje Elting. Witnesses : Jacob Low and Rebecca Van Wagen.

Born June 23. Rebecca, child of Jacob Dubois and Lidia Jumens. Witness : Rebecca Van Wagene.

August 8 ; born July 9. Catrina, child of Petrus Lefever, Jr., and Magdalena Elting. Witnesses : Daniel Lefever and Catrina Cantine.

Born Oct. 29, 1790. Sara, child of Jacob Wilkelo and Elizabeth Hood.

Born Feb. 15, 1791. John, child of Lucas Terwilger and Hester Frere. Witnesses : John, Jr., and Jannetje Terwilger.

Born June 5. Catrien, child of Dennis Colman and Tjatje Roos. Witnesses : Methusalem Dubois and Catrien Bevier.

August 21 ; born July 24. Isack, child of Laurence Hood and Sara Walron.
Witnesses : Johannes Walron and Elizabeth Een.

Born July 9. Maria, child of Joseph Coddington and Meriba Hardford.

Born July 24. Hester, child of Wauter Sluyter and Margriet Barton.

August 28 ; born August 11. David, child of Edward Kyser and Maria Sluiter.
Witnesses : Jacob Sluiter and Rachel Stooks.

Sept. 18 ; born August 16. Abram, child of Elias Ein and Elizabeth Hasbrouck.
Witnesses : Abram Ein and Catrina Van Wagenen.

Oct. 2 ; born Sept. 5. Hester, child of Benjamin H. Frere and Eva Eccer.

Born August 27. Eliza, child of Samuel Bovier and Rachel Achmody.

Born Sept. 12. Catrina, child of Benjamin Hasbrouck and Elizabeth McCinly.

Oct. 16 ; born Sept. 4. Nancey, child of Jonas Smith and Dina Van Ostrant.

Born Sept. 15. Sara, child of Rolof Hasbrouck and Jannetje Elting.

Born Sept. 27. Maria, child of Elias Bovier and Sara Lefever.

Oct. 30 ; born Sept. 24. Maria, child of James Achmody and Elizabeth Smith.

Nov. 21 ; born July 23. Bregje, child of Cornelius Kern and Elsje Kyser.
Witnesses : Charles Kyser and Bregje Etkens.

Born Oct. 8. Elisabeth, child of Isack Hardenberg and Rachal Graham.

Dec. 26 ; born June 17. David, child of Hugo Doio and Catrina Bush.

Born Sept. 17. Charles, child of John Slott, Jr., and Geertruy Van Vliet.

Born Dec. 6. Margarita Salome, child of Step^s. Goetschius and Elizabeth Dubois.
Witnesses : Gerret Blinkerhof and Margrita Goetschius.

1792, Jan. 1 ; born Nov. 25, 1791. Hendricus, child of Jacob Bovier and Maria York.

Jan. 8 ; born Dec. 24, 1791. Nathan, child of Levi Doio and Margriet Pawling.

Jan. 22 ; born Nov. 14, 1791. Jennet Blare, child of James Gallasbie and Elizabeth Brown.

Born Dec. 3, 1791. Rebecca, child of Charles and Maria Dubois.
Witnesses : Jacob Low and Rebecca Van Wagene.

Born Nov. 23, 1791. Peter, child of David Handmore and Nelly Ellenor.

Jan. 29 ; born Dec. 27, 1791. Evert Terwilger, child of Matheus Blonjan and Jacoba Borhans.
Witnesses : Bodowyn Terpenning and Rachel Terwilger.

March 4 ; born Feb. 6, 1792. Gertruy, child of David Low and Rachel Lemerter.
Witnesses : Cornelius Dubois and Gertruy Bruyn.

Born Dec. 29, 1791. Jeny, child of Simon Frere and Phebe Kitcham.
Witnesses : Elisa Frere and Martha Everet.
(A leaf in the original seems here to have been lost.)

Nov. 11 ; born Oct. 8, 1792. Hendricus, child of Isack Dubois and Rebecca Doio.

Born Oct. 23. Nella, child of Lowis Hardenberg and Catrien Daly.

Nov. 18 ; born Oct. 16. Jonas, child of Noagh Lefever and Cornelia Bovier.
Witness : Jonas Bovier.

Born Oct. 26. Alida, child of Ambrose Elmore and Maria Doio.
Witnesses : Christian Doio and Alida Terwilger.

Nov. 23 ; born Nov. 21. Catrina, child of Jeremias Frere and Sara Van Wagenen.

Nov. 30 ; born. Dec. 4 (?). Sarah, child of Benjamin Doio and Susanna Kritzinger.
Witnesses : Willem Doio and Sara Elting.

Born Nov. 11, 1792. Nathanel, child of Wessel Dubois and Catrien Lefever.

Nov. 27 ; born Nov. 11. Daniel, child of Isack Low and Francisca Everet.

1793, Jan. 14 ; born Dec. 15, 1792. Coenraad Lefever, child of Abram Sluiter and Elisabeth Davis.

Born Oct. 17, 1792. Stephen, child of Isack Sluiter and Sara Kritsinger.

Born Dec. 8, 1792. John, child of John Windfield and Jenny Van Ostrant.

Born Oct. 18, 1792. Jacob, child of Ephraim Kyser and Lena Klyn.
Witnesses : Jacob Kyser and Amalyma Sluiter.

Born Oct. 11, 1792. Catrina, child of Gerret Vanbunschoten and Rebecca Tatton.
Witness : Catrina Van Wagene.

Jan. 20 ; born Dec. 6, 1792. Abram Bovier, child of Daniel Van Wagene and Catryntje Low.
Witnesses : Abram Bovier and Sara Low.

Feb. 3 ; born Nov. 17, 1792. Andries, child of Josia K. ? Elting and Sara Lefever.
Witness : Andries Lefever.

Born Aug. 21, 1792. Gabriel, child of Elisa Frere and Martha Everet.

Born Dec. 8, 1792. Matheus, child of Simon Lefever and Jenneke Zwart.

Feb. 10 ; born Jan. 24. Catrien, child of Philip Doio and Gertruy Lefever.

Feb. 14 ; born Jan. 17. George, child of Piter Ostrander and Clarissa Fortham.

Born Jan. 30. Benjamin, child of Jacob Van Keuren and Elisabeth Terwilger.

March 17 ; born Feb. 15. Daniel, child of Timothy Branen and Maria York.
Witnesses : Daniel York and Maria Van Aken.

Born Feb. 4. Christoffel, child of David Doio and Rachel Ein.
Witness : Debora Van Vliet.

March 23. Jacobus, child of Jacobus Myers and Catrina Snyder.

Born Jan. 21. Elisabeth, child of Denie Raljie and Annatje Van Vliet.
Witnesses: Benjamin Raljie and Elisabeth Van Vliet.

March 31; born March 11. Ester, child of Ezechiel Van Wagene and Rachel Janson.

April 7; born Feb. 18. Rachel, child of Johannes Lefever and Elisabeth Dubois.

April 28; born May (?) 16. Betcy, child of Jonathan Tamkins and Peggy Heffy.

Born March 31. Eva, child of James Achmody and Elisabeth Smith.
Witness: Eva Smith.

Born April 18. John Dubois, child of Lowis and Maria Hardenberg.

Born March 28. Cornelis Dubois, child of Henry Green and Maria Doio.

Born Jan. 12. Adam, child of Christoffel Green and Catrina Eccert.

Born March 11. Tjark, child of Jonathan Traphagen and Maria Terwilger.
Witnesses: Elisa Ostrander and Sally Simson.

May 11; born Jan. 24. Jonathan, child of Jonathan Lefever and Catrina Frere.

May 12; born Feb. 17. Joseph, child of Edward Wood, Jr., and Anna Westleake.
Witnesses: Joseph Klarwater and Lidia Wood.

Born March 12. Eva, child of Thomas Klarwater and Lea Wood.

Born April 5. Salomon, child of Ezechiel and Magdalena Elting.
Witnesses: Salomon Elting and Catrina Van Deusen.

Born March 17. Rachel, child of Salomon Elting and Catrina Lefever.

Born March 29. Sara, child of Art Terwilger and Sara Saxon.

May 18; born March 9. Margrietje, child of Jesaias Hasbrouck and Maria Bovier.

June 9; born May 16. Daniel, child of Petrus Lefever, Jr., and Magdalena Elting.

June 16; born Feb. 20. William, child of Jacob Wilkelo and Elisabeth Hood.

Born June 3. Christoffel, child of Solomon Low, Jr., and Hester Low.

July 7. Jannetje, child of Matheus Hess and Martha Litz. Witness: Janetje Wekman.

Born June 7. Dirk, child of Jacob Kyser and Amalyna Sluiter.

Born June 18. John, child of James Mahony and Mary Decker.

July 21; born June 25. Abraham, child of Abraham Doio and Maria Lefever.

Born June 24. Maria, child of Johannes Wilkelo and Jackemyntje Strawbridge.

Born June 16. John Everse, child of Evert I. Terwilger and Maria Frere.

Sept. 1; born Aug. 16. John, child of Laurence Hood and Sara Walron.

Sept. 22; born June 26. Annatje, child of Philip Lemonjon and Mary Wells.

Born Aug. 29. John, child of Adam Jepold and Arriantje Hendrick.

Oct. 6; born Aug. 13. Elisabeth, child of Jacob Lefever and Lidia Doio.
Witnesses: Petrus Lefever and Elisabeth Vernoy.

Oct. 27; born Aug. 28. Wyntje, child of Cornelius Krom and Maria Doio.
Witnesses: Jonathan Krom and Maria Morris.

Born Sept. 25. Christian, child of Johannes Doio and Catrien Kritzinger.

Born Sept. 13. Maria, child of Jacob Green and Rachel Sammons.

Nov. 25; born Oct. 30. Dina, child of Philip and Catryntje Elting.
Witness: Abram Elting.

Dec. 25; born Nov. 21. Maria, child of Charles Hardenberg and Annatje Lefever.

Dec. 24 ; born Nov. 25. Jane, child of Zacharias Burger and Elisabeth Windfield.

1794, Jan. 1 ; born Nov. 23, 1793. Levi, child of Jonathan Frere and Margrietje Doio.

Born Oct. 21, 1793. Mary, child of Jonas Smitt and Dina Van Ostrant.

Born Nov. 30, 1793. Lewis Hardenberg, child of John Van Ostrant and Anna Catong.
Witness : Eva Vrelinghuise.

Born Dec. 4, 1793. Rebecca, child of Elias Bovier and Sara Lefever.

Jan. 19 ; born Nov. 9, 1793. Titus, child of Simon Frere and Phebe Kitcham.

Born Dec. 11, 1793. Catryntje, child of Rolof Hasbrouck and Jannetje Elting.
Witnesses : Jacobus Hardenberg and Catryntje Elting.

Born Sept. 9, 1793. Jemes Gilbert, child of Francis Handmore and Phebe Gilbart.

Born Aug. 19, 1793. James, child of Daniel Sluiter and Sara Bovier.

Born July 17, 1793. Elisabeth, child of Jesse Cool and Jenny Frere.

Born Aug. 22, 1793. Lena, child of Abram Wesmiller and Hester Raljie.

Feb. 9 ; born Jan. 4. Maria, child of Johannes Walron, Jr., and Marretje Herres.

Born Jan. 1. Albert, child of Lambert Jinkins and Annatje Bartolf.

Born Dec. 30, 1793. Catarine, child of Isack Hardenberg and Rachel Graham.

Born June 13, 1793. Elisabeth, child of Robert Claton and Mary Revoe (?)

March 27 ; born Feb. 14. Petrus, child of Jehu Low and Elisabeth Snyder.

March 30 ; born Feb. 15. Elisabeth, child of Moses and Anatje Frere.
Witnesses : Paulus Frere and Elisabeth Van Wagenen.

Born Feb. 9. Sara, child of Hugo Sluiter and Sara Frere.

April 20; born March 25. Stephanus, child of Marcus Wecman and Jenny Kool.

May 11; born April 28. Jeremias, child of Daniel Frere, Jr., and Rachel Devaal.

Born Oct. 1, 1793. Jannetje, child of Jordan Pulhemus and Lidia Doio.

May 18; born March 19. Maria, child of Salomon Doio and Bregje Frere.
Witnesses: Simeon Doio and Maria Depue.

Born May 23. Annatje, child of Jacob Blonjan and Maretje Hermanse.
Witnesses: Edward Hermanse and Anatje Blonjan.

June 22; born May 3. Mary, child of John Dun and Sarah Lockwood.

Born April 21. John, child of William Hood and Sarah Caddington.

July 21; born May 30. John, child of Arie Myer and Santje Sturn.

Aug. 24; born July 13. Johannes, child of Eliphas and Sara Smitt.

Born July 8. Marytje, child of Cornelius Connency and Annatje Sluiter.

Born June 15. Johannes, child of George Vansyl and Catrien Wilkelo.

Aug. 31; born Oct. 16, 1793. Anatje, child of John Keter and Rebecca Elmore.
Witnesses: Simon Elmore and Annie Frere.

Sept. 14; born Aug. 7. Jacobus, child of Simion Frere and Elisabeth Elmondorph.
Witnesses: Jacobus Elmondorph, Jr., and Maria Terwilger.

Oct. 5; born Sept. 10. Wyntje, child of Willem Smitt and Magdalena Aghmody.

Born Sept. 8. Maria, child of Benjamin H. Frere and Eva Eccert.

Born Aug 20. Cornelius, child of Simon Helm and Maria Schonmaker.

Born July 30. Maria, child of Benjamin I. Terwilger and Elisabeth Bindfield.

Born Aug. 27. Rachel, child of Lowis Hardenberg and Catrina Daly.
Witnesses: Henry Daly and Catrina Terwilger.

Born Sept. 17. Willem, child of Moses Doio and Maria Ostrander.
Witness: William Delemerter.

Born Sept. 9. Elsje, child of Isack Frere and Maria Terwilger.

Born Oct. 15. Sara, child of James Weldon and Lidia Litz.

Born Sept. 8. Maria, child of Josia Elting and Sara Lefever.
Witnesses: Rolof Eling and Maria Low.

Nov. 2; born Sept. 27. Philip, child of Johannes Hasbrouck and Caty McDonald.

Born Sept. 25. Eva, child of Jesaias Sluiter and Guirtry Van Ostrant.

Born Sept. 17. Polly, child of Timothy Branen and Polly York.

Born Oct. 6. Nathanel, child of Charles and Polly Dubois.
Witnesses: Nathanel and Ann Dubois.

Nov. 9; born Oct. 11. Jannetje, child of John I. Frere, Jr., and Margrita Bennet.

Nov. 23; born Nov. 2. Petrus Ostrander, child of David Raljie and Laura Ostrander.

Dec. 14; born Oct. 18. Maria, child of Christoffel Green and Catrina Eccert.

Born Nov. 4. Christoffel, child of Ezechiel Low and Eva Stryker.

Born July 5. Mills, child of Peter Wells and Osseltje Schryver.

Dec. 26; born Nov. 13. Johannes, child of Daniel and Sarah Bovier.

1795, Jan. 4; born Nov. 19, 1794. Maria, child of Johannes Lefever and Elisabeth Dubois.

Jan. 25; born Dec. 29, 1794. Abram Van Wagene, child of Levi Van Wagene and Elisabeth Low.

Born October 20, 1794. Daniel, child of Benjamin Hasbrouck and Maria Bovier.

Born Dec. 21. Jannetje, child of Willem Doio and Sarah Elting.
Witnesses: Benjamin Doio and Jannetje Van Vliet.

Born Sept. 29. Peter, child of Isack Bodoin and Rachel Dubois.

Born Oct. 16. Sartje, child of John Barret and Seletje Palmetier.

Born Nov. 30. Lena, child of Robert Leroy and Blandina Palmetier.

Jan. 26; born Nov. 22, 1793. Jacob, child of David Goff and Johanna Devoe.

Born Feb. 24, 1788, Gabriel; born Jan. 12, 1794, Mary, children of Nowell Forman and Margriet Hoff.

Feb. 8; born Jan. 10. Benjamin, child of William Davis and Catrina Smitt.

Born July 31, 1794. Phebe, child of Hendric Wicman and Lidia Hart.

Born Nov. 25, 1794. Johannes, child of Jacobus Devenport and Maria Muul.

Born Jan. 19. Josia, child of Salomon and Hester Low.

Feb. 15; born Jan. 28. Josia Doio, child of Ambrosius Elmore and Maria Doio.
Witnesses: Josia Doio and Catrina Blonjan.

April 19; born Jan. 20. Magdalena, child of Noagh Lefever and Cornelia Bovier.
Witnesses: Andries and Magdalena Lefever.

Born Feb. 26. Maria, child of Petrus Lefever, Jr., and Magdalena Elting.

Born Feb. 1. Rachel, child of Stephanus Schryver and Sara Stenberg.
Witnesses: Matheus and Margriet.

May 10; born Jan. 18. Benjamin, child of Evert Burger and Maria York.

Born April 7. Jacobus, child of Elias Ein and Elisabeth Hasbrouck.

Born April 13. Lucas, child of Daniel Van Wagene and Catryntje Low.

Born March 18, at 12 o'clock M., John Henry ; born March 18, at 3 o'clock P.M., Steven Zobriskie, children of Steph. Goetschius and Elisabeth Dubois.

May 22 ; born March 18. Rachel, child of Casparus Van Ostrant and Eva Vrelinghuisen.

May 24 ; born April 26. Catrina, child of Jonathan Dubois and Rachel Goetschius.

Born Feb. 14. Jannetje, child of Denie Raljie and Annatje Van Vliet.
Witnesses : Dirk Van Vliet and Anatje Raljie.

Born Sept. 21, 1794. Magdalena, child of Benjamin Wood and Eva Smitt.
Witnesses : Willem Smitt and Magdalena Aghmody.

June 14 ; born March 15. Neltje, child of Mynert Vilie and Johanna Parmetier.
Witnesses : Simon Vilie and Neltje Parmetier.

Born April 12. Elisabeth, child of John Lemonjon and Elisabeth Wells.

Born Feb. 23, Sara and Cornelia, children of Philip Doio and Guirtruy Lefever.

Born May 8. Richard, child of Josia Ab.? Elting and Ester Broadhead.

July 5 ; born June 6. Jonas, child of Ezechiel Frere and Elisabeth Sluiter.
Witnesses : Jonas Frere and Maria Sluiter.

Born May 10. Jonathan Terwilger, child of Jonathan Traphagen and Maria Terwilger.

Aug. 16 ; born July 24. Maria, child of Ezechiel and Magdalena Elting.

Born July 12. Peter, child of Simon Vilie and Neltje Palmetier.

Born July 22. Polly, child of David Philips and Polly Swarthout.

Sept. 3 ; born July 13. John, child of Edward Wood and Ann Westlake.

Sept. 7 ; born June 13. Petrus, child of Petrus Crouter and Catrina Steveson.

Born Aug. 27. Henry, child of Adam Jepold and Arriantje Hendricson.

Born July 13. Lourence, child of Jacob Wilkelo and Elisabeth Hood.
Witness : Rachel Hood.

Born Aug. 10. John, child of William Geding or Gedney and Betcy Leroy.

Born July 13. Daniel, child of Isack Dubois and Rebecca Doio.
Witness : Daniel Dubois.

Born Aug. 11. Daniel, child of Johannes Berenhart and Sara Sluiter.
Witnesses : Daniel Dubois and Tryntje Lefever.

Sept. 27; born Sept. 15. Elisabeth, child of Piter Cetur and Gertje Roos.
Witnesses : Jacob Ketur and Elisabeth Constable.

Oct. 18; born Aug. 25. Andries Lefever, child of Andries Dubois, Jr., and Elisabeth Lefever.
Witnesses : Andries and Lena Lefever.

Oct. 25 ; born July 21. Johannes, child of Charles Hardenberg and Annatje Lefever.

Born Oct. 9. Benjamin, child of Johannes B. Doio and Catrien Kritsinger.

Born June 10. Sara, child of Jacob Van Keuren and Elisabeth Terwilger.
Witnesses : Jesaias Doio and Annatje Terwilger.

Born Aug. 31. Sara, child of Isack Dubois and Debora Raljie.

Oct. 27 ; born Sept. 14. Jannetje, child of Johannes, Jr., and Jannetje Terwilger.

Tjatje, child of Cornelius Frere and Margrietje Weller.
Witnesses : Johannes Weller and Tjatje Masten.

Born Oct. 7. Jonas, child of John J. Slott and Gertje Van Vliet.
Witnesses : Jonas Slott and Abigael Longsberry.

Nov. 7 ; born July 16. Maria, child of Jordan Purhemus and Lidia Doio.

Nov. 8 ; born Oct. 22. Peter, child of Evert Terwilger and Maria Frere.
Witnesses : Samuel Terwilger and Elisabeth Frere.

Born Sept. 15. Catrina, child of George Baster and Hannah Helm.

Nov. 29 ; born Oct. 27. Jeremias, child of Jeremias Frere and Sara Van Wagene.

Born Oct. 26. Wyntje, child of Jonas Smith and Dina Van Ostrant.

Born Oct. 27. Rolof, child of Jonathan Frere and Margriet Doio.

1796 ; Jan. 10, born Nov. 29, 1795. Maria, child of Abram Wesmiller and Hester Raljie.

Feb. 15 ; born Dec. 12, 1795. Maria, child of Daniel Sluiter and Sara Bovier.

Born Nov. 28, 1795. Abram Ein, child of Benjamin Hasbrouck and Annatje Ein.
Witnesses : Abram Ein and Catrina Van Wagene.

Born July 9, 1795. Elisabeth, child of Jeremia Ellis and Susanna Brown.

Born Jan. 17. Thomas, child of Jacobus Elmondorph and Bregje Etkins.
Witness : Nella Samons.

Born Jan. 18. Maria, child of Philip Lefever and Elsje Dubois.
Witnesses : Daniel Dubois and Tryntje Lefever.

Feb. 18 ; born Jan. 10. Elias, child of Josia Depue and Rachel Hardenberg.

March 13 ; born Feb. 22. Magdalena, child of Philip and Catrina Elting.
Witnesses : Petrus Lefever, Jr., and Magdalena Elting.

April 3 ; born Feb. 12. Sarah, child of Benjamin Terwilger and Maria Frere.
Witnesses : Isack Frere, Jr., and Sara Terwilger.

Born Feb. 26. James, child of Petrus Helm and Elisabeth Parrine.

April 17 ; born Dec. 1, 1795. Louis, child of Jacob J. Hasbrouck and Margrietje Hardenberg.

Born March 17. Rachel, child of Abram P. Schonmaker and Catrina Frere.
Witness : Rachel Schonmaker.

Born March 7. Magdalena, child of Elias Bovier and Sara Lefever.

Born March 16. Zacharias, child of Abram Bovier and Marytje Frere.
Witnesses: Zacharias Frere and Jannetje Dubois.

May 8; born March 17. Arriantje, child of Jacobus Vilie and Catryntje Palmetier.

Born April 9. Sartje, child of Simon Raljie and Lena Doio.

Born Feb. 2. Jonas, child of Simon Frere and Elisabeth Elmondorph.
Witnesses: Jonas Frere and Magdalena Bovier.

May 16; born April 25. Dennis, child of Dennes Coleman and Tjatje Roos.
Witness: Maria Hasbrouck.

Born Feb. —. Johannes, child of Johannes Wilkelo and Jackemyntje Trowbridge.

Born March 16. Elisa, child of Zacharias Burger and Elisabeth Windfield.
Witnesses: Elisa Ostrander and Selly Simson.

Born April 8. Simon, child of Abram Sluiter and Elisabeth Davis.
Witnesses: Simon Hendricse and Lea Sluiter.

June 5; born Feb. 17. Maria, child of Jesaias Hasbrouck and Maria Bovier.

Born Jan. 11. Benjamin, child of William Hood and Sarah Caddington.

Born April 6. Charles, child of Francis Handmore and Phebe Gilbert.

Born May 21. Ester, child of Elisa Frere and Martha Everet.

Born April 2. Rachel, child of Noel Forman and Margriet Hoff.

July 19; born June 3. Johannis, child of Johannes York and Jannetje Bovier.

Born June 6. Maria, child of Jonathan Lefever and Catrina Frere.

Sept. 28; born Aug. 25. Rachel, child of Josua R. Eltinge and Sarah Lefefer.

Born May 25, 1796. Magdelena, child of Rolof Haasbroek and Janetie Eltinge.

Born Sept. 10. Catrina, child of David Deyoo and Rachel Ien.
Witnesses : Abraham Ien and Catrina Vanwagene.

Born Dec. 10. Elizabeth, child of Jeremiah Low and Weyntie Wieler.

Born Aug. 23. Petrus, child of Jonathan Deyoo and Maria Lefefer.

Oct. 27 ; born Sept. 22. Andrew, child of Johannes Hasbrouck and Caty McDonald.

Dec. 15 ; born Oct. 6. Hendric, child of Timothy Branen and Maria York.
Witnesses : Hendric Van Wagenen and Margriet York.

Born Nov. 5. Benjamin, child of Lucas Vanwagenen and Cornelia Merkil.
Witness : Benjamin Merkil.

Born Aug. 28. Elisabeth, child of Jonathan, Jr., and Maria Terwilger.

Born Nov. 4. Rachel, child of Paulus Frere and Elisabeth Van Wagene.
Witnesses : Petrus Schonmaker and Rachel Vanwagene.

Born Nov. 24. Benjamin, child of John Z. Flaglor and Anne Bogert.
Witness : Mary Sluiter.

1797, Jan. 29 ; born Nov. 24, 1796. Elias, child of Philippus Schonmaker and Rachel Frere.

Born Jan. 23. Elisabeth, child of Matheus Hess and Martha Litz.

Born Oct. 22, 1796. Gertruy, child of Hendric Wekman and Lidia Hert.

Born Nov. 12, 1796. Susanna, child of William Litz and Elisabeth Palmetier.

Jan. 30 ; born Sept. 15, 1796. Maria, child of John France and Sara Elting.
Witness : Elisabeth Depuy.

Born Jan. 27, 1797. Paul, child of Job Tilson and Hester Frere.
Witnesses : Paulus Frere and Elisabeth Vanwagene.

Born Dec. 30, 1796. Jinny, child of Christoffer Green and Catrina Eccert.

Born No. 16, 1796. Krynus, child of Lambartus Jinkins and Annatje Bartolf.

Born Dec. 20, 1796. Elisabeth, child of Simon Raljie and Maria Divine.

April 17 ; born Feb. 17. Maria, child of David Low and Rachel Delemerter.
Witnesses : Methusalem D—— and Catrina Bovier.

Born Feb. 8. Rolof, child of Piter Lefever, Jr., and Magdalena Elting.
Witnesses : Rolof Elting and Maria Low.

Born April 6. Elias, child of Moses and Annatje Frere.
Witnesses : Jacob J. Frere and Grietje Ein.

Born Jan. 27. Pitronella, child of Johannes Lefever and Elisabeth Dubois.
Witnesses : Andries and Lena Lefever.

Born Jan. 28. Grietje, child of Jost Ekhart and Grietje Roos.

Born Sept. 22, 1796. Forman, child of Samuel Budd and Polly Leroe.
Witness : Jenny Wertz.

Born Feb. 20. Petrus, child of Matheus Doio and Selly Hasbrouck.
Witnesses : Petrus Hasbrouck and Selly Bovier.

Born Jan. 18. John, child of Jacob Roos and Selly Yelverton.
Witnesses : John Roos and Catrina Pekker.

Born Feb. 3. Hendric, child of Gerret Dubois and Maria Elting.

Born Jan. 22. Jannetje, child of Salomon Elting, Jr., and Rachel Eccert.

Born April 12. Sara, child of William Doio and Sara Elting.

Born Jan. 5. Mathew, child of Petrus Hardenberg and Jenny Armstrong.

Born Sept. 24. (1796?) Polly, child of George Vansyl and Catrina Wilkilo.

Born Jan. 15. Rolof Hasbrouck, child of Simeon Shorger and Enne Eccert.

Born April 3. Ezechiel, child of Benjamin Sluiter and Elisabeth Nies.

June 18; born May 15. Salomon, child of Daniel Vn Wagenen and Tryntje Low.

Born May 22. Jacob, child of Petrus York and Margritta Vn Leuven.

Born May 13. Jacamyntje, child of Peter Elting and Cornelia Wyncoop.
Witnesses: Derick Wyn—— and Annatje El——.

Sept. 3; born July 11. Catrina, child of Noah Le Fever and Cornelia Bovier.
Witnesses: Daniel ——— and Catrina Lef——.

Born July 12. Christina, child of David Reljea and Laura Ostrander.

Born May 24. Andreas, child of Philip Doyo and Geertruy Lefever.

Born Aug. 12. Francis, child of William Kidney and Elizabeth LeRoi.

Sept. 19; born May 5. Hester, child of Zacharias Frere and Jenneke Dubois.

Born July 16. Elsje, child of Simon Frere and Phebe Katcham.

Born April 9. Gerret, child of Daniel Hasbrouck and Margrietje Frere.

Born April 8. Abram, child of David Philips and Polly Swartwout.

Sept. 27; born Feb. 1. Rachel, child of John Lemonjon and Elisabeth Wells.

Born Aug. 1. Abram, child of Dirk Johnson and Margrietje Stenberg.

Oct. 22; born Sept. 22. Daniel, child of Simon Roos and Maria Van Wagenen.

— 21; born Oct. 14. Maria, child of Isaac Bodine and Rachel Dubois.

Born July 22. Daniel, child of Nathaniel Deyoe and Lea Dewitt.
Witness: Daniel Deyoe.

Born Sept. 12. William, child of Abraham Hood and Rachel Feelie.

1798, Jan. 4; born Jan. 1, 1797. Myndert, child of Jacobus Viele and Catharina Palmetier.

Jan. 4; born Dec. 3, 1797. Jonas, child of Abraham P. Schoonmaker and Catharina Freer. Witnesses: Jonas and Lena Freer.

Born Aug. 22, 1797. Joseph, child of Isaac Debois and Rebecca Deyoe.

April 29; born April 10. Sarah, child of Ezechiel and Magdalena Elting.

Born Sept. 25, 1797. Maria, child of Peter Wells and Osseltje Schryver.

Born March 18. Polly, child of Ambrose Elmore and Maria Doio.

Born March 4. Sara, child of Smith? Holsted and Maria Schriver. Witnesses: Stephen Schriver and Sara Stenberg.

Born April 7. Sara, child of Philip Lefever and Elsje Dubois. Witness: Sara Lefever.

Born March 9. Thejrk, child of Jacob Lefever and Lidia Doio.

Born April 13. Peter, child of John Fleger and Charity Vandebogert.

April 11; born March 25. Antje, child of Benjamin Hasbroeck and Maria Bevie.

No date of baptism. Born May 14. Stephanus, child of Johannes B. Dejoo and Catharina Kritsingen.

Born Jan. 31. Jacobus, child of Levi Van Waagene and Elizabeth Law.

Born April 4. Rebecka, child of Ezechiel Van Wagene and Rachel Janse.

Born May 9. Hannah, child of John Dunn and Sarah Lockwood.

Aug. 12; born June 15. Hanna, child of Johannes Wilkelo and Jackemyntje Trowbridge.

Born July 28. Sara, child of Mynert Vilie and Johanna Palmetier.

Born July 14. Lena, child of Marynus Terpenning and Debora Raljie.
Witnesses : Willem Raljie and Lena Ostrander.

Born July 14. William, child of Amassa Michel and Mary Bovier.

Born July 4. Jenneke, child of Elias Bovier and Sara Lefever.
Witnesses : Samuel Dubois and Jenneke Lefever.

Born July 23. Gamaliel, child of Marcus Wekman and Jannetje Kool.

Born Jan. 22. Hennery, child of Samuel Crissel and Ame Polhemus.

Born July 20. Johannes, child of Isack Dubois and Debora Raljie.

Born May 12. Isack, child of Benjamin B. Frere and Maria Terwilger.

Born May 30. Annatje, child of Hendricus Goetschius and Margriet Masten.

Born Dec. 12, 1797. Elisabeth, child of Abram Wesmiller and Hester Raljie.

Aug. 22 ; born July 28. Thomas, child of Thomas Owens and Caty Vanwagene.

Born July 26. Arriantje, child of Dennis Colman and Tjatje Roos.
Witness : Arriantje Schonmaker.

Oct. 21 ; born Sept. 24. Polly, child of Johannes Hasbrouck and Kete McDonald.

Oct. 24 ; born Sept. 15. Lewis, child of Charles and Maria Dubois.
Witness : Lewis Dubois.

Born Sept. 28. Treyntie, child of Garret Dubois and Maria Elting.

Born Sept. 9. Henry, child of Hendrick Werkman and Lidia Hert.

Born Aug. 23. Benjamin, child of Phillip Schoonmaker and Rachel Freer.

Born Sept. 7. Moses, child of Phillip and Tryntie Elting.

1799, Jan. 2 ; born Nov. 13, 1798. Annatje, child of Samuel Dubois and Jenneke Lefever.
Witnesses : Petrus Frere and Annatje Dubois.

Born Dec. 20, 1798. Methusalem, child of Jacob Doio and Rachel Wood.

Born Nov. 26, 1798. Abram Een, child of David Doio and Rachel Een.

Born Nov. 10, 1798. Timothy Frere, child of Job Telson and Hester Frere.

Born Nov. 8, 1798. Hester, child of John Elting and Jannetje Wertz.

Born Dec. 6, 1798. Rachel, child of Christoffer Green and Catrina Eccert.

Born Dec. 7, 1798. Maria, child of Josia Hasbrouck and Sara Decker.

Born Sept. 13, 1798. Caty, child of Samuel Budd and Polly Leroe.

Born Oct. 18, 1798. Jacob, child of Timothy Brannen and Polly York.
Witnesses : Jacob Crispel and Polly Schoonmaker.

Born Aug. 20, 1798. Anne, child of Gideon Ostrander and Elisabeth Dusenberg.

Born Sept. 1, 1798. Benjamin Frere, child of Benjamin Terwilger, Jr., and Maria Frere.

Feb. 7 ; born June 26, 1798. Salomon, child of Salomon Doio and Bregje Frere.

Born Jan. 12. Lowis, child of Jonas Dubois and Rachel Lefever.
Witness : Louis Dubois.

Born Dec. 20, 1798. Margriet, child of Levi Doio and Margrietje Paling.

Born Dec. 11, 1798. Maria, child of Jonathan, Jr., and Maria Terwilger.

May 8 ; born March 5. Jonathan, child of Lucas Van Wagene and Cornelia Merkil.

Born March 7. Daniel, child of Matheus Blonjan and Maria Dubois.
Witnesses : Daniel Dubois and Tryntje Lefever.

Born Feb. 23. Annatje, child of Benjamin Sluiter, Jr., and Elisabeth Nies.

Born March 15. Jonas, child of Daniel Hasbrouck and Margrietje Frere.
Witnesses : Jonas and Wyntje Hasbrouck.

Born Feb. 23. Margrietje, child of Moses Dewitt and Elisabeth Doio.
Witnesses : Daniel Doio and Catrina Dewitt.

Born Aug. 25. David, child of Charles Mackey and Rachel Baker.

Born Sept. 22. Jemes Burnet, child of Lucas Billyou and Mary Burnett.

Aug. 11 ; born March 7. Hendric, child of Hendric Raljie and Elisabeth Wesmiller.

Born May 14. Annatje, child of Moses Frere, deceased, and Annatje Frere.
Witnesses : Benjamin Frere and Elisabeth Terwilger.

Born Sept. 3, 1798 ? Elisabeth, child of William Erwin and Jane Ennes.

Born May 27. Johannes, child of Elias and Elisabeth Ein.

Born May 10. Horatio Nelson, child of Levi P. McDonald and Enne Wood.
Witnesses : William and Elisabeth McDonald.

Born June 4. Jannetje, child of Piter Lefever, Jr., and Magdalena Eltinge.

Born May 11. Gertje Wynkop, child of Petrus Eltinge and Cornelia Wynkop.
Witness : Gertje Wynkop.

Born May 3. Polly, child of Peter Johnson, Jr., and Nancy Saxon.

Born May 22. Catryntje, child of Daniel Van Wagene and Catryntje Low.

Born May 20. Elisabeth, child of Simon Frere, Jr., and Phebe Ketcham.

Sept. 25 ; born Aug. 22. Catrina, child of Jonathan Doio, Jr., and Catrina Ein.
Witnesses : Abram Ein and Catrina Van Wagene.

Born Aug. 6. Ezechiel, child of William Doio and Sara Eltinge.

Born Aug. 23. William, child of William Doio and Elisabeth Palmetier.

Born April 16. Abram, child of John Barret and Seletje Palmetier.

Born June 10. Jacob, child of Robert Leroy and Dintje Palmetier.

Oct. 13; born Sept. 1. Isaac, child of Zacherias Freer and Yannetie Dubois.
Witness: Isaac Freer.

Born Aug. 17. Margaret, child of Wilhelmus Hasbrouck and Alida Frere.

Born Aug. 28. Sarah, child of Ezegiel Van Wagenen and Rachel Johnsen.

Nov. 3; born July 4. Garret, child of Jonathan Lefever and Catharina Freer.

Born Sept. —. Margaret, child of Mathew Dejo and Sally Hasbrook.

Born 1799. John Waldron, child of Jacob Wilkeloo and Margaret Harris.

Born Sept. 7. Abraham Dubois, child of Simeon Shuragen and Anne Akker.

Nov. 17; born Oct. 23. Maria, child of Abraham P. Schoonmaker and Catarina Freer.
Witness: Maria Freer.

Born July 30. Meynderd, child of Abraham Hood and Rachel Veley.

Born Oct. 3. Abraham, child of Ann Bogart, wife of John Flagler, Quaker.

Born Sept. 11. Phebe, child of William Hood and Anne Simons.

Born Sept. 13. James, child of James Soper and Margaret Dunn.

Dec. 8; born Oct. 9. Alida, child of James Russel and Lambertha Ostrander.

Dec. 29; born Nov. 30. Cornelia, child of Johannes Lefevre and Elizabeth Dubois.

Born Oct. 24. Peter, child of Simon Rose and Maria Van Wagenen.

1800, Jan. 12 ; born Dec. 18, 1799. Sarah, child of Zacharias Sluyter and Elizabeth Freer.
Witnesses : Jeremy Freer and Sarah Van Wagenen.

Born May 10, 1797, Simon ; born Sept. 16, 1799, Peter, children of Jeremiah Hasbrook and Anne Masten.
Witness : Sarah Bevier.

Jan. 26 ; born Dec. 15, 1799. George Washington, child of Sheffield Forster and Ann Lowe.

Feb. 22 ; born Feb. 1. Gertrude, child of Levi Van Wagenen and Elizabeth Lowe.

Feb. 23 ; born Jan. 19. Nathaniel Lefevre, child of Jonas Dubois and Rachel Lefevre.

Born Feb. 4. Maria, child of Ezechial Lowe and Eva Stryker.

Born Oct. 8, 1799. Benjamin, child of Jonathan Traphagen and Maria Terwilliger.
Witnesses : Benjamin Terwilliger and Maria Freer.

March 9 ; born Jan. 17. Mary, child of Josiah Eltinge and Hester Broadhead.

Born Jan. 31. Jacobus, child of Johannes York and Jane Bevier.

March 16 ; born Feb. 10. Janitye, child of David and Elizabeth Terwilliger.

April 2 ; born Feb. 16. Hiram, child of Isaac Bodine and Rachel Dubois.

May 11 ; born March 6. Moses, child of Job Tilson and Hester Freer.

Born Feb. 27. George, child of Jonathan Dubois and Rachel Goetschius.

Born April 4. Levi, child of Edward Edmundus Schoonmaker and Lea Rose.

Born April 16. Rachel, child of John I. Freer and Margarit Bennet.

Born April 15. Johannis, child of Philip Schoonmaker and Rachel Freer.

June 22 ; born May 10. Petrus Lefever, child of Charles Hardenbergh and Anne Lefever.

Born May 28. Rachel, child of Noah Lefever and Cornelia Bevier.

Born April 14. Helena, child of Charles Broadhead and Anne Schoonmaker.

Born May 27. Levi, child of Jacobus Rosa and Sarah Van Wagenen.

Born May 31. Elihu, child of Jacob Dejo and Rachel Hood.

Born May 17. Derick Wynkoop, child of Thomas Owens and Catharina Van Wagenen.

July 6; born May 24. Maria, child of Isaac Van Wagenen and Else Freer.
Witnesses: Garret and Maria Freer.

Born Feb. 25. Rhodi, child of Howell? Furman and Margaret Huff.

Born May 5. Cornelius, child of Abraham Hardenbergh and Margaret Dubois.

July 20; born April 4. Jacob, child of Amasy Mitchell and Mary Bevier.
Witnesses: Jacob Bevier and Mary York.

Born June 18. Isaac, child of Benjamin Terwilliger and Maria Freer.

Elliot, child of John Halstead and Sarah Meyers.

Aug. 10; born July 8. Seyntie, child of Peter Auchmoudy and Eva Smith.

Aug. 24; born May 4. Josia, child of Abraham Wessimiller and Hester Relyea.

Born June 13. Alexander, child of Samuel and Elizabeth Coe.

Sept. 21; born Aug. 17. Maritie, child of David Rilyea and Loura Ostrander.

Born June 30. Jacobus, child of Meyndert Veley and Johanna Palmitier.

Born Aug. 12. Sally, child of Timothy Brannen and Mary York.

Born Jan. 25. Peter, child of Peter Wells and Osseltie Schryver.

Born April 1. Maria, child of Evert Terwilligen and Maria Freer.

Nov. 2; born Sept. 15. Jonathan, child of Jonathan and Maria Terwilligen.

Nov. 30; born Sept. 25. Moses, child of Johannis B. Dojo and Catharine Critsinger.

Born Oct. 23. Catharine, child of Ezekiel and Magdalen Eltinge.

Dec. 8; born Oct. 3. Simon, child of Lewis Hardenbergh and Caty Daily.

Born Nov. 26. Derick Wynkoop, child of Peter Elting and Cornelia Wynkoop.
Witnesses: Derick Wynkoop and Anatie Elting.

Dec. 21; born Oct. 16. Cornelius, (or Cornelia?) child of Josiah R. ? Eltinge and Sarah Lefevre.

Born Sept. 14. Sabrea, child of William Irwin and Jane Ines.

Dec. 25; born Dec. 9. Maria, child of Abraham Shut and Margaret Myer.

Born Oct. 21. Charick, child of Benjamin Dojo and Susannah Critsinger.

Born Nov. 26. Maurus, child of Jacob J. Hasbrook and Anne Dubois.

1801, Jan. 18; born Dec. 12, 1800. Rebecca, child of Christopher Green and Catharina Ackert.

Born Dec. 18, 1800. Sarah, child of Josiah Dojo and Maria Terwilliger.

Born Dec. 18, 1800. Magdalena, child of Arche P. Van Wagenen and Maria Freer.

Feb. 1; born Dec. 14, 1800. Johannis, child of Jeremiah Freer and Sarah Van Wagenen.
Witnesses: Johannis Van Wagenen and Jane Crom.

Born Dec. 27, 1800. Anatje, child of Solomon Eltinge and Rachel Acker.
Witnesses: Derick Wynkoop and Anatje Eltinge.

Born Nov. 21, 1800. Jacob, child of Peter Johnson and Nancy Saxon.

Feb. 15; born Jan. 13. Solomon, child of Philip Lefevre and Else Dubois.
Witness: Solomon Lefevre.

March 1; born Jan. 26. Josiah Dubois, child of Samuel Budel and Mary LeRue.

March 15 ; born Jan. 21.   Daniel, child of Jacob Wilkeloo and Margaret Harris.

Born Jan. 25.   Lydia, child of Elias Bevier and Sarah Lefevre.

April 1 ; born Sept. 27, 1800.   Gamaliel, child of Henry Wakeman and Lydia Hart.

Born Jan. 19.   Jacob Lowe, child of Cornelius Bruyn Dubois and Rebecca Dubois.
Witnesses : Jacob Lowe and Rebecca V. Wagenen.

April 12 ; born Feb. 20.   Elisha Ostrander, child of Benjamin Sluyter and Elizabeth Neise.
Witnesses : Elisha Ostrander and Sarah Simpson.

Born Feb. 19.   Methuselah, child of Philip Eltinge and Catharine Eltinge.
Witnesses : Methuselah Dubois and Catharina Bevier.

April 15 ; born Feb. 27.   Jacob, child of Garrit Dubois and Maria Eltinge.

Born Dec. 22, 1800.   Marinus, child of Timothy Wheeler and Mary Nostrand.

April 28 ; born July 19, 1798, Andrew ; born Aug 24, 1800, David, children of Allen Irwin and Ester Townsend.

May 3 ; born April 1.   Samuel Dubois, child of Ezekiel Freere and Elizabeth Sluyter.
Witnesses : Samuel Dubois and Jane Lefevre.

Born Jan. 7.   Annatje, child of David Dojo and Rachel Ein.
Witnesses : Benjamin I. Hasbrook and Anatje Ein.

Born April 5.   Jannitje, child of Luke Van Wagenen and Cornelia Merkel.

Born April 19.   Jacobus, child of Richard McKinley and Deborah Rose.

May 17 ; born April 18.   Catharine, child of Daniel Louwe and Elizabeth Gerow.

Born Feb. 8.   Caleb Simmens, child of William Hood and Anne Simmons.

June 21 ; born Oct. 1, 1798, Peter ; born Oct. 8, 1800, George Clinton, children of George Dill and Lena Burhanse.

July 5 ; born May 11.   George, child of Jacob Wirtz and Treynte Dubois.
Witnesses : George Wirtz and Hester Hasbroek.

July 19; born June 14. Elizabeth, child of James Scott and Hannah Keyser.

Aug. 2; born June 24. Philip, child of Philip Schoonmaker and Rachel Freer.

Aug. 15; born July 14. Dubois, child of Wm. N. McDonald and Mary Dubois.

Aug. 16; born July 12. Moses, child of Peter Lefevre, Jr., and Magdalen Eltinge.

Born July 14. Gilbert, child of Benjamin U. Terwilliger and Sarah Saxon.

Born July 9. David, child of James Soper and Margaret Dunn.

Sept. 6; born Aug. 4. Jacob, child of Charles and Maria Dubois.

Born Aug. 19. Garret, child of Jonas Freer and Wyntie Hasbrook.
Witnesses: Garret and Maria Freer.

Born June 19. Andries Dewitt, child of Isaac Dubois, Jr., and Deborah Relyea.

Sept. 27; born Aug. 27. Cornelius, child of William Dojo and Sarah Eltinge.

Born Sept. 3. Petrus Een, child of Jonathan Dojo and Catharina Een.
Witnesses: Peter Een and Maria Dojo.

Born Aug. 10. Aldert, child of Edward E. Schoonmaker and Lea Rose.

Sept. 27; born Aug. 29. Elizabeth, child of Moses Lefevre and Margaret Vernoy.
Witnesses: Mathew and Elizabeth Lefevre.

Oct. 11; born Sept. 28. James, child of Isaac Lowe, Jr., and Anne York.

Born Sept. 11. Lefevre, child of Jonas Dubois and Rachel Lefevre.

Oct. 25; born Sept. 21. Josiah Hasbrook, child of Robert LeRue and Dinah Palmatier.

Nov. 8; born Sept.—. Sarah, child of Wilhelmus Hasbrook and Agetta Freer.

Nov. 22; born Oct. 17. Josiah, child of Roelef and Dinah Eltinge.

Born Oct. 27. Simon, child of Simon Rose and Maria Van Wagen, dec'd.

Dec. 6 ; born Oct. 23. Rachel, child of Johannis Hasbrook and Caty McDonald.

Dec. 20 ; born Oct. 8. Delilah, child of Levi P. McDonald and Anne Wood.

Born Oct. 31. Maria, child of Henry Dubois and Elizabeth Dojo.
Witnesses : Jonth. Dojo and Maria Lefevre.

1802, Jan. 1 ; born Nov. 12, 1801. Ariantje, child of Abraham P. Schoonmaker and Catharina Freer.
Witnesses : Petrus P. Schoonmaker and Else Terwilliger.

Feb. 8; born Oct. 4, 1801. Margaret Hasbrook, child of Robert Hood and Martha Wakman.
Witness : Margt. Hasbrook.

Born Dec. 29, 1801. Sarah, child of Jonathan Traphagen and Maria Terwilliger.

March 7 ; born Dec. 23, 1801. Mary, child of Aamasy Mitchell and Mary Bevier.

Born Feb. 6. Maria, child of Johannis I. Lefever and Jane Louw.
Witnesses : Sim Low and Christina McMullen.

Born Jan. 28. Joshaphat, child of Daniel Hasbrook and Margaret Freer.
Witnesses : Joshaphat Hasbrook and Cornelia Dubois.

Born Sept. 19, 1801. John, child of Daniel Wilkeloo and Sally Palmatier.

Born Feb. 13. Anne, child of David and Elizabeth Terwilliger.

Born Dec. 18, 1801. Hannah, child of Stephen Terwilliger and Wyntie Freer.

April 18 ; born March 9. Rebecca, child of Zacharias Freer and Jane Dubois.
Witnesses : Jacob Lowe and Rebecca Van Wagenen.

April 24 ; born Jan. 23. Ester, child of Josiah Hasbrook and Sarah Decker.

Born Nov. 14, 1801. Charles Wessel, child of Charles Broadhead and Ann Schoonmaker.

May 9 ; born March 25. Paulus, child of Zacharias Sluyter and Elizabeth Freer.

Born April 11. Derick Wynkoop, child of Peter Eltinge, Jr., and Cornelia Wynkoop.
Witnesses : Derick Wynkoop and Anatje Eltinge.

Born March 28. Johannis Dewitt, child of Nathaniel Dojo and Lea Dewitt.

Born Feb. 2. George, child of Jacob Dojo and Rachel Hood.

Born Aug. 24. Phebe, child of John Dun and Sarah Lockwood.

Born April 10. Maria, child of Ezekiel Van Wagenen and Rachel Johnson.

Born Feb. 7. Anne, child of Ambrose Elmore and Mary Dojo.
Witnesses : Simon Elmore and Anne Freer.

Born Jan. 1. Johannis, child of Samuel Dubois and Janneke Lefever.
Witnesses : Johannis Lefever and Mary Hardenbergh.

June 13 ; born April 8. Rachel, child of Alexander Coe and Elizabeth Dubois.

Born May 6. Jacob, child of Methuselah Dubois and Maria Low.
Witnesses : Jacob Low and Rebecca Van Wagenen.

Born April 23. Jonathan, child of Benjamin Terwilliger and Maria Freer.

Born April 27. Anne, child of Isaac Bodine and Rachel Dubois.

Born May 14. James, child of Jacobus Rose, Jr., and Sarah Van Wagenen.

Born May 11. Andries, child of Moses Dewitt and Elizabeth Doyo.
Witnesses : Andries Dewitt and Maria Depuy.

June 23 ; born March 17. William, child of William Irwin and Jane Ennis.

Born Feb. 16. Mary, child of Margaret Irwin, wife of Jacobus Achmoedy (infidel).

June 27 ; born April 30. Henderick, child of William Smith and Magdalen Achmoody.

July 11; born June 21. Catharine, child of Johannes Eltinge and Jane Wirtz.

Born June 4. Anatje, child of Thomas Owens and Catharina Van Wagenen. Witnesses: D. Wynkoop and Anatje Eltinge.

Born March 11. Isaac, child of John Wilkeloo and Jemimie Trowbridge.

Born June 7. Charles, child of Abraham Hardenbergh and Margaret Dubois.

Born March 15. William Hill, child of Jacobus Bevier and Mary Yandel.

Sept. 5; born July 21. Grietje, child of Peter York, Jr., and Sarah Freer.

Born Aug. 16. Sarah, child of Elizabeth Nees, wife of Anthony Bullet (absent, beyond sea).

Sept. 19; born Aug. 21. Samuel Hasbrook, child of Mathew Doyo and Sara Hasbrook.

Oct. 10; born Sept. 16. Maretje, child of John I. Freer and Margaret Bennet.

Nov. 15; born Sept. 11. Abraham, child of Ez. Low and Eve Stryker.

Letty, child of Elizabeth Ostrander, wife of (husband's name destroyed).

Nov. 28; born Oct. 23. Geertye, child of Petrus P. Schoonmaker and Else Terwilliger. Witnesses: Josua and Rachel Freer.

Born Oct. 2. Jonas, child of Arche P. Van Wagenen and Mary Freer.

1803, Jan. 1; born Nov. 7, 1802. Jonas Dubois, child of Daniel Hasbrook and Margaret Schoonmaker.

Born Nov. 15, 1802. Catharine, child of Solomon Eltinge, Jr., and Rachel Acker.

Jan. 27; born Dec. 14, 1802. Catharine, child of Jacob I. Hasbrouck and Anne Dubois.

Feb. 27; born Dec. 24, 1802. Jonathan, child of Peleg Stephens and Hannah Moore.

Born Jan. 16. Simion, child of Daniel Low and Elizabeth Jerow. Witness: Simion Low.

Born Jan. 10. Fanny, child of Isaac Low, Jr., and Anna Yorke.

March 20. Henry (baptized), a black man, aged twenty-six years.

Born Feb. 4. Methuselah, child of Cornelius Bruyne Dubois and Rebecca Dubois.
Witnesses : Methuselah Dubois and Catharine Bevier.

Born Feb. 6. Abraham, Isaac, children of Henry Goetschius and Margaret Master (or Masten).

Born Feb. 9. Jonathan Terwilger, child of Isaac Freer and Sarah Terwilliger.
Witnesses : Jonathan Terwilliger and wife.

April 3 ; born Sept. 7, 1802. Lena, child of Abraham Wussimiller and Hester Rilyea.

Born Feb. 5. Jonas, child of Philip Schoonmaker and Rachel Freer.
Witnesses : Jonas Freer and Magdalena Bevier.

Born Dec. 20, 1802 ? Margaret, child of Jonathan Dubois and Rachel Goetschius.

Born Feb. 26. Johannis Smith, child of Peter Achmudy and Eve Smith.

Born Aug. 28, 1802. Catharine, child of John Holstead and Sarah Meyer.

Born Jan. 30. Maria, child of David Doyo and Rachel Een.
Witnesses : Petrus Een and Maria Freer.

Born Jan. 21. Maria, child of Edward Ed. Schoonmaker and Lea Rose.

Born Nov. 24, 1802. Ester, child of Peter R. Johnson and Jane Deyo.

April 10. Isaac De Moorman, a black man, aged sixty-three years.

Samuel Samaria, a black man, aged fifty-four years.

Born March 27. Jacob, child of Ezekiel and Magdalen Eltinge.

April 24 ; born Dec. 17, 1802. Elizabeth, child of Jacob Wilkeloo and Margitje Harris.

Born March 20. Ibbe, child of Ambrose Seaman and Anne Constable.

Born March 22. Peter, child of Mathew I. Blanshan and Mary Dubois.

Born March 18. Hetty, child of William Hood and Anne Simmons.

May 17 ; born April 18. Johannes Moul, child of Levi Van Wagenen and Elizabeth Louw.

Born March 22. Lydia, child of Jacob Le Fevre and Lydia Doyo.

June 5 ; born May 11. Henry, child of Christoffel Green and Catharina Ecker.

June 12 ; born May 4. Benjamin Haesbroeck, child of Isaac and Maria Bevier.

Born May 8. Sarah, child of William N. and Polly McDonald.

Born May 15. James, child of William and Sally Jenkins.

Sept. 3 ; born July 26. Magdalena, child of Josia R. Elting and Sarah Lefever.

Born July 13. Hiram, child of Samuel Bud and Mary Larow.

Born July 27. Jeremia, child of Benjamin H.? Terwilliger and Sarah Saxton.

Born Jan. 16. Sarah, child of Peter Johnston, Jr., and Nancy Saxton.

Sept. 8 ; born July 18. Yannetie, child of Roelef and Dina Elting.

Born July 5. Maria, child of Wilhelmus Haasbrouck and Agetta Freer.

Oct. 9 ; born Aug. 13. Jacob, child of Simon Rose and Ruth Williger.
Witnesses : The parents.

Born Aug. 26. Elisabeth, child of Abraham Harris and Mary Waldron.

Dec. 4 ; born Sept. 22. Simeon, child of Methusalem Dubois, Jr., and Maria Low.

Born Sept. 9. Abram, child of William Deyoe and Sarah Eltinge.

Born Oct. 5. Cornelia, child of Moses Lefever and Margret Vernoy.
Witnesses : Cornelius and Elizabeth Vernoy.

Born Sept. 19. Elizabeth, child of Jonathan Deyoe, Jr., and Cathrina Een.
Witnesses : Elias and Elizabeth Een.

Born June 3. John, child of Timothy Brannen and Mary York.

Born Nov. 17. Nancy, child of Richard McKinley and Debora Rose.

Born Aug. 31. Moses, child of Ambrose Elmore and Mary Deyoe.

Born Nov. 8. Henricus, child of Joshua Freer and Rachel Schoonmaker.

Born Nov. 16. Maria, child of Lucas Van Wagenen and Cornelia Merkel.

Born Aug. 25. Merrit, child of Josia Deyoe and Annatye Merrit.

Born Oct. 19. Greitye, child of Jonathan Trophagen and Maria Terwilleger.

Born Oct. 8. Isaac, child of Jonathan and Maria Terwilleger.

Dec. 22 ; born Nov. 15. Hester, child of Zacharias Sluiter and Elisabeth Frere.

Sept. 28 ; born Sept. 30. Josaphat, child of Jonas Frere, Jr., and Wyntje Hasbrouck.
Witnesses : Josaphat Hasbrouck and Cornelia Dubois.

1804, Jan. 29 ; born Dec. 28, 1803. Gertruy, child of Jacob Wirtz and Tryntje Dubois.

Born Nov. 24, 1803. John Hasbrouck, child of Abram P. Schonmaker and Catrina Frere.

Born Dec. 20, 1803. Jesse, child of Philip and Catryntje Eltinge.

Jan. 28 ; born Nov. 22, 1803. Elias, child of Elias Ein and Elisabeth Hasbrouck.

Born Nov. 19, 1803. Magdalena, child of Philip Lefever and Elsje Dubois.

April 15 ; born Jan. 12. David, child of David Ralyea and Laura Oostrander.

Born March 19. Benjamin Freer, child of Benjamin Terwilleger, Jr., and Maria Freer.

Born Feb. 23. Sarah, child of Isaiah Terwilleger and Freelove Saxon.

Born Feb. 2. Elizabeth, child of David Terwilleger, Jr., and Maria Vandemerke.

Born Jan. 25. William Irwin, child of Jacobus Achmude and Margret Irwin.

May 6 ; born March 17. Henry, child of Thomas Owens and Catharina Van Wagenen.

Born Feb. 17. Maria, child of Jonas Dubois and Rachel Lefever.

June 24 ; born Nov. 25, 1803. Jacob, child of Jacob Hardenberg (deceased) and Jean Dubois.

Born March 28. Johan Vernoy, child of Elias Bevier and Sarah Lefever.

Born March 18. Daniel, child of Robert Hood and Martha Weckman.

Born April 16. Blandina, child of Johannis Elting and Yannetje Wirts.

Born May 14. Jonas, child of Elias Freer and Cathrina Teerpenning.

Born Feb. 15. Benjamin Winfield, child of Jacobus Bevier and Mary Yandel.

Sept. 23 ; born July 25. Annatye Dubois, child of Abraham and Rachel Hood.

Born May 20. Josiah, child of Elias and Dolly York.

Born Sept. 6. Methuselah, child of Jacob D. and Hester Freer.

Born Aug. 8. Sarah, child of Jacobus, Jr., and Sarah Rose.

Dec. 17 ; born Oct. 2. Noah, child of Peter Elting and Cornelia Wynkop.

Born Nov. 26. Thomas, child of Zacharias Frere and Jannetje Dubois.
Witness : Thomas Frere.

Born June 21. Rebecca, child of Stephen Terwilger and Wyntje Frere.

Born Aug. 17. Roloff, child of Gerret Dubois and Maria Eltinge.

Born Oct. 28. Bregje, child of John Aghmody and Lea Windfield.

Born Oct. 23. David, child of Salomon Eltinge, Jr., and Raghel Eccert.

Born Sept. 23. Ira, child of Isack Bodoin and Rachel Dubois.

Born Aug. 10. Anny, child of Allen Irwin and Ester Townsend.

No dates of baptism to the above two entries, both entered on margin of page in original.

Born Nov. 15, 1803. George Washington and Ambrose Elmore, children of Christoffel Van Bommel and Sara Terwilger.

Dec. 17 ; born Sept. 27. Eliza Bridget, child of Isaac Lefever and Catherine Burhans.

1805, Feb. 5 ; born Jan. 22. Jenny, child of Isack Bovier and Maria York.

Born Dec. 17, 1804. Johannes, child of Isack Low and Anne York.

Born Oct. 14, 1804. Martin Ryerson, child of Myer Hardenberg and Elsje Hasbrouck.

Born July 1, 1803. Catarine, child of John Johnson, Jr., and Jenny Concking.
Witness : Hanah Johnson.

Born Oct. 15, 1804. Sartje, child of Benjamin A. Doio and Sara Frere.
Witnesses : Abram Doio and Bregje Frere.

Born Dec. 24, 1804. Henry, child of Peter Achmody and Eva Smith.

Born Jan. 6. Peter, child of Job Telson and Ester Frere.
Witnesses : Peter Een and Maria Frere.

Born Dec. 14, 1804. Jacob, child of Wilhelmus Hasbrouck and Agetta Frere.

Feb. 17 ; born Jan. 19. Anny Dunn, child of Samuel Terwilger and Susanna Dunn.

May 14 ; born Feb. 23. Philip, child of Ezechiel Van Wagene and Rachel Johnson.

Born Feb. 18. Sarah, child of Ezechiel Low and Eva Stryker.

Born April 11. Jemes, child of Jonas Dubois and Rachel Lefever.

Born Feb. 13. Catrina, child of Cornelius B. and Rebecca Dubois.

Born April 11. Simon, child of Timothy Brannen and Maria York.

Born Feb. 11. Jacob, child of Jacob J. Hasbrouck and Ann Dubois.

Born Dec. 29, 1804. Wilhelmus, child of Philip Schonmaker and Rachel Frere.

Born March 3. Rachel, child of Peter Shoonmaker and Elsje Terwilger.

Born March 9. Elisabeth, child of Simon Roos and Ruth Terwilger.

Born March 12. Elisabeth, child of Peter Lefever, Jr., and Magdalena Eltinge.

July 14; born April 12. Margarat, child of Benjamin Terwilgar and Sally Saxon.

Born June 18. Henry, child of Methusalem Dubois, Jr., and Mary Low.

Born May 19. Jacob Hasbrook, child of Benjamin Schoonmaker and Sally Van Bumbler.

Born June 10. Gitty, child of Simon M. La Fever and Elizabeth Deyo.

Born May 5. Elizabeth, child of Hugo B. and Elizabeth Fraer.
Witness : Elizabeth Fraer.

Born Sept. 6, 1803. Rachel, child of Simon Fraer, Jr., and Pheba Ketcham.

Born Sept. 14, 1804. Zachariah, child of Elijah Weldin and Jane Fraer.

Born Feb. 23. Cornelia, child of Daniel Hasbrouck and Gerritie Fraer.

Born May 8. Jefferson, child of Benjamin Terwilligar, Jr., and Mary Fraer.

Born April 21. Gilbert Sexton, child of Isaiah Terwilligar and Frelove Sexton.

Born June 11. Mary, child of Elias York and Dolly Geers.

Born Feb. 7. David, child of Jacob Goetchius and Arntie Schoonmaker.

Aug. 11; born July 18. Charles Brodhead, child of Roelif and Dinah Eltinge.

Born April 1. Catriena, child of Johannis and Jacomyntye Wilkelow.

Born May 3. Johathan, child of Nathaniel and Leah Deyo.

Sept. 8 : born Aug. 2. Simon Le Fever, child of Abraham and Anne Dubois.

Dec. 15 ; born Oct. 12. Geertruy, child of Joshua R. Elting and Sarah Lefever.

Born Sept. 9. Mary Magdeline, child of Levi Van Wagenen and Elizabeth Low.

Born Oct. 5. Alexander, child of Archa (?) P. Vanwagenen Maria Freer.

Born Sept. 29. Jenny Ralyee, child of Marinus Teerpenning and Debra Ralyee.
Witnesses : William Ralye, Jr., and wife, Jenny Deyo.

Born Nov. 21. Elizabeth, child of Ezechiel Freer and Elizabeth Sluyter.
Witnesses : David Etkins and Grietye Sluyter.

Born Nov. 29. Sarah Van Wagenen, child of Richard McKinly and Debra Roos.

Born Aug. 4. Charles Broadhead, child of Evert I. Terwilliger and Maria Freer.
Witness : Charles Broadhead.

1806, Jan. 26 ; born Dec. 9, 1805. Jemimy Rosekrans, child of Robert Moule and Aplony Oosterhoudt.

Born Dec. 22, 1805. Josiah Hasbrouck, child of Abraham P. Schoonmaker and Catherine Freer.
Witness : Josieh Hasbrouck, Jr.

Born Dec. 14, 1805. Johannis, child of Zecheriah York and Mary Geer.

Jan. 20 (*sic*); born Jan. 18. Daniel Hasbrouck, child of Jonas Freer and Wyntje Hasbrouck.
Witnesses : Daniel Hasbrouck and Margret Schonmaker.

Jan. 26 ; born Jan. 6. Sarah, child of Abram Wood and Rachel Velie.

April 20 ; born Feb. 22. Bregje, child of William Doio and Sara Eltinge.
Witnesses : Abram Doio and Bregje Frere.

Born Feb. 6. Johannes Waldron, child of Abram Herres and Mary Waldron.
Witness : Johannes Waldron.

Born Jan. 25. Charles Dubois, child of Pelegh Stephens and Anna Moor.

Born March 20. Stephen, child of Josia Doio and Hannah Meret.

Born Nov. 27, 1805. Hester, child of Jonathan and Maria Terwilger.

Born Feb. 11. Elsje, child of David and Elisabeth Terwilger.

Born Aug. 17, 1805. James, child of John Dunn and Sarah Lockwood.

July 20 ; born May 27. Jeremiah, child of Zacharias Sluyter and Elizabeth Freer.

Born June 21. Maria, child of Charles Broadhead and Antye Schoonmaker.

Born May 18. Peter Edward, child of Isaac Lefever and Cathrina Burhanse.

Born June 10. Mehaley, child of John Van Garden and Neelye Van Vliet.

Born May 19. Rachel, child of William Hood and Anna Simmons.

Born July 13. Samuel, child of Elias Bevier and Sarah L. Fever.

Oct. 14 ; born Aug. 18. Jane, child of Ezekiel and Magdalene Eltinge.

Born Aug. 28. Maria, child of Matthew Deyo and Sarah Hasbrouck.

Born Aug. 27. Sally, child of Methuselem Hasbrouck and Maria Deyo.

Dec. 16 ; born Oct. 19. Anna Maria, child of John Elting and Jane Wertz.

Born Oct. 6. Margarat and Benjamin, twins of Hugo B. and Elizabeth Frear.

Born Nov. 16. Rachel, child of Jonathan Deyo, Jr., and Catharine Een.
Witness: Rachel Deyo.

Born Sept. 16. Marian, child of Stephen Trewilligar and Winche Freer.

Born Sept. 10. Marian, child of Samuel Trewilligar and Sukey Dun.

1807, Feb. 22; born Jan. 7. Marian, child of Simon Roos and Ruth Terwilger.

Born Sept. 17, 1806. Getty Lefever, child of Samuel Bodd and Polly Lerue.

Born Jan. 18, 1806. Rachel Maria, child of Hendrick Wockman and Lidea Hart.

Born Dec. 15, 1806. Maria, child of Jerimie Raljie and Debora Lefever.

Born Nov. 4, 1806. Jannetje, child of Peter Elting and Cornelia Wynkop.

Born Nov. 12, 1806. Ann Maria, child of Andries Bovier and Mary Doio.

Feb. 22; born Dec. 12, 1806. Isack, child of Isack Bodoin and Rachel Dobois.

Born Sept. 29, 1806. Henry, child of Isack Dubois and Catarina Terwilger.

Born Nov. 10, 1806. Elisabeth, child of Amasa Michel and Maria Bovier.

Born Nov. 6, 1806. Sarah, child of Josia Dubois and Elisabeth Hasbrouck.

Born Oct. 25, 1806. Sally, child of Thomas Owens and Caty Vanwagene.

Born Oct. 25, 1806. Sara Ann, child of Jacob I. and Arriantje Schonmaker.

Born Oct. 2, 1806. Elias, child of Elias York and Dolly Geers.

Born Oct. 20, 1806. Moses, child of Elias Frere and Catrina Terpenning.

Born Nov. 7, 1806. Methusalem, child of Jacob Wertz and Tryntje Dubois.

June 7; born Feb. 11. Catherine, child of Charles and Maria Dubois.

Born March 12. Maritye, child of Zecheriah and Jannetye Freer.

Born Jan. 27. Catharine Dubois, child of Teunis and Maria Terwilliger.

Born Sept. 14. Garret Dubois, child of Marcus, Jr., and Laura Wackman.

Born Jan. 17. Jane, child of Isaac and Anna Louw.

Born April 28. Jane, child of Benjamin and Sarah Terwilliger.

Born Jan. 24. Rachel, child of Adam and Maria Yaple.

Born Feb. 22. Mary, child of Abraham, Jr., and Sarah Achmoedie.

Born Nov. 20, 1806. Matthew, child of Moses and Margaret Lefever.
Witnesses: Matthew and Elizabeth Lefever.

Born May 6. Jane, child of Daniel and Elizabeth Louw.
Witness: Simon Louw.

Born April 1. Arietta Mary, child of Jacobus and Brachy Elmendorf.

June 28; born March 26. Samuel Dewett, child of Cristopher Green and Catrina Eckert.

Born March 8. Rebecah, child of Salomon Elting, Jr., and Rachel Eckert.

Born Feb. 6. Elizabeth, child of Simon N. (or M.) Lefever and Elizabeth Deyoe.
Witnesses: Mathew and Elizabeth Lefever.

Born March 26. Jane, child of William Erwin and Jane Innes.

Born Nov. 7. John Lefever, child of Peter Johnson, Jr., and Nancy Saxon.

Born May 24. James, child of Archable Chittick and Rachel Miller.

Sept. 20; born July 25. Magdalen, child of Peter and Magdalene Lefevre.

Born Aug. 5. Hester, child of Roelif and Dinah Elting.

Born July 3. Mary, child of Isaac and Mary Bevier.

Born July 21. C—i, child of Jacob J. and Ann Haesbrouck.

Born May 29. David, child of Philip and Rachel Schoonmaker.

Born July 30. Catrina, child of Peter and Mary Ean. Witness : Catrina Ean.

Born May 16. Abraham, child of Simon and Catriena Vannoy.

Born Aug. 2. Jonathan Vanwagenen, child of Jacobus and Saertye Rose.
Witnesses : Jonathan and Hester Vanwagenen.

Born March 30. Maria, child of Benjamin, Jr., and Maria Terwilliger.

Born May 9. James Morris, child of James and Johanna Dumond.

No dates of baptism ; born June 15. Conelius Dubois and Gitty Jane, children of Timothy and Maria Branan.

Born Oct. 19. Sally, child of Ezekiel and Esther Freer.
Witnesses : Daniel and Sally Van Wagener.

Born Oct. 27. Wessel, child of Jonas Debois and Rachel Lefever.

No date of baptism ; born Nov. 4, 1807. Rebecca, child of Garrit Debois and Maria Eltinge.

1808, March 27 ; born Feb. 10. Bridget Ann, child of John Whitaker and Elizabeth M. Danold.

Born Jan. 24. Cornelius Delemater, child of Ezekiel Deyoo and Deborah Low.

Born Feb. 25. Alida, child of Christian and Annaatie Freer.

Born March 24. John Van Wagenen, child of Richard McKinnelly and Deborah Rose.

May 8 ; born May 22, 1807. Rebecca, child of Cornelius Freer and Rachel Weller.

Born March 20. Caty Ann, child of Lewis B. Dubois and Phabe Coe.

Born Jan. 27. Caty Maria, child of Lewis W. Dubois and Bridget Jenkins.

Born Dec. 30, 1807. Agnes, child of Coenraed Fryziner and Lea Soper.

Born Nov. 20, 1807. Catherine, child of Abraham P. Schoonmaker and Catrina Freer.

Born April 3. John, child of James Ridney or Kidney and Lanah Bunton.

Born Feb. 26. Johannes, child of Peter P. Schoonmaker and Elschie Terwilliger.

Born Feb. 26. Henry * Doremus, child of Peter Roos and Rachel Traphagen.

Born March 7. Peter Benjamin, child of James Perrine and Catrina Freer.

Born Dec. 23, 1807. Zachariah, child of Zachariah York and Mary Years.

May 22 ; born April 22. Broadhead, child of Jonathan Dubois and Rachel Goetchius.

Born Feb. 27. Simeon, child of Daniel Hasbrook and Margaret Freer.

Born Feb. 2. James, child of Peleg Stevans and Hannah Moor.

Born May 22. James, child of Allen Irwin and Esther Townsend.

Born March 15. Maria, child of Jacobus Bovier and Mary Yendell.

Born April 16. Rebeccah, child of Cornelis Bruyn Dubois and Rebeccah Dubois.
Witnesses : Jacob ——— and Rebeccah Vanwag———

Born Feb. 24. Catharine, child of Ambrose Elmore and Mary Deyoo.

Born Dec. 24, 1807. Elner, (or Anna ?) child of Jacob Carman and Mary Hess.

Born Feb. 10. James, child of Robert Hood and Martha Wackman.

Born June 26, 1807 (?). Ann Eliza, child of John Van Garde and Agnes Van Vliet.

June 12 ; born May 21. Philip, child of Josua Freer and Rachel Schoonmaker.

* The name John in the original had been crossed out and Henry inserted in a different handwriting.

Born Jan. 25. Catherine and Elizabeth, children of Henry V. W. Terwilliger and Rachel Frederick.

Born Jan. 6. Catherine Sattles, child of Amasa Mitchel and Maria Bovier.

Born April 12. Smith, child of William Hood and Anny Simmons.

Born Nov. 16, 1807. Nelly, child of Benjamin Schoonmaker and Maria Van Bombele.

Born —— 19, 1807. Jane Hardenbergh, child of Marcus Wyckman, Jr., and Laura Van Ostrant.

Born May 18. Elizabeth Bodine, child of Walter Dubois and Hannah Bodine.

July 17 ; born June 2. Jonathan Deyoo, child of William Dubois and Catrina Deyoo.
Witnesses : Jonathan Deyoo and Maria Lefever.

Aug. 19 ; born March 12. Moses, child of Wilhelmus Hasbrook and Agetta Freer.

July 31 ; born Aug. 15, 1807. Hannah, child of John Johnson and Jane Concklin.

Aug. 14 ; born May 18. Levi, child of Levi Van Wagener and Elizabeth Louw.

Aug. 28 ; born Aug. 3. Elizabeth, child of Charles Broadhead and Antie Schoonmaker.

Born Aug. 7. Benjamin, child of Jonas Freer, Jr., and Wyntie Hasbrook.

Born July 22. Lewis, child of Jacob and Ariantie Schoonmaker.

Born July 18. Maria Ann, child of Methuselah Hasbrook and Maria Deyoo.

Sept. 11 ; born Aug. 3. Daniel Johnson, child of Dr. Mauritius Werts and Maria Johnson.

Oct. 10 ; born Aug. 30. Elizabeth, child of Elias Ean and Elizabeth Hasbrook.

Oct. 30 ; born Sept. 25. Cornelius Dubois, child of Andrew I. Lefever and Hannah Dubois.

Nov. 11 ; born Oct. 2. Hannah, child of Gordon Kraig and Margaret Lemunger (or Lemanyen ?).

Dec. 25; born Oct. 19. Albertus Schryver, child of Abraham Halstead and Magdalena Schryver.

1809, Jan. 8; born Oct. 3, 1808. Jane Hardenbergh, child of Jonathan Deyoo and Maria Hardenbergh.

Born Nov. 19, 1808. John, child of Abraham Lefever and Ann Bell.

Born Nov. 19, 1808. John, child of Abraham Steen? and Elizabeth Freer.

Born Dec. 9, 1808. Ann Maria, child of David Aghmody, Jr., and Maria Van Keuren.

Born Oct. 28, 1808. Harvey, child of Daniel Galey and Elizabeth Brown.

Born June 23, 1808. Jane, child of Philip Schoonmaker and Rachel Freer.

Jan. 29; born Nov. 22, 1808. Cornelius, child of Moses Lefever and Margaret Vanoy.
Witnesses: Cornelius and Elizabeth Vanoy.

Born Nov. 14, 1808. Mathew, child of Simon Lefever and Elizabeth Deyoo.
Witnesses: Mat. and Elizabeth Lefever.

Born Nov. 6, 1808. Levi, child of Zachariah Sluyter and Elizabeth Freer.

Feb. 9; born Sept. 26, 1808. Marinus Vanaker, child of Frederick F. Van Ostrand and Maria Tearpenning.

Feb. 12; born July 14, 1808. Solomon, child of James Waring and Jane Van Hoovenberg.

Feb. 26; born Jan. 24. Sally Jane, child of Hendricus Goetchius and Margaret Mastin.

Born Jan. 19. David, child of Isaac Louw and Anny York.

Born Jan. 22. Caty Maria, child of Ezekiel Sparks and Deborah York.

Born Jan. 21. Methusalem, child of Jacob Goetchius and Ariantie Schoonmaker.

Born Sept. 10, 1808. Caty Maria, child of William Jenkins and Sally Goetchius.

March 1; born Jan. 17. Roilif, child of Josiah R. Eltinge and Sarah Lefever.

March 12; born Feb. 8. Catherine Maria, child of Abraham Dubois and Anny Lefever.

Born Jan. 10. Elizabeth, child of Samuel Danelson and Elenor Hood.

Born Jan. 19. Catherina, child of Charles Wells and Anny Hood.

Born Feb. 11. Hugo Freer, child of Benjamin Sluyter and Elizabeth Neice.

Born Dec. 31, 1808. Catherine Maria, child of Jacob J. (?) Hermance and Anny Deyoo.

March 19; born Feb 19. Abraham, child of Elias Freer and Caty Tearpenning.

April 2; born March 12. Caty, child of Isaac Bovier and Mary York.

April 30; born April 2. Sarah, child of Peter Eltinge and Cornelia Wynkoop.

Born March 21. Richard Broadhead, child of Benjamin Terwilliger and Maria Freer.

Born Feb. 19. Jonathan, child of William Traphagen and Rachel Freer.

May 14; born March 2. Susannah, child of Smith Halstead and Mary Schryver.

Born April 11. Christian, child of Jonathan Deyoo, Jr., and Catrina Ean.

Born April 8. Gitty Jane, child of Dr. Jacob Wirtz and Tryntye Dubois.

Born April 16. Isaac, child of Benjamin H. (?) Terwilliger and Sarah Saxon.

Born April 20. Jeremiah, child of Robert Dunn and Lucy Freer.

Born April 24. Ezzekiel Eltinge, child of William Duvall and Sarah Freer.

Born April 24. Chadock, child of Simon Johnson and Maria Traphagen.

Born Feb. 24. Cornelia, child of Solomon Eltinge, Jr., and Rachel Ekker.

Born April 20. (No name), child of Benjamin Decker and Anny Terwilliger.

Born April 18. Cornelia, child of Henry Schoonmaker and Jane Hornbeek.

June 4; born Feb. 18. Abraham Bovier, child of Josua Hasbrook and Ann Viele.
Witnesses: Maria Bovier, widow of Isaack Hasbrook.

Born April 13. Sarah, child of David Ostrander and Margaret Masten.

June 18; born May 20. Anna Maria, child of Daniel Low and Betsy Geroe.
Witness: Simeon Low.

July 2; born June 4. Jacob, child of Christian and Annatye Freer.

Born May 17. Jane, child of Coenrad Vrysyn and Lea Soper.

July 30; born June 12. Catrina, child of William Deyoo and Sarah Eltinge.

Born June 12. Jonathan, child of Hugo and Elizabeth Freer.

Born June 3. David, child of Abraham Hardenbergh and Margaret Dubois.

Born June 12. Catherine Maria, child of Daniel I. Hasbrouck and Margaret Freer.
Witnesses: Jonas Freer, Jr., and Catrine Freer, wife of Jonathan Lefever.

Sept. 10. Alexander, child of Ezekiel and Magdalina Eltinge.

Born Aug. 8. Daniel, child of Roelif and Dinah Eltinge.

Born Aug. 8. Ruth, child of Isaac Halstead and Sarah Wilkelo.

Sept. 24; born Aug. 1. Jane, child of Cornelius Ostrander and Elenor Emerett.

Born July 31. Ezekiel, child of Ezekiel Freer, Jr., and Esther Van Wagenen.
Witnesses: Ezekiel Freer and Elizabeth Slouter.

Born Aug. 13. Phebe, child of Jacob D. and Esther Freer.

Oct. 7; born Sept. 7. John, child of Isaac Bodine and Rachel Dubois.

Born Aug. 21. Elizabeth Maria, child of Christopher Green and Catherine Ekkert.

Oct. 28 ; born Sept. 20. Jacob, child of Jacob Halstead and Charity Van Aker.

Born Sept. 18. George, child of John Eltinge and Jane Wertz.

Nov. 12 ; born Sept. 30. Maria, child of Zachariah Freer and Jane Dubois.

Born Sept. 21. Garrit, child of Methusalem Dubois, Jr., and Maria Louw.

Born Oct. 12. Alexander, child of Solomon P. Hasbrouck and Magdalena Lefever.

Born Oct. 4. Catherine Maria, child of James Lefever and Elizabeth Johnson.

1810, Jan. 7 ; born Nov. 12. 1809. Margaret, child of Jacob J. Hasbrouck and Ann Dubois.

Feb. 5 ; born Dec. 3, 1809. Abraham, child of Benjamin A. Deyoo and Sarah Freer.
Witnesses : Abraham Deyoo and Brachy Freer.

Feb. 11; born Jan. 6. Zachariah, child of Charles and Mary Dubois.

Born Dec. 27, 1809. William McDonald, child of John Whitaker and Betsy McDonald.

Born Jan. 4. Peter, child of John P. Lefever and Mary Hardenbergh.

Born Jan. 9. Hetty Jane, child of John I. Freer and Margaret Bennet.

Born July 14, 1809. Henry Bodine, child of Water Dubois and Hannah Bodine.

Feb. 25 ; born Jan. 5. Elizabeth, child of Peter Ean and Mary Freer.

Born Nov. 18, 1809. Fanny, child of Abraham Aughmoedy, Jr., and Sarah Louw.

Born Nov. 2, 1809. Caty Maria, child of Isaac T. Dubois and Catharina Terwilliger.

March 11 ; born Jan. 25. Annatie, child of James Kidney and Lanah Banton.

Born Nov. 9, 1809. Magdalena, child of Abraham P. Schoonmaker and Trina Freer.

Born Jan. 14. Richard Brinckerhoff, child of William and Rachel Hasbrouk.

Born Dec. 31, 1809. Rachel, child of Lewis W. Dubois and Bridget Jenkins.

Born Sept. 19, 1809. Eliza Catherine, child of Tim Branin and Maria York.

March 25 ; born Nov. 2, 1809. George Washington, child of Simeon Shurager and Anny Acker.

Born Jan. 27. Esther, child of Isaiah and Jemimah Freer.

May 13 ; born April 3. Caty Maria, child of Lewis Hardenbergh and Caty Daily.

Born March 20. Philip, child of Adam Yaple and Maria Davenp.

Born April 16. Daniel, child of Jonathan D. D. Deyoo and Maria Hardenbergh.

Witnesses : Daniel Deyoo and Catherine Dewitt.

Born April 8. Caty Jane, child of Frederick and Sally Stokes.

May 27 ; born Dec. 18, 1809. Jane, child of Peleg Stevans and Hannah Moore (unbaptized).

Born March 19. Catherine Eliza, child of Jonas Dubois and Rachel Lefever.

Born Jan. 19. Peter, child of Zechariah York and Mary Geers (unbaptized).

Born Feb. 22. Lea, child of Henry V. W. Terwilliger and Rachel Frederick.

Born May 16. Bridget Maria, child of Jacobus Bovier and Maria Yendell.

June 10 ; born May 7. Peter Ditmasse Fraligh, child of Jacobus Roose, Jr., and Sarah Van Wagener.

Born April 7. Andrew, child of William Louw and Anny Bern (unbaptized).

June 24 ; born March 5. Henry, child of John Polhemus and Margaret Keyser.

Born March 5. Laura Wadsworth, child of Samuel Budd and Polly Laroe.

Born April 24. Jacob, child of Simon Roose and Elizabeth Hasbrouck.

July 8 ; born April 8. Cornelius, child of William Hood and Anny Simmons.

Born May 5. Mary Strattin, child of James Terwilliger and Bridget York.

Born May 17. Methusalem, child of William Dubois and Catherine Deyoo.

Jan. 8, 1809 ; born Sept. 26, 1808. Rachel, child of Archibald Chittuck and Rachel Miller.

July 8, 1810 ; born May 5, 1810. Sarah, child of Archibald Chittuck and Rachel Miller.

Anny Simmons, who is the wife of William Hood.

July 29 ; born July 4. Susan Banks, child of Peter D. Freeligh, V. D. M. and Nelly Bogart.

Born Feb. 5. Henry, child of Marcus Wackman, Jr., and Laura Van Ostrant.

August 12 ; born July 1. Ebby, child of Ambrose Simmons and Anny Constable.

Born June 20. Abraham, child of Cornelius B. and Rebecca Dubois.

Born June 18. Solomon, child of Garrit Dubois and Mary Eltinge.

Born June 20. Paulus, child of Abraham Steen and Elizabeth Freer.

August 26 ; born July 28. Catherine Dubois, child of Simion Roose and Ruth Terwilliger.

Born July 7. Josiah, child of James N. and Sarah Lefever.

Sept. 9 ; born July 27. Isaac Dubois, child of James Perine and Caty Freer.

Born August 3. Rachel Ann, child of Abraham Lefever and Ann Bell.

Sept. 21 ; born August 21. Sally Amanda, child of Ambrose Elmore and Mary Deyoo.

Born July 23. Joseph, child of Charles Wells and Anny Hood.

Sept. 23 ; born August 19. Daniel Coe, child of Louis B. Dubois and Phabe Coe.

Born August 8. David, child of James McCollogh and Catherine Louw.

Born August 14. Esther, child of Allan Irwin and Esther Townsand.

Oct. 14; born Aug. 30. Esther, child of Dr. Mauritius Wirtz and Maria Johnson.

Nov. 4; born Aug. 28. Elihu, child of Jacob I. and Ariantje Schoonmaker.

Born Oct. 2. Jonathan Van Wagenen, child of Jonathan Clayton and Rebeccah Johnson.

Nov. 18; born Oct. 2. Johannes, child of Andries Lefever and Hannah Dubois.

Nov. 22; born Sept. 21. Hulda Jane, child of Peter Rose and Rachel Traphagen.

Dec. 4; born Aug. 27. Thomas, child of Philip Bunten and Lanah Kidney (unbaptized).

Born Oct. 27. Susanah Jane, child of David Deyoo and Catherine Freer.

Dec. 23; born Nov. 11. Catherine, child of Ezekiel Deyoo and Deborah Louw.

1811, Jan. 6; born Dec. 2, 1810. Jeremiah, child of Christian and Annatie Freer.

Born Oct. 28, 1810. Jane, child of Ezekiel Sparks and Deborah York.

Jan. 20; born Oct. 25, 1810. Luther Hasbrouck, child of Paulus Countryman and Margaret Wood.

Born Nov. 12, 1810. James Jenkins, child of David Terwilliger, Jr., and Mary Van Demerk.

Born Nov. 12, 1810. Wessel, child of Abraham Traphagen and Catherine Dubois.

Feb. 10; born Jan. 19. Gidion Van Aken, child of Jacob Halstead and Charity Van Aken.

Born Dec. 25, 1810. Catherine, child of Methusalem Hasbrouck and Maria Deyoo.

Born Dec. 4, 1810. Philip Deyoo, child of Simon M. Lefever and Elizabeth Deyoo.

Born Dec. 27, 1810. Rachel, child of Smith Halstead and Mary Schryver.

Feb. 24; born Jan. 6. Levi, child of Elias York and Dolly Greer (unbaptized).

Born Dec. 14, 1810. Lydia Jane, child of Peter P. Schoonmaker and Elschie Terwilliger.

March 10 ; born Dec. 29, 1810. Sarah, child of Solomon Eltinge and Rachel Acker.

Born Jan. 23. Abraham and Isaac, children of Isaac Louw and Anny York.

Born Dec. 7, 1807. Roelif, child of John Wilkelow and Jemimy Trowbridge.

March 24 ; born Feb. 23. Rachel Ann, child of Isaac Bovier and Maria York.

March 31 ; born Feb. 26. Maria Jane, child of Henry Schoonmaker and Jane Hornbeek.

March 22 ; born Feb. 24. David, child of Isaac Halstead and Caroline Linkester.

April 14 ; born March 10. John Saxen, child of Benjamin U. ? Terwilliger and Sally Saxon.

April 19 ; born March 12. Cornelia, child of Charles C. Broadhead and Antje Schoonmaker.

May 11 ; born April 19. Isaac, child of Jonathan Deyoo, Jr., and Catrina Ean.

May 27 ; born April 2. Johannes Johnson, child of Peter Eltinge and Cornelia Wynkoop.
Witnesses : Johannes Johnson and Catherin Eltinge.

Born March 12. George, child of Benjn. Terwilliger, Jr., and Maria Freer.

Born April 23. Jacob Hasbrouck, child of Amasa Mitchel and Maria Bovier.

Born April 14. Anny Hasbrouck, child of Ez. Bovier and Nelly Van Bommelle.

Born April 24. Addison, child of Jacob P. Hermance and Anny Deyoo.

June 9 ; born May 2. Abraham Dubois child of Josiah R. Eltinge and Sarah Lefever.

Born May 11. Thomas, child of Robert Dunn and Lucy Freer.

June 30 ; born June 2. David Deyoo, child of Abraham Harris and Mary Waldron.
Witness : Rachel Ean, wife of Abraham Relyea.

Born May 7. Jane, child of John H. Barnard and Mary Sluyter.

Born May 28. Dewitt, child of Benjamin Deyoo and Sarah Dewitt.

Born June 5. Art Freer, child of William Duval and Sarah Freer.

Born May 14. Mary, child of Paulus Freer and Polly Weast.

Born May 2. Moses, child of Zachariah Sluyter and Elizabeth Freer.

Born May 26. Jane, child of Solomon P. Hasbrouck and Magdaline Lefever.

July 14; born June 1. Hiram, child of David Ostrander and Margaret Masten.

Born June 14. Sally Maria, child of Jonathan Bovier and Judith Louw.

Born May 10. James, child of Jonathan Freer and Syntye Agmoedy.

Born May 28. Abner, child of Joseph Hasbrouck, Jr., and Jane Hasbrouck.

Born June 24. Matthew, child of David Agmoedy and Mary Van Keuren.

Aug. 25; born July 15. Catherine Magdaline, child of Elias Freer and Catherine Teerpenning.

Sept. 15; born Aug. 10. Josiah, child of Peter Lefever, Esq., and Magdalena Eltinge.

Born July 7. Hiram, child of Peter P. Hasbrouck and Anny Freer.

Born July 25. Johannes, child of Natl. I. Lefever and Lany Hornbeck.

Sept. 23; born June 22. William Radcliff, child of Henry Goetchius and Margaret Mastin.

Sept. 23; born June 22. Maria, child of Josiah Hasbrouck and Anny Viele.

Oct. 13; born Aug. 19. Ann Eliza, child of Ezekiel Freer, Jr., and Esther Van Wagenen.
Witnesses: Ezekiel Freer and Elizabeth Sluyter.

Nov. 7 ; born Oct. 19. Jehosaphat, child of Jonas Freer and Wyntye Hasbrouck.

Born Sept. 9. Isaac, child of Abraham Halsted and Magdaline Scryver.

Born Sept. 10. Rebecca, child of Archibald Chittuck and Rachel Miller.

Born Sept. 10. Joseph Dubois, child of Cornelia Markel, widow of Lu. Van Wagenen.

De'c. 15 ; born Aug. 25. Deyoo, child of Jonas Dubois and Rachel Lefever.

Born Nov. 11. Ezekiel, child of Roelef and Dinah Eltinge.

Born Oct. 10. Milton, child of Abraham P. Hasbrouck and Mary Blenchan.

Dec. 29 ; born Nov. 13. Mary Magdalena, child of Peter Agmoedy and Eve Smith.

1812, Jan. 12 ; born Dec. 7, 1811. Wessel, child of Lewis W. Dubois and Bridget Jenkins.

Jan. 25 ; born Dec. 23, 1811. Elisah, child of William W. Deyoo and Sarah Hasbrouck.

Born Dec. 19, 1811. Rachel, child of Simon Johnson and Maria Traphagen.

Born Dec. 15, 1811. Eley, child of Hugo B. and Elizabeth Freer.

Feb. 16 ; born Jan. 27. Anny Hasbrouck, child of John I. Freer and Margaret Bennet.

Born Jan. 13. Nathaniel, child of Abm. N. and Sarah Lefever.

Born Jan. 6. Eliza Jane, child of Richard Hardenbergh and Maria Crispel.

Born Nov. 7, 1811. Mary, child of Henry V. W. Terwilliger and Rachel Frederick.

March 6 ; born Jan. 14. Rachel, child of Daniel Hasbrouck and M. Freer.

April 18 ; born Feb. 23. Samuel, child of Peter Dubois and Anna Blenchan.

Born Dec. 16, 1811. James, child of Marcus Wackman and Laura Van Ostrant.

Born Dec. 8, 1811. Myndert, child of James Kidney and Lany Bunton.

April 4; born March 18. Anny Osylla, child of Charles Wells and Anny Hood.

Born Feb. 28. Maria Wintfield, child of Jacob Hendrickson and Bridget Wintfield.

Born April 1. Maria, child of Jacob D. Freer and Esther Freer.

Born Sept. 2, 1811. Eliza, child of Peleg Stevans and Hanah Moor (unbaptized).

May 22; born Feb. 12. Hyram, child of Jesaias and Jacemyntie Freer.

May 31; born March 31. Hasbrouck, child of Jonathan I. Lefever and Dinah Hasbrouck.

Born May 3. John Hardenbergh, child of Jonathan D. Deyoo and Maria Hardenbergh.

Born March 10. Blandina, child of Jacobus Lefever and Elizabeth Johnson.

Born May 6. Esther, child of Abraham Steen and Elizabeth Freer.

July 12; born April 29. Magdalene, child of Abraham Dubois and Anny Lefever.

Born May 31. Jane, child of Ezek. Elting and Magdaline Eltinge.

Born May 31. Sally Maria, child of Samuel Hasbrouck and Lydia Crispel.

Born May 21. Sally Maria, child of Peter Stryker and Anny Dunn.

Born April 28. Eli, child of Stephen Schryver and Hannah Purdee.

July 26; born June 22. Jemimy, child of Wilhelmus Dubois and Catrina Duyoo.

Aug. 9; born July 4. Pamilla, child of Josiah Dubois and Elizabeth Hasbrouck.

Born June 27. John Bogardus, child of Methusalem Dubois, Jr., and Maria Louw.

Born July 6. Thomas, child of William Traphagen and Rachel Freer.

Born April 16. Catherina, child of Daniel Deyoo and Maria Eltinge.

Aug. 23 ; born July 29. Dirk Wesbrook, child of Charles and Polly Dubois.

Born July 29. Isaac, child of William Hood and Anny Seaman.

Sept. 6 ; born May 24. Ann Maria, child of Daniel Frieligh and Ann Buga.

Born Aug. 3. Sally Jane, child of Simon Roose and Ruth Terwilliger.

Born Aug. 13. Jane Ann, child of Matthew I. Blenchan and Anny Turk.

Born Aug. 3. Johannes Johnson, child of Zechariah Freer and Jane Dubois.

Born July 17. Jeremiah, child of Amasa Mitchel and Maria Bovier.

Born July 7. Maria, child of Zechariah York. (his wife unbaptized).

Born July 26. Catrina, child of Christian and Annatye Freer.

Sept. 26 ; born Aug. 24. Charles Bruyn, child of Roelef Hasbrouck and Maria Dewitt.

Born Aug. 13. Margaret Magdaline, child of Timothy Branin and Maria Yerk.

Aug. 26 ; born May 28. Peggy, child of John Rim, absent, and Wyntje Hasbrouck.

Sept. 26 ; born Sept. 12. John Yerk, child of Ezekiel Sparks and Deborah Yerk.

(No name) child of James Perine.

(No name) child of Paulus Freer.

(No name) child of Aart Freer.

Nov. 1 ; born Sept. 10. Ezekiel, child of Garrit Dubois and Maria Eltinge.

Nov. 16 ; born Sept. 17. Samuel Dubois, child of Frederick Stokes and Sarah Keyser.

Born Oct. 14. Jane Dubois, child of John Witaker and Elizabeth McDonald.

Born Sept. 27. Daniel, child of John Sexton and Caty Yerk.

Born Sept. —. John Bogardus, child of Henry Dunn and Elizabeth Terwilliger.

Dec. 14; born Nov. 11. Simon Hardenbergh, child of Joseph Dubois and Maria Hardenbergh.

Born Oct. 28. Jemima, child of Peter P. Hasbrouck and Anny Freer.

Dec. 25; born Nov. 20. Albina, child of Jacob J. Hasbrouck and Ann Dubois.

Dec. 27; born Nov. 13. Eve, child of Thomas Sammons and Maria Freer.
Witness: Eve Acker, widow of Ben. Freer.

Dec. 27; born Oct. 23. Ezekiel, child of Jonathan Louw and Jane Yendel.

Born Nov. 22. Gilbert, child of Charles Eltinge and Helen Bovier.

Born Nov. 26. Henry, child of David Terwilliger and Mary Van de Merk.

Born Oct. 28. Martinus Freer, child of Martinus Freer and Margaret Freer, adopting.

1813, Jan. 10; born Nov. 19, 1812. Catherine Dubois, child of Henry Schoonmaker and Jane Hornbeek.

Born Dec. 2, 1812. Jacob, child of Jonathan Bovier and Judith Louw.

Born Nov. 17, 1812. William, child of John Halsted and Maria Terwilliger.

Jan. 22; born Nov. 3, 1812. Jane, child of James McCollogh and Catherine Louw.

Born Oct. 6, 1812. Eliza, child of John E. Freer and Eve Agmoedy.

Born Dec. 18, 1812. Abraham Deyoo, child of Jacobus Roose and Sarah Van Wagenen.

Feb. 7; born Aug. 11, 1812. Jonathan Wintfield, child of John Agmoedy and Lea Wintfield.

Born Aug. 25, 1812. Jemima Ann, child of Christopher Green and Catherine Acker.

Born Jan. 4. Margaret Ann, child of Abrm. H. Traphagen and Catherine Dubois.

Feb. 14; born Oct. 12, 1812. Rebecca, child of Allen Irwin and Esther Townsend.

March 7 ; born Feb. 4. Jonas, child of Jonathan Freer, Jr., and Syntje Agmoedy.

March 21 ; born Jan. 22. Catherine, child of Elias Yerk and Dolly Geers, unbapt.

April 11 ; born Feb. 10. Nathaniel, child of Simon M. Lefever and Elizabeth Duyoo.

Born Feb. 28. Anna Maria, child of Isaac Louw and Anny Yerk.

Born March 30. Ann Eliza, child of J. Terwilliger and Bridget York.

Born March 30. Abraham Hasbrouck, child of Jonathan Deyoo, Jr., and Caty Ean.

May 7 ; born April 8. Gitty, child of Philip and Catherine Eltinge.

Born March 22. Philip, child of Abraham J. and Maria Deyoo.

May 23 ; born Feb. 19. Archibald, child of Archibald Chittuck and Rachel Miller.

Born April 17. Margaret, child of John H. Bernhart and Mary Sluyter.

Born April 10. Rachel, child of Ezekiel Deyoo and Deborah Louw.

Born April 28. Sally Maria, child of Robert Dunn and Lucy Freer.

Born Jan. 8. Peggy Annetta, child of Adam Yaple and Maria Davenport.

June 21 ; born May 7. Ida, child of Paul Countryman and Margaret Wood.

Born May 2. James Bayard, child of Jacob Schoonmaker and Ann Bayard, unbapt.

Born May 2. James, child of James Van Ostrandt and Rachel Hill, unbapt.

July 4 ; born May 27. Matthew, child of Moses Lefever and Margaret Vanoy.
Witnesses : Mat. Lefever and Eliz. Lefever.

Born May 13. John, child of Lewis B. Dubois and Phœbe Coe.

Born Jan. 9. Hannah, child of Jacs. Elmendorf and Brachy Atkins.

Born May 24. Sarah Meyers, child of Isaac Halsted, Jr. and Sarah Wilkelow.

Born May 17. Cornelius Hornbeek, child of Natl. J. Lefever and Helen Hornbeek.

Born May 9. Ezra, child of Joseph, Jr., and Jane Hasbrouck.

Born June 6. Maria, child of Ezekiel Bovier and Nelly Van Bomelle.

Born May 25. Gitty, child of Isaac Bovier and Maria York.

Born Jan. 10. Joshua, child of Philip Schoonmaker and Rachel Freer.

Born May 10. Benjamin Layton, child of David Atkins and Maria Van Leuwen.

July 18; born May 6. Charles, child of Peleg Stevans and Hannah Moor, unbapt.

Born June 1. Peter, child of Jacob E. Heermance and Hannah Deyoo.

Born June 25. Jacob, child of Peter Dubois and Hannah Blenchan.

Born June 23. Charles, child of John A. Bodley and Elizabeth Freer.

Born June 20. Harvey, child of John N. Lefever and Sarah Dubois.

Born June 17. Catharine Jane, child of Dr. Mauritius Wirtz and Maria Johnson.

Born May 23. Jane, child of Abraham Agmoedy and Sarah Louw.

Aug. 1; born July 19. Garrit Freer, child of Abraham Harris and Mary Waldron.

Born June 30. Eltinge, child of William W. Deyoo and Sarah Hasbrouck.

Born April 17. Eliza, child of Abraham S. Hasbrouck and Elener Minickhouse.

Aug. 5 ; born July 23. Jane, child of Methusalem Hasbrouck and Maria Deyoo.

Aug. 29 ; born July 2. Jane, child of Samuel Van Leuwen and Rachel Clearwater.

Sept. 12 ; born July 16. David, child of Dr. Jacob Wertz and Catharina Dubois.

Born April 25. Johannes, child of Peter Kyser and Elizabeth Broom.

Born Aug. 12. Nathan, child of Stephen Terwilliger and Wyntje Freer.

Born July 29. John, child of Caleb Simmons, unbaptized, and Esther Simmons.

Oct. 22 ; born Jan. 1. Abraham, child of John Van Voorhees and Phoebe Flucwelling, unbapt.

Born Sept. 7. Tryntje Wertz, child of William Duvall and Sarah Freer.

Born July 22. Catherine Dubois, child of Richard McKinnelly and Deborah Roose.

Born Sept. 17. Calvin, child of Johannis Hornbeek and Gitty Dubois.

Nov. 7 ; born Sept. 23. Gertrude, child of Andries Lefever and Hannah Dubois.

Born Sept. 25. James, child of Myndert Kidney, unbapt., and Hannah Bunten.

Born Oct. 10. David, child of John Sexton and Catherine York.

Nov. 21 ; born Nov. 14. Gilbert, child of Benjamin U. Terwilliger and Sarah Saxon.

Born Aug. 14. Jacob, child of Isaac T. Dubois and Catherine Terwilliger.

Born Oct. 16. Richard Harrison, child of Abraham P. Hasbrouck and Mary Blenchan.

Born Oct. 10. Solomon, child of Solomon Eltinge and Rachel Acker.

Dec. 5 ; born Oct. 20. Wade Hampton, child of Samuel Budd and Mary Laroe.

Born Nov. 2. Mathew, child of Frederick Atkin and Rachel Countryman.

Born Nov. 4. Peter, child of Abraham Steen and Elizabeth Freer.

Dec. 25; born Oct. 15. Levi, child of Abraham Relyea and Rachel Ean.

Born Oct. 6. Sarah Magdaline, child of Jacob Freer and Hannah Smith.

Born Nov. 8. Elias, child of Elias Freer and Catherine Tearpenning.

1814, Jan. 2; born Dec. 5, 1813. Caty Maria, child of Isaac Hood and Elizabeth Freer.

Born Dec. 4, 1813. Sally Jane, child of John Hood and Rachel Freer.

Jan. 30; born Oct. 6, 1813. Peter Delemater, child of David Agmoedy and Mary Van Keuren.

Feb. 13; born Dec. 20, 1813. Elijah, child of Hugo and Elizabeth Freer.

Feb. 27; born Dec. 28, 1813. Josiah, child of John Beesemere and Margaret Van Steenbergh.

March 13; born Jan. 26. Ezekiel, child of Cors. Brodhead and Dinah Eltinge.

Born Feb. 11. Oliver Perry, child of Jonathan J. Lefever and Dinah Hasbrouck.

April 10; born Dec. 22, 1813. Rachel Ann, child of Jeremiah Freer, Jr. and Maria Van De Mark.

April 24; born March 15. Henry Snyder, child of John E. Hasbrouck and Ann Snyder.

Born March 25. Harriet, child of Simeon Freer and Maria Agmoedy.

Born March 15. Margaret, child of Loewis Atkins and Ruth Freer.
Witnesses: Martinus and Margaret Freer.

April 20; born Nov. 24, 1813. Sarah Dubois, child of James Kidney and Leany Bunten.

May 22; born April 14. Almira, child of Abraham P. Schoonmaker and Catrina Freer.

Born April 14. Esther, child of Benjamin Wood and Esther Davenport.

Born April 11. Nelly Fraligh, child of Simon Roose and Ruth Terwilliger.

May 8. Maria, child of Roelif and Dinah Eltinge.

June 25; born May 11. Jacob Smedes, child of Matthew I. Blenchan and Anny Turk.

Born June 18. Peter, child of William Delemater and Jane Hardenbergh. Witness: John C. Hardenbergh.

July 10; born May 16. L. Nathaniel, child of Jonas Dubois and Rachel Lefever.

Born May 12. Elmira Jane, child of Peter Stryker and Anny Dunn.

Rebeccah Ann, child of Jacob Halsted and Charity Vanaken.

Born Feb. 20. Richard Brinkerhoff, child of Marcus Wakman and Laura Van Ostrandt.

July 22; born June 25. Samuel, child of Abraham Dubois and Anny Lefever.

Aug. 14; born July 3. Ann Broadhead, child of Abraham A. and Margaret Deyoo.

Sept. 18; born July 3. Sally Jane, child of John Agmoedy and Lea Wintfield.

Born Aug. 2. Matthew, child of Solomon P. Hasbrouck and Magdaline Lefever.

Born Aug. 3. John Henry, child of John Van Voorhees and Phoebe Flewilling, unbaptized.

Born Aug. 1. Eliza Jane, child of Jonathan Bovier and Judith Louw.

Born Aug. 9. Julian, child of Zachariah York and Mary Geer.

Born July 5. James Henry, child of James Terwilliger and Bridget York.

Oct. 4; born Aug. 30. Catherine Maria, child of Christian I. Deyoo and Nelly Hardenbergh.

Born July 30. Sarah, child of Daniel D. Bernhart and Maria Countryman.

Oct. 16; born Aug. 26. Levi Hasbrouck, child of Ambrose Simmons and Anny Constable.

Born Sept. 4. Cornelia, child of Samuel Hasbrouck and Lydia Crispel.

Born Aug. 18. Brachy Deyoo, child of Christian and Annatje Freer.

Oct. 30 ; born Sept. 5. Catherine, child of John W. Schoonmaker and Maria Deyoo.

Born Oct. 6. Gertrude Bruyn, child of John N. Lefever and Sarah Dubois.

Oct. 30 ; born Oct. 3. Rebeccah Dubois, child of Timothy Branin and Maria Yerk.

Born Oct. 31. Ditmasse, child of Abraham J. Hardenbergh and Margaret Dubois.

Nov. 11 ; born July 27. Huldah, child of Samuel Danelsen and Elaner Hood.

Born July 30. Corinus Jenkins, child of Lewis W. Dubois and Bridget Jenkins.

Nov. 27 ; born Oct. 27. Eli, child of Jonathan Freer and Syntje Agmoedy.

Dec. 11 ; born Oct. 14. Daniel Johnson, child of Jacobus Lefever and Elizabeth Johnson.

Born Nov. 2. Cornelia, child of Joseph Dubois and Maria Hardenbergh.

Born Oct. 16. Jacob, child of Ezekiel Sparks and Deborah York.

Dec. 25 ; born Oct. 23. Peter, child of Peter Agmoedy and Eve Smith.

Born Nov. 2. Ann Eliza, child of Art Freer and Maria Smith.

1815, Jan. 8 ; born Nov. 25, 1814. Maria, child of Wilhelmus Dubois and Catherine Deyoo.

Born Nov. 4, 1814. Hugo, child of Charles B. Van Wagenen and Sarah Sluyter.

Born Nov. 3, 1814. Ennes, child of Joseph and Jane Deyoo.

Jan. 12 ; born Dec. 16, 1814. Luther, child of Joshua Freer and Rachel Schoonmaker.

Born Nov. 21, 1814. Blandina Elmendorf, child of Abraham P. Lefever and Margaret Johnson.

Feb. 5 ; born Oct. 25, 1814. Ezekiel, child of Josiah Hasbrouck, Jr., and Anny Viele.

Born Dec. 16, 1814. William Henry, child of Abraham Traphagen and Catherine Dubois.

Born Dec. 22, 1814. Harriet, child of Jacob Schoonmaker.

Born Dec. 3, 1814. Catherine Maria, child of Edward Klaerwater and Elizabeth Freer.

Born Jan. 1. Anny, child of Peter Ean and Maria Freer.

Born Dec. 21, 1814. Peter, child of John Burger and Catherine Van Vliet.

July 30 ; born June 19. Eliza, child of Charles Eltinge and Magdalene Bovier.

Aug. 4 ; born July 3. Rachel, child of Henry Dunn and Elizabeth Terwilliger.

Born May 2. Henry, child of Henry Schoonmaker and Jane Hoornbeek.

Aug. 18 ; born July 10. Noah Eltinge, child of William Hood and Anny Simmons.

Born July 24. Josiah, child of Mathusalem Hasbrouck and Maria Deyoo.

Born June 8. Magdaline, child of Paulus Freer and Mary Weest.

Born July 23. Hiram, child of James Perine and Catherine Freer.

Born July 7. Garrit Dubois, child of Peleg Stevans.

Born July 30. Almira, child of Garrit I. Freer and Maria Waldron.

1816, Feb. 11 ; born Jan. 7. Catherine, child of Matthew I. Blanshane and Anna Turk.

Born Dec. 26, 1815. Livina, child of Simeon Freer and Mary Achmudy.

Born Nov. 7, 1815. Jonathan, child of Abram J. and Maria Deyo.

Born Sept. 15, 1815. Tobias, child of Solomon Eltinge and Rachel Eckert.

Born Jan. 11. Juliann, child of David Atkins and Maria Van Luvan.

Born Nov. 2, 1815. John, child of Joseph Yaple and Sarah Stokes.

Born Nov. 9, 1815. Elvy, child of William W. Deyo and Sarah Hasbrouck.

Born Aug. 31, 1815. Ann, child of Isaiah and Jemima Freer.

April 28 ; born Sept. 14, 1815. Magdalene, child of Simon M. Lefever and Elizabeth Doio.

Born Apr. 5. Jane, child of Elias Frere and Catarine Terpenneng.

Born Jan. 16. Jonathan Lefever, child of Smith Ransom and Maria Lefever.

Born Apr. 15. Catarine, child of David Parker (not baptized) and Elizabeth Van Ake.
Witness : Gideon Van ——

Born Apr. 7. Mauritius, child of Jacob Wirtz and Catrina Dubois.

Born Feb. 29. Jacob, child of Jeremia Bovier and Wyntje Smith.

No date of baptism ; born Apr. 16. William Barns, child of Lewis Atkins and Ruth Freer.

Born Apr. 19. Cornelia, child of Ezekiel Deyoe and Deborah Louw.

Born Apr. 4. Solomon, child of Roelof S. Eltinge and Catherine Lefever.

Born Apr. 29. Catherine, child of Philip Dubois and Hester Freer.

Oct. 13 ; born Aug. 18. William, child of Christopher Lefevre and Sara Doyo.

Born May 30. Jonathan, child of Jacob Freere, Jr., and Anna Smith.

Born July 10. Elias, child of Zacharia Yark and Mary Geers.

Nov. 3 ; born June 24. Magdalin, child of Rolof Elting and Dina Eltinge.

Born June 2. Sarah, child of Salomon P. Hasbrouk and Magdalen Lefever.

Born Sept. 5. Peter, child of Daneel Bernhardt and Maria Contriman.

Born Sept. 15. Jane, child of Abram S. Dubois and Magdalin Jinkins.

Born Sept. 21. Catarine Dubois, child of Daniel Rosa and Jane Saxton.

Born Aug. 12. Nathaneel, child of Jonathan J. Lefever and Dina Hasbrouck.

Born July 15. Eva, child of Jonathan Bovier and Judic Low.

Born Jan. 30. Elisa, child of David Doio and Catrina Frere.

Born June 24. Mary Ann, child of Cornelius Terwilger and Polly Wilkelo.

Born Aug. 2. Louis, child of Richard Hardenberg and Maria Crispel.

Born Sept. 7. Jesse, child of John W. Schonmaker and Maria Doio.

Born July 17. Crinis, child of Lewis W. Dubois and Bridget Jenkins.

Born May 4. Dolly Jane, child of James R. Terwilger and Bridget York.

Born July 6. Christoffel Doio, child of Christian and Annatje Frere.

Born Oct. 7. Miamy Ann, child of John Van Voorhees and Phebe Fluellen.

INDEX.

There was some question as to the best mode of preparing this index, inasmuch as there are so many variations in spelling the cognomens as well as the baptismal names in these records. The dominies, voorlezers, or whoever acted as scribe, appear to have exercised their own judgment as to orthography, and frequently varied it without apparent reason. For example, the name of Ann Westluck is found on page 139, on page 146 it is Wesley, on page 152 it is Wesly, on page 162 it appears as Weslyk, on page 170 it is written Weslye, on page 179 it is Westleake, and on page 185 it was put down as Westlake. Yet all of these several names belong to the same person. If all the names were indexed separately just as they appear in the records with the original spelling, it is evident that the work of tracing family lineages by the unskilled searcher would be greatly increased. It was concluded, therefore, that it would facilitate reference by embracing under one heading all names evidently belonging to one family, and indexing them, as far as practicable, under that form which is now in most common use.

Appended will be found a list of some of the most numerous variations in the surnames that appear in these records :

Acker, Akker, Eccert, Ackert, Ekkert, Eccer, Ekker, Eckerd.
Alsdorf, Aalsdorf, Alsdorpf, Alsdorpt, Alsdorph, Alsdorp, Alstorf, Altsdorf, Asdraugh, Alsdorff, Aelsdorf.
Atkins, Etkens, Etkins, Atkin.
Auchmoedy, Achmoody, Ackmoedy, Agmoedy, Aughmoedy, Aghmody, Achmudy, Achmody, Eckmoedy, Ecmoedy, Auchmoetie, Agmoedy, Achtmoethe, Acmoidec, Achmudi, Auchmutie, Auchmoudy, Achmude, Achmoedy, Achmoedie.
Baker, Bakker, Beeker, Beker.
Barton, Barten, Bartin, Berton.
Bessemer, Beesimere, Besmer, Beesemere.
Bevier, Bevie, Bayvyer, Bovie, Bevirs, Bovier, Bevir, Bavier, Beviere, Beviers, Bevieer, Baivyer, Bayvier, Beuvier.
Blanchan, Blonjan, Blanjan, Blancon, Blenchan, Blonchan, Blanchou, Blaynjohn, Blanjohn, Blanshane.
Bosch, Bosh, Bush, Bos, Boss.
Broadhead, Broded, Broedhead, Brodhead, Brades.
Bruyn, Bruin, Breun, Brown, Broune, Brouwn.
Burhans, Borhans, Borehans, Burhanse.
Cantyn, Contyn, Conteyn, Canteyn.

Countryman, Contryman, Kontryman, Contriman.
Danielson, Dannelson, Donaldson, Danelson, Donalson, Donnolson.
Davenport, Davenpoort, Denport, Davenp, Devenport.
Decker, Dekker, Deccer, Deckers.
Degraff, Degraef, Degraaf, Degroof, De Graaf.
Delamater, Delemetre, Delemerter, Lamerter, Lemerter, Delemeter, Lamater, Delemater.
Deyo, Deyoo, Dioo, Doyo, Du Jo, De Yoo, Dojou, De Joo, De Yo, Dejo, Duyo, Dojo, Doieie, Deyoe, D'Oyaux, De Jo, Duyoo, Doiau, Do Joy, Dejoo, De Joy, Dojau, Doioo, Doeau, De Joe, Douo, Doio, Dio, Doyou, D'Oyaeux, Doioie, Do Yoo, Dujo, Doyaux, Dojouw, Dojoux, Doye, Dejou, D'Oyo, Dyo, Doiaa.
Dubois, Duboy, De Boes, DeBoey, Du Boys, De Boi, Duboys, De Boy, De Booy, De Boeys, Debois, Dubois.
Ean, Een, Ein, Un, Enn, Eyn, Yn, Ien.
Elmendorp, Elmondorph, Almendorf, Elmondorf.
Eltinge, Elting, Elinge, Eltig, Eling.
Elton, Elten, Elte, Eltinge.
Everett, Emerett, Everit, Evert, Beverit, Evered.
Freeligh, Frieligh, Freligh, Vreligh, Fraligh.
Frelinghuisen, Vrelinghuisen, Frelinghuysen, Frielinghuysen.
Freyer, Frere, Freer, Freres, Frerers, Freeres, Frear, Fraer, Vreer, Freere, Frers, Freures, Frair.
Geer, Geers, Greer, Years.
Griffin, Griffens, Griffen, Griffing.
Hasbrouck, Hasbrouque, Assebroucq, Hasebroek, Hasbroucq, Hasbrook, Hasebrouck, Housbrouck, Haas Douk, Harsbrook, Haasbrouque, Haasbrook, Hasbrouk, Haasbroek, Hasbrouq, Haasebroek, Haesbroek, Haesbrouek, Hasebroucq, Hasbrouc, Hasbroek, Haasbroeck.
Hendriks, Hendrickson, Hendrikson, Hendricks, Hendricse.
Hoogteling, Hooghteyling, Hogteling, Van Hoogteelink.
Hoornbeek, Hornbeek, Hornbeck, Hoornbeck.
Huy, Huey, Hue, Heuwe.
Jansen, Janson, Johnson, Janse, Johnsen, Jonson (see also Johnston).
Jeple, Jepole, Jepold, Yaple.
Keyser, Kyser, Keizer, Ceyzer, Keiser, Kyzer, Keyzer.
Klaarwater, Klaarwaater, Claarwaater, Claerwater, Claarwater, Clarvater, Klarwater, Clearwater.
Kritzinger, Critsinger, Kritsingen, Kritsinger.
Lefever, Lefeber, Le Fever, Lefeve, Leffeber, Lefevre, Levever, Le Feur, Fever, Lefefer, Le Fevre, Le Vewer, Lafever, Le Febre, Lefevour, Feaver, Feber, Lafaver, Lefaver, L. Fever, Le Febvre.
Le Munyer, Lemonjon, Monjon, L. Monjon, Lemungen, Lemunger, Leminger, Lamonjon, Lemunyen.
Louw, Low, Lowe, Law, Lau, Lauw.
McAvey, McKaby, McCaby, McCavy, McAvie.
McKinley, McCinly, McCenly, McKinnelly.
McMollin, McMullen, McMullan, McMollen.
Masten, Maasten, Mastin, Maste, Maesten.
Meier, Meyer, Myer, Myers.
Newkerk, Nieuwkerk, Neuwkerk, Newkirk.
Nice, Nees, Nies, Neice, Neise, Niess, Niec, Neas.

Palmatier, Palmetier, Parmetier, Palmiteer, Palmitier.
Parrine, Perrine, Perine, Parrain.
Polhemus, Perhemes, Purhemus, Pulhemus.
Ralyea, Relyea, Raljie, Rilyea, Reljea, Relyee, Reille, Ralyee, Rellie, Relie, Rallie, Relje, Ralyie, Rally, Ralye.
Rang, Rank, Ranck, Rand, Rhauk, Rong, Rauck.
Roberson, Robbertson, Robbersen, Robinson.
Roose, Rooza, Rosa, Rose, Roosa, Roos.
Rutan, Rutampt, Rutemp, Rutemps.
Schryver, Scryver, Schreyfer, Schriver.
Schut, Shut, Scutt, Chut.
Shurager, Skurigan, Shuragen, Shorger.
Sluyter, Sluiter, Slouter, Sluuter.
Smith, Smitt, Shmith, Smit, Schmit, Smits, Shmidt.
Soper, Sopier, Sope, Sopus, Sooper.
Stokes, Stoks, Stooks, Stocks.
Stokraed, Stokkraed, Stokkerat, Stokraad, Stockeraat.

Teerpenning, Terpenneng, Tearpenning, Terpenning, Teerpenningh, Terpening.

Terwilger, Terwilge, Terwilliger, Terwilgen, Terwilligen, Ter Wellinge, Terwilleger, Terwillingh, Terwille, Trewilligar, Terwiliger.

Van Aken, Van Aaken, Van Aker, Van Ake, V. Aake, Van Aake, Aaken.

Van Bommel, Van Bommele, Van Bombele, Van Bomelle, Van Bumbler.

Vandemark, Vander Merken, Van de Merk, Vandemerker, Van der Merke, Van de Merke, Vandermerk, Vandemerken.

Van Leuwen, Van Leuve, Van Leuven, Van Leuwe, Van Luvan.

Van Steenberg, Steenberg, Van Stienbergh, Steenbergh, Van Steenbergh, Van Steenhergen, V. Steenbergen, Stenberg, Van Steenberghen, Van Steenberge.

Van Wagenen, Van Wagene, Van Wagener, Van Waigan, Van Wag, Van Wagen, V. Wagenen, Van Wagena.

Vernoy, Vernoej, Vannoy, Vernooy, Vanoy, Van Noy, Fernooi, Vernooi.
Viele, Vilie, Vielie, Veley, Fiele, Feelie, Velie.
Wackman, Werkman, Wecman, Wieman, Wakman, Wakeman, Wockman, Wekman, Wyckman.
Waldron, Walron, Walran, Walderon, Walderaan.
Wesmiller, Wessimiller, Wussimiller, Welmiller, Wesemiller, Wesmuller.
Westluck, Weslyk, Westlake, Wesley, Westleake.
Wheeler, Wieler, Whielcr, Willer, Whiler, Whiller, Whehler, Weeler, Weler, Wiler.
Wilkenlow, Wilkelo, Wilkilo, Wilkeloo, Wilkeloe, Wilkelow.
Windfield, Wintfield, Windtfield, Wembfield, Winfield, Windield, Windfiel, Witfield, Windfeald, Wildfield, Wintfiel, Viltfil.
Wirtz, Wertz, Wirts, Werts.
York, Yerk, Jork, Yurk, Yurry, Yark.

A

Aarsdalen, Catarina, 102.
    Elisabeth, 102.
    Philip, 102.
Abrams, Isaac, 58.
Acker, Anna, Enne, 191, 196, 222.
    Catrien, 170, 179, 183, 190, 194, 199, 206, 214, 221, 230.
    David, 112, 119.
    Eva, 75, 129, 176, 182, 230.
    Johannis, 42, 51, 129.
    John, 91.
    Rachel, 190, 199, 204, 209, 214, 219, 225, 233, 237.
    Stephanus, 127.
    William, 92.
Ackerman, Gerloin, 58.
Albartus, Nicolaas, 123.
Allen, Ellen, Dina, 127.
    Matheus, Mathew, 99, 103.
Alliger, Aliger, Benjamin, 137.
    Elijah, 91.
    John, 60, 171.
Alsdorf, David, 93.
    Elizabeth, 81, 105, 107, 111, 119, 123.
    Henry, 86.
    Johannes, 83, 153.
    Lea, 90.
    Lourentz, Lorantz, Lowrance, 4, 12, 19, 73, 75, 95, 96, 100.
    Maria, 86, 95, 96, 131.
    Peter, 91.
    Philip, 109.
    Simon, 105, 110, 123.
    Tempy, 93.
Ancton, Petrus, 83, 121.
Anderson, Enderson, Jane, 92.
    William, 10.
Archbald, Widow, 89.
Archer, Daniel, 90.
Armstrong, Jenny, 190.
    Sarah, 149, 153.
Aswin, Phebe, 150.
Atkins, Bregje, Brachy, 176, 187, 232.
    David, 59, 110, 141, 149, 211, 232, 237.
    Elizabeth, 136.
    Elsje, 134, 141, 149.
    Frederick, 233.
    John, 101, 110.
    Joseph, 104.
    Loewis, 234, 238.
    Maria, 101.
    Thomas, 104.
    Widow, 92.
Auchmoedy, —— 88.
    Abraham, 58, 71, 78, 214, 221, 232.
    Christian, 42, 49, 53, 56.
    David, 109, 152, 218, 226, 234.
    Dorkas, 161.
    Elizabeth, 103, 104, 106, 109.

Auchmoedy (Con.).
    Eve, 91, 230.
    Hester, 109.
    Jacobus, Gemes, James, 54, 56, 74, 76, 79, 80, 94, 163, 166, 176, 179, 203, 208.
    John, 209, 230, 235.
    Magdalena, Lena, 74, 100, 152, 154, 162, 169, 173, 182, 185, 203.
    Maria, Mally, 74, 91, 100, 234, 237.
    Peter, 198, 205, 209, 227, 236.
    Rachel, 76, 130, 132, 135, 139, 146, 151, 152, 160, 166, 176.
    Sarah, 214.
    Syntye, 226, 231, 236.
Avry, Susanna, 161.

B

Baker, Elizabeth, 165.
    Jacob, 108.
    Philip, 107.
    Rachel, 195.
Banker, Salomon, 85.
Banks, Benks, Caty, 87.
    Ester, 84.
Barley, —— 89.
Barnard, John, 226.
Barret, John, 59, 143, 149, 157, 161, 184, 196.
Bartolf, Annatje, 181, 190.
Barton, Margriet, 126, 132, 136, 140, 149, 156, 164, 169, 176.
    Maria, 149.
Baster, George, 187.
Baxter, Abraham, 92.
Bayard, Anny, 91, 231.
    Catherine, 91.
    Zechariah, 91.
Baylree, John, 93.
Bearns, John, 91.
    William, 92.
Becker, Bekker, Joh. Hannese, 10.
    Johannes, 10.
Beem, Elizabeth, 161.
    Marietje, 100, 104.
Bell, Ann, 218, 223.
Bennet, Lena, 85.
    Margrietje, Margaret, 154, 161, 171, 183, 197, 204, 221, 227.
Berchal, Hannah, 91.
Berger, Jacob, 109, 110, 118, 124.
Bern, Anny, 222.
Berner, Bernert, Margritt, 84, 125, 128, 139.
Bernet, Catrin, 125.
Bernhart, Bernhardt, Berenhart, Daniel, 235, 239.
    Johannes, 166, 186.
    John, 231.
Bessemer, Ann, 78, 92.
    Dorothe, 85, 157.
    Elizabeth, 89.

Bessemer (Con.).
John, 78, 234.
Maria, 88.
Bever, Beaver, Beever, John, 158, 170.
Piter, 170.
Sara, 75, 108, 110, 118, 121, 124, 126, 135.
Tjatje, 141.
Bevier, Bayvyer, Abraham, 64, 66, 67, 73, 75, 76, 84, 94, 97, 98, 100, 102, 103, 106, 119, 123, 126, 132, 140, 144, 153, 156, 161, 166, 174, 178, 188.
Andres, 3, 110, 137, 213.
Antje, 101.
Catrina, Catryntje, 75, 138, 144, 147, 150, 156, 158, 162, 170, 175, 190, 200, 205.
Christian, 89.
Conraed, 145.
Cornelia, 85, 155, 162, 164, 167, 173, 177, 184, 191, 197.
Daniel, 183.
David, 48, 51, 137.
Elias, 69, 70, 71, 76, 137, 146, 158, 163, 170, 176, 181, 188, 193, 200, 208, 212.
Elizabeth, 76, 92, 105, 107, 128, 137, 143, 150, 158, 166.
Esther, Hester, 48, 62, 73, 100.
Ezzekiel, Ez., 89, 225, 232.
Helen, 230.
Hetty, 89.
Isaac, 79, 87, 105, 107, 206, 209, 215, 219, 225, 232.
Jacob, 68, 76, 105, 124, 130, 131, 132, 135, 139, 145, 152, 159, 168, 177, 198.
Jacobus, 4, 12, 41, 66, 67, 74, 98, 100, 101, 102, 104, 105, 106, 108, 111, 121, 126, 204, 208, 216, 222.
Jacomeyntie, 84, 122, 133, 136, 140, 153, 173.
Jan, Yan, 64.
Jannetje, Jane, 137, 140, 146, 151, 157, 165, 188, 197.
Jeremiah, 91, 238.
Johanna, 74, 105, 107.
Johannes, 4, 12, 19, 73, 74, 81, 96, 97, 98, 99, 100, 101, 102, 103, 106.
Jonas, 177.
Jonathan, 90, 226, 230, 235,239.
Louis, Lovye, Loejs, Lowies, etc., 2, 3, 42, 60, 61, 62, 63, 106, 121.
Magdalena, Lena, Lany, 73, 74, 75, 83, 84, 90, 91, 94, 101, 122, 126, 127, 130, 131, 132, 137, 143, 147, 150, 159, 164, 166, 188, 205, 237.
Margrietje, Margerita, 42, 47, 49, 53, 80, 96, 136, 144.

Bevier (Con.).
Maria, Mareytje, 78, 87, 93, 97, 98, 100, 101, 103, 104, 105, 106, 110, 126, 129, 131, 132, 140, 143, 145, 146, 149, 153, 158, 160, 161, 162, 166, 174, 179, 183, 188, 192, 193, 198, 202, 206, 213, 215, 217, 220, 225, 229.
Matheus, 75, 84, 133, 136, 140, 153, 173.
Petrus, 48, 68, 76, 117, 155, 162, 167, 173.
Philip, Philippus, 48, 51, 74, 107, 150.
Rachel, 88, 138.
Samuel, 2, 4, 47, 50, 53, 56, 65, 67, 68, 74, 75, 76, 94, 130, 132, 135, 139, 146, 151, 152, 160, 166, 176.
Sara, Selly, 82, 85, 110, 118, 119, 123, 126, 127, 129, 132, 136, 145, 151, 161, 163, 168, 169, 175, 181, 183, 187, 190, 197.
Solomon, 42, 130, 131, 133, 136, 141, 145, 151, 154, 162.
Billigee, John, 89.
Billyou, Lucas, 195.
Bindfield (Windfield?), Elisabeth, 182.
Bishop, Sally, 87.
Blanchan, Anny, Annatje, Hannah, 90, 131, 133, 141, 147, 155, 164, 182, 227, 232.
Caterien, 60, 61, 159, 164, 170, 184.
Jackemyntje, Jacemyntje, 85, 92.
Jacob, 86, 182.
Johannes, 107, 124.
Mary, 89, 227, 233.
Mathew, 71, 78, 177, 194, 206, 229, 235, 237.
Rachel, 107.
Blecker, Jean, 62.
Blinkerhof, Gerret, 176.
Bodine, Bodoin, Bodyne, Caty, 87.
Hannah, 86, 217, 221.
Isaac, 54, 57, 70, 71, 78, 184, 191, 197, 203, 209, 213, 220.
Sally, 90.
Bodley, John, 232.
Bogardus, John, 88.
Bogert, Bogart, Anne, 189, 196.
Nelly, 79, 223.
Bonrepo, Bon Repos, 60, 64, 65.
Bosch, Annatje, 113.
Catarina, 155, 176.
Hendricus, 143.
Johannes, 143.
Mary, 143.
Sarah, 79, 116, 167, 174.
Boyd, Boid, Jean, Jane, Jenny, 117, 132, 136, 139, 146.

Brandel, Thimothy, 165.
Branin, Brannen, Maria, Polly, 93, 215.
   Timothy, 174, 178, 183, 189, 194, 198, 207, 210, 215, 222, 229, 236.
Brewster, Clara, 89.
Brink, Cornelius, 59, 110, 163.
   Magdalena, 159.
Broadhead, Anne, 85, 156, 164.
   Catharina, 107, 113, 120, 126, 129, 133, 150, 153.
   Charles, Charols, 94, 113, 142, 156, 164, 198, 202, 211, 212, 217, 225.
   Cornelius, Cors., 91, 234.
   Daniel, 163.
   Geertruyd, 113.
   Hester, Ester, 84, 153, 162, 185, 197.
   John, 142.
   Lewis, Louis, 42, 48, 129.
   Mary, Maretie, 86, 94, 142.
   Samuel, 163.
   Wessel, 74, 80, 107.
Broom, Elizabeth, 233.
Bross, Townsend, 92.
Brown (see also Bruyn), Broune, etc., Andrew, 92.
   Edward, 95.
   Elizabeth, 177, 218.
   Henry, 87.
   John, 89.
   Phebe, 83.
   Susanna, 95, 172, 187.
   William, 86.
Bruyn (see also Brown), Cathrina, Tryntje, 95, 100, 128.
   Gertruyt, Gertruy, 77, 116, 117, 128, 139, 145, 149, 154, 170, 177.
   I., 4, 12.
   Jacobus, 15, 48, 72, 95, 100, 116.
   James S., 87.
   Maria, 98, 105, 116.
Budd, Budel, Bodd, Samuel, 190, 194, 199, 206, 213, 222, 233.
Buga, Ann, 229.
Buling, Experience, 161.
Bullet, Anthony, 204.
Bunton, Banton, Bunten, Hannah, 91, 233.
   Lanah, 216, 221, 228, 234.
   Philip, 89, 224.
Burger, Cathrin, 111.
   Coenrad, Koenerad, 84, 111, 147, 165.
   Evert, 184.
   Hyeronymus, Hieronimus, Jeronimus, 108, 111, 118, 121, 124, 129, 141, 144.
   John, 92, 237.
   Lisabeth, 109, 157.
   Margaret, 93.
   Petrus, Pitter, 84, 105, 109.

Burger (Con.).
   Sarah, 148,
   Zacharias, 181, 188.
Burhans, Catherine, 209, 211.
   Deborah, 111.
   Jacoba, 177.
   Lena, 200.
   Petrus, 120.
Burian, Thomas, 172.
Burnett, Mary, 195.
Burwell, Henna, 85.
Bussy, Enos, 157.
Buyker, Buiker, Ester, 75.
   Lise, 75.
   Syntje, 76.
Byk, Ann, 60.
Byram, Sally, 89.

C

Cameron, Christina, 87.
Campbell, Camble, Jenie, 146.
   John, 90.
Camzon, John, 84.
Cantyn, Catharina, Catryntje, 81, 101, 106, 113, 128, 142, 154, 155, 175.
   Cornelia, 101.
   Mathewes, 32.
   Pieter, Petrus, 101, 113.
Carman, Anne, 160.
   Cornelius, 92.
   Jacob, 216.
Carner, Antje, 169.
Carson, Samuel, 150.
Cassman, Elisabeth, 83.
Catong, Anna, 181.
Celden, Johannes, 97.
   Mary, 97.
Chalker, Chelker, Isaac, 96, 97.
Chambers, Richard, 89.
Cherry, Abraham, 85.
Chiedly, Jacob, 115.
Chittick, Chittuck, Archable, Archibald, 214, 223, 227, 231.
Clark, Clerk, Abigael, 170.
   Elizabeth, 81.
   Sibel, 144.
Clayton, Claton, Klayton, Jonathan, 89, 224.
   Nancy, 89.
   Robert, 181.
Clearwater, see Klaarwater.
Coader, John, 101.
Cock, Cok, Gerhard Daniel, G. D., 72, 79, 82.
   Margrita, 116.
Coddington, Caddington, —— 57.
   Catarina, 144.
   Joseph, 42, 47, 56, 59, 75, 104, 106, 108, 110, 112, 118, 122, 125, 127, 130, 144, 151, 155, 163, 168, 176.
   Maria, Pally, 159, 164.
   Sarah, 152, 159, 172, 182, 188.

Coe, Alexander, 86, 203.
  Elizabeth, 198.
  Phebe, Phabe, 78, 215, 223, 232.
  Samuel, 198.
Coleman, Colman, Dennis, 85, 175, 188, 193.
Collier, Sarah, 87.
Comfort, Hannah, 116.
Concklin, Concking, Jenny, Jane, 87, 209, 217.
Consalis, Emanuel, 145.
Constable, Abraham, 89.
  Anny, Anne, 205, 223, 235.
  Benjamin, 86, 89.
  Elisabeth, 186.
Coneway, Canneway, Cornelius, 129, 169, 182.
  Maria, 169.
Cool, see Kool.
Cooper, Philip, 56, 85.
Cornwell, Soloman, 90.
Corson, Samuel, 59.
Cosens, —— 91.
Cosselin, Jane, 87.
Cottin, Jean, 62.
Countryman, Eliza, 92,
  Hendricus, 169.
  Laura, 167.
  Maria, 235, 239.
  Mathew, Matheus, 59, 167, 173.
  Paulus, Paul, 224, 231.
  Rachel, 233,
Couwle, Catharine, 95.
  Meyls, 95.
Crappel, Hillegont, 104.
Crispel, Krispell, Chrispel, Abram, 85.
  Antoni, 103.
  Catrina, 103.
  Jacob, 194.
  Johannes, 103.
  Lena, 98, 101.
  Lydia, 90, 228, 236.
  Maria, 90, 227, 239.
  Neeltje, 98.
Crissel, Samuel, 193.
Crom, Abraham, 118.
  Mary, 90.
Crouse, Hannah, 92.
Crouter, Petrus, 185.
Crowes, Elizabeth, 87.

D

Daillie, Dailliez, Pierre, Mr., 1, 62, 63.
Daly, Daily, Catrien, Cate, 174, 177, 183, 199, 222.
  Henry, 183.
D'Amour, Anne, 63.
Danielson, Abraham, 103, 104, 106, 109.
  James, 157.

Danielson (*Con.*).
  Lany, Lena, 90, 173.
  Margrita, Margret, 99, 103.
  Samuel, 219, 236.
  Solomon, 89.
  William, 140, 142, 157, 170.
Davenport, Caty, Catrien, 92, 162.
  Deborah, 87.
  Esther, 234.
  Gerret, 59, 160.
  Jacobus, 184.
  Maria, 116, 222, 231.
Davis, Davids, Davisse, Abigael, 141, 146.
  Caty, 89.
  Elias, 59, 162.
  Elizabeth, Lisabeth, 94, 95, 102, 109, 129, 130, 133, 141, 168, 178, 188.
  Eve, 89, 154.
  Jan, John, 131, 154.
  Martinus, 92.
  Petrus, 154, 167.
  Richard, 94, 95.
  William, 154, 169, 173, 184.
  Wyntie, 86.
Debaen, Ester, 96.
  Benjamin, 96.
Decker, Abram, 80.
  Alida, 104.
  Benjamin, 219.
  Efraim, 171.
  Elizabeth, 88.
  Elsje, 96.
  Garret, 116.
  Hannah, 91.
  Henderik, 62.
  Jacob, 62, 80.
  Johannes, 122.
  Joseph, 15.
  Lena, 94.
  Levi, 91.
  Maria, 104, 127, 128, 180.
  Matheus, 83, 122.
  Reuben, 90.
  Sarah, 157, 175, 194, 202.
Deen, Dean, Jannetie, Jane, 119, 143, 157.
  Jorsy, 119.
Degraff, ——, 92.
  Annatje, 143, 152.
  Cornelius, 171.
  Elisabeth, 117, 119, 123.
  Hannah, 88.
  Jacobus, 119.
  Jannetie, 119.
  John, 130.
  Maria, 152.
De Hart, James, 93.
DeLange, DeLang, Frans, 127.
  Nelly, 126.
  Sarah, 110, 126, 131.
Delemater, Benjamin, 117.
  Catherin, Katherin, 90, 147.
  Cornelius, 86, 89, 171.

Delemater (*Con.*).
Elizabeth, 117.
Jan, 114, 147.
Margrita, 155.
Rachel, 76, 116, 117, 141, 147, 155, 160, 171, 177, 190.
William, 79, 183, 235.
De Moorman, Isaac, 205.
Demorest, Jacobus, 77.
Demsy, Charles, 159.
Depui, Depuy, Depue, Cornelius, 138.
Elizabeth, 135, 189.
Elsje, 138.
Josia, 187.
Maria, 182, 203.
Moses, 135.
Devaal, Rachel, 182.
Deven, Abraham, 97.
Margaret, 97.
Devoe, Jeremia, 173.
Johanna, 170, 184.
Michel, Michael, 42, 50.
De Vroom, Louwra, 105.
Dewitt, De Wit, Andries, 52, 68, 69, 76, 118, 150, 152, 203.
Annatje, 75, 114, 140, 150, 159, 166.
Catharine, 77, 195, 222.
Egbert, Ebbert, 86, 152.
Jan, John, 96, 138.
Jenneke, 162, 167.
Lea, 191, 203.
Levi, 162.
Maria, 229.
Moses, 195, 203.
Petrus, 59, 160.
Ruben, 135.
Sarah, 89, 226.
Tjerck, 138.
William, 85.
Deyoo, ——, 93.
Aaltie, Eltie, 57.
Abraham, 2, 3, 5, 38, 39, 40, 44, 46, 47, 48, 51, 53, 58, 64, 66, 67, 68, 69, 73, 75, 82, 85, 91, 94, 95, 96, 99, 104, 105, 110, 119, 120, 122, 126, 138, 144, 148, 151, 155, 156, 164, 168, 180, 209, 212, 221, 231, 235, 237.
Agetta, 74, 83, 139, 153.
Alfred, 58.
Anne, Hannah, 60, 61, 62, 63, 64, 82, 120, 122, 128, 131, 141, 153, 156, 158, 164, 169, 219, 225, 232.
Benjamin, Benjamen, 18, 41, 49, 51, 53, 66, 67, 68, 69, 74, 86, 89, 102, 104, 105, 108, 122, 135, 151, 153, 164, 173, 177, 184, 199, 209, 221, 226.
Betsy, 91.
Catharina, 74, 84, 217, 223, 228, 236.

Deyoo (*Con.*).
Christian, Crystyan, Christyiaan, 2, 3, 41, 47, 50, 55, 57, 64, 65, 66, 67, 69, 74, 80, 92, 111, 118, 121, 122, 125, 127, 132, 141, 170, 177, 235.
Christophel, Christoffel, Stophel, 41, 47, 50, 51, 54, 55, 57, 66, 67, 68, 74, 92, 103, 105, 112, 120, 133, 136, 156.
Claartje, Klaartie, 41, 50, 94, 95.
Cornelius, 58.
Daniel, 41, 47, 75, 77, 81, 110, 113, 120, 122, 125, 128, 136, 164, 191, 195, 222, 229.
David, 69, 74, 77, 89, 174, 178, 189, 194, 200, 205, 224, 239.
Debora, 101, 103, 133.
Elisabeth, 73, 85, 93, 95, 96, 104, 105, 138, 146, 148, 195, 202, 203, 210, 214, 218, 224, 231, 238.
Elzie, Elsy, 73, 92.
Eva, 136.
Ezekiel, 78, 215, 224, 231, 238.
Henry, Hendrick, 2, 3, 60, 64, 74, 84, 92, 94, 124, 127, 146, 155, 161, 167.
Hester, Ester, 98, 100, 104, 106, 133, 162.
Hugo, 150, 155, 176.
Isaak, Isack, 82, 100, 105, 110, 118.
Jacob, 168, 194, 198, 203.
Jane, Jannetje, Jenneke, Jenny, 87, 91, 151, 153, 158, 173, 205, 211, 236.
Jesaias, 186.
Johannes, Hannes, 4, 12, 41, 50, 66, 68, 69, 76, 77, 83, 100, 104, 107, 111, 118, 120, 129, 153, 164, 169, 180, 186, 192, 199.
John, 69, 70, 78, 89, 90, 92.
Jonathan, 68, 69, 70, 71, 74, 142, 148, 154, 161, 170, 189, 195, 201, 202, 207, 213, 217, 218, 219, 222, 225, 228, 231.
Joseph, 77, 91, 236.
Josiah, 87, 159, 164, 170, 184, 199, 207, 212.
Leah, 211.
Levi, 141, 156, 166, 177, 194.
Lidia, 140, 145, 149, 155, 156, 161, 164, 167, 174, 180, 182, 186, 192, 206.
Lysbet, Lisbette, 61, 63.
Magdalena, Lena, 86, 116, 127, 128, 131, 134, 145, 160, 171, 188.
Margarit, Margareta, Margaret, Marghriet, Margritta, 61, 62, 63, 73, 74, 83, 84, 91, 94, 95, 98, 118, 121, 139, 147, 151, 161, 163, 173, 181, 187, 235.

Deyoo (*Con.*).
　Mary, Marie, Mareytie, Maria,
　　60, 61, 62, 63, 64, 73, 77, 80,
　　82, 84, 91, 95, 112, 119, 120,
　　121, 122, 124, 125, 126, 127,
　　128, 129, 131, 134, 136, 138,
　　142, 144, 147, 148, 155, 156,
　　159, 164, 166, 177, 179, 180,
　　184, 192, 201, 203, 207, 212,
　　213, 216, 217, 223, 224, 231,
　　233, 236, 237, 239.
　Matheus, Mathew, 190, 196,
　　204, 212.
　Moses, 74, 94, 95, 111, 183.
　Nathan, 170.
　Nathaniel, 92, 191, 203, 211.
　Peter, Pieter, Pierre, Pier, 42,
　　47, 58, 61, 62, 74, 96, 98, 102,
　　103, 104, 105, 106, 109, 110,
　　111, 120, 122.
　Philip, 58, 145, 148, 155, 168,
　　169, 175, 178, 185, 191.
　Rachel, 84, 90, 213.
　Ralph, 57.
　Rebecca, 144, 146, 152, 160,
　　165, 172, 177, 186, 192.
　Salomon, 156, 168, 182, 194.
　Sara, 238.
　Simon, 90, 93, 130, 132, 138,
　　144, 182.
　Vuyne, 95.
　William, 57, 70, 71, 78, 90, 165,
　　173, 177, 184, 190, 195, 196,
　　201, 206, 212, 220, 227, 232,
　　238.
　Wyntie, Wyntje, 80, 94, 96.
Dickensen, Augustine, 88.
Dickinson, Polly, 91.
Dill, George, 200.
Dinghee, John, 87.
Diver, Dyver, Daniel, 52, 56, 130,
　134, 140, 167.
　Margriet, 140.
Divine, Elizabeth, 170.
　Maria, 190.
Doean, Abraham, 96.
　Elisabeth, 96.
Don, Joseph, 83.
Dotting, Rachel, 83.
Dowden, John, 42, 46.
Dubois, Abraham, 2, 3, 61, 62, 63,
　80, 93, 132, 211, 219, 228,
　235, 239.
　Andries, 58, 107, 113, 121, 138,
　　142, 148, 156, 186.
　Anna, Anny, Ann, Hannah, 25,
　　28, 76, 84, 85, 89, 132, 183,
　　194, 199, 204, 210, 211, 217,
　　221, 224, 230, 233.
　Arriantje, 145.
　Benjamin, 42, 49, 50, 53, 66,
　　74, 92, 95, 97, 99, 100, 103,
　　105, 110, 126, 129, 132, 143,
　　158, 161.
　Catharina, Trynte, 73, 80, 82,

Dubois, Catharina, Trynte (*Con.*).
　　86, 94, 145, 200, 207, 213,
　　219, 224, 230, 233, 237, 238.
　Caty, 89.
　Charles, 71, 79, 177, 183, 193,
　　201, 214, 221, 229.
　Cornelia, 75, 83, 113, 121, 124,
　　127, 128, 131, 136, 144, 153,
　　202, 207.
　Cornelius, 5, 42, 47, 56, 68, 69,
　　70, 71, 76, 77, 78, 80, 81,
　　116, 117, 128, 139, 145, 149,
　　154, 165, 170, 177, 210, 223.
　Cornelius Bruyn, 85, 200, 205,
　　216.
　Daniel, 2, 3, 41, 49, 64, 65, 73,
　　84, 93, 94, 122, 129, 135,
　　143, 158, 186, 187, 194.
　Dina, 79, 114, 163.
　Elenor, 58.
　Elizabeth, Lizabeth, 73, 76, 80,
　　84, 86, 94, 95, 96, 99, 126,
　　144, 150, 155, 159, 160, 166,
　　167, 172, 176, 179, 183, 185,
　　190, 196, 203.
　Elschie, Else, 78, 187, 192, 199,
　　207.
　Ester, 103, 106.
　Garrit, 71, 78, 190, 193, 200,
　　208, 215, 223, 229.
　Gertrude, Geertruy, 91, 99.
　Gitty, 233.
　Henricus, Henry, Hendrick, 6,
　　7, 16, 22, 23, 24, 25, 26, 27,
　　31, 34, 44, 45, 58, 72, 74, 76,
　　79, 80, 82, 85, 114, 115, 116,
　　117, 150, 202.
　Isaac, Is, Isaque, 60, 61, 62, 65,
　　144, 146, 152, 160, 164, 165,
　　171, 172, 177, 186, 192, 193,
　　201, 213, 221, 233.
　Jacob, 6, 7, 15, 22, 24, 25, 26,
　　27, 44, 58, 61, 72, 76, 79, 80,
　　150, 164, 175.
　Jacobus, 46.
　Jakemyntje, 137.
　Janetje, Jenneke, Jane, Jean,
　　81, 86, 98, 101, 104, 106, 121,
　　129, 143, 188, 191, 196, 202,
　　208, 221, 229.
　John S., 58.
　Jonas, 194, 197, 201, 208, 210,
　　215, 222, 227, 235.
　Jonathan, 73, 80, 94, 97, 167,
　　172, 185, 197, 205, 216.
　Joseph, 88, 90, 230, 236.
　Josia, 213, 228.
　Lea, 79, 85.
　Lefever, 93.
　Lewis, Louys, Luiis, Luys,
　　Leuwies, Loys, etc., 2, 3, 40,
　　48, 54, 55, 57, 58, 60, 61, 63,
　　64, 65, 66, 67, 68, 69, 70, 74,
　　78, 94, 103, 107, 113, 120,
　　126, 129, 133, 150, 153, 193,

Dubois, Lewis, Louys, Luiis, Luys,
Leuwies, Loys, etc. (Con.).
194, 215, 222, 223, 227, 232,
236, 239.
Magdalena, 6, 76, 79, 114.
Margaret, 198, 204, 220, 236.
Mary, Polly, Maria, Mareytie,
2, 3, 73, 84, 86, 93, 94, 99,
123, 126, 177, 183, 193, 194,
201, 206, 214, 221, 229.
Methusalem, 45, 54, 55, 57, 68,
69, 70, 71, 76, 86, 116, 117,
144, 145, 150, 156, 158, 162,
170, 175, 200, 203, 205, 206,
210, 221, 228.
Nathaniel, 41, 48, 55, 67, 68,
69, 75, 92, 94, 99, 113, 183.
P., 58.
Peter, 58, 90, 227, 232.
Philip, 2, 3, 22, 23, 24, 25, 33,
44, 46, 62, 93, 99, 113, 238.
Rachel, 79, 81, 99, 101, 106,
108, 112, 113, 119, 123, 140,
153, 170, 184, 191, 197, 203,
209, 213, 220.
Rebecah, Rebecca, 78, 85, 89,
200, 205, 210, 216, 223.
Rulof, 58.
Salomon, 2, 3, 60, 62, 63, 145.
Samuel, 161, 166, 174, 193, 194,
200, 203.
Sarah, 58, 64, 87, 90, 161, 232,
236.
Simon, 4, 5, 12, 38, 39, 41, 46, 51,
56, 65, 66, 67, 73, 81, 91, 97,
100, 103, 106, 110, 119, 121.
S. L., 58.
Walter, 86, 217, 221.
Wessel, 58, 84, 153, 159, 164,
172, 177.
Wilhelmus, William, 101, 217,
223, 228, 236.
Dumond, Dumand, James, 215.
Johanna, 215.
Dunn, Dun, Anny, 88, 90, 228, 235.
George, 89.
Henry, 90, 230, 237.
James, 132, 152, 160.
John, 171, 182, 192, 203, 212.
Joseph, 87, 160.
Margaret, 196, 201.
Mary, Polly, 86, 93.
Rachel, 87.
Robert, 219, 225, 231.
Susannah, Sukey, 209, 213.
Thomas, 91.
Dusenberg, Elizabeth, 194.
Dusenbury, ——, 92.
Duseney, Catey, 131.
Duvall, William, 219, 226, 233.

E

Ean, Abraham, 22, 24, 25, 26, 34,
42, 44, 45, 50, 52, 57, 58, 78,

Ean, Abraham (Con.).
114, 128, 131, 133, 145, 163,
176, 187, 189, 195.
Annatje, 187, 200.
Catherine, Caty, 78, 195, 201,
207, 213, 215, 219, 225, 231.
Eli, Elias, 2, 3, 69, 70, 71, 77,
166, 176, 184, 195, 207, 217.
Elisabeth, 83, 120, 124, 129,
132, 176, 195, 207.
Geesje, 42.
Jan, 95.
Margritt, Grietje, 84, 120
125, 127, 132, 190.
Maria, 95, 215.
Mrs. Peter, 57.
Peter, 78, 87, 201, 205, 209,
215, 221, 237.
Rachel, 174, 178, 189, 194, 200,
205, 225, 234.
Sarah, 89, 129.
Ekhart, Jost, 190.
Ellenor, Nelly 177.
Ellis, Elles, Eunice, 90.
Jeremia, 172, 187.
Mary, 170.
Owen, 170.
Elmendorph, Blandina, 117, 141,
147, 163.
Brachy, 214.
Coenraet, 117.
Elisabeth, 182, 188.
Jacobus, 182, 187, 214, 232.
Wilhelmus, 117.
Elmore, Ambrosius, 77, 177, 184,
192, 203, 207, 216, 223.
Huldah, 91.
Rebecca, 182.
Simon, 182, 203.
Elsworth, Joseph, 143.
Willem, 119, 143, 157.
Eltinge, Abraham, 16, 22, 24, 25, 33,
44, 45, 58, 68, 72, 76, 79, 80,
85, 114, 153, 157, 180.
Annatien, Hanna, 79, 165, 199,
203, 204.
Catharina, Tryntje Catharintje,
57, 77, 79, 114, 168, 175, 180,
181, 187, 193, 200, 207, 225,
231.
Charles, 57, 91, 230, 237.
Cornelius, 45, 76, 79, 117, 141,
147.
Dinah, 86, 91, 201, 206, 211,
214, 220, 227, 234, 235, 238.
Ezekiel, Ezechiel, 44, 70, 71,
77, 78, 164, 173, 179, 185,
192, 199, 205, 212, 220, 228.
Gilbert, 58.
Henry Deyoo, 89.
Jacobus, 88.
Jacomyntje, 6, 79.
Jannitje, 153, 169, 176, 181,
189.
Johannes, 204, 208.

Eltinge (Con.).
John, 57, 70, 71, 77, 194, 212, 221.
Joseph, 90.
Joshua, 97, 188, 211.
Josia, 6, 7, 22, 23, 24, 25, 27, 28, 33, 44, 45, 46, 58, 70, 71, 76, 77, 79, 84, 97, 114, 153, 162, 178, 183, 185, 197, 199, 206, 218, 225.
Mrs. Louis, 58.
Magdalen, Lanah, Lena, 77, 78, 142, 164, 168, 173, 175, 179, 184, 185, 187, 190, 192, 195, 199, 201, 205, 210, 212, 220, 226, 228.
Margrita, 100, 103, 106, 130, 140, 143, 156.
Maria, 58, 78, 190, 193, 200, 208, 215, 223, 229.
Methusalah, 57.
Noach, 6, 7, 20, 22, 23, 24, 25, 26, 29, 30, 31, 33, 44, 45, 58, 72, 79, 56, 164, 169.
Peter, Petrus, 70, 71, 77, 191, 195, 199, 203, 208, 213, 219, 225.
Philip, 71, 77, 78, 168, 175, 180, 187, 193, 200, 207, 231.
Rebecca, 130.
Roelof, Rolif, 44, 45, 57, 58, 71, 72, 76, 78, 86, 92, 100, 114, 115, 116, 165, 168, 174, 183, 190, 201, 206, 211, 214, 220, 227, 235, 238.
Roelof I. or J., 45, 46, 115, 131.
Roelof Josias, 15, 22, 24, 25, 32, 58, 72, 79, 114, 115.
Salomon, 16, 25, 26, 45, 72, 78, 79, 80, 86, 114, 174, 179, 190, 199, 204, 209, 214, 219, 225, 233, 237.
Sarah, 58, 76, 78, 79, 114, 115, 165, 173, 177, 184, 189, 190, 195, 201, 206, 212, 220.
Elton, Margriet, 97, 98, 100, 102.
Ely, Montgomery, 144.
Emson, Leentje, 140.
Ennes, Ines, Innes, Jane, 195, 199, 203, 214.
Everett, Emerett, Daniel, 84, 148.
Elenor, 88, 220.
Fenny, 121.
Francisca, 115, 117, 145, 174, 178.
Martha, 84, 124, 131, 135, 142, 148, 155, 164, 171, 177, 178, 188.
Eversbach, Catharina, 75.

F

Farrington, Maragrieta, 106.
Thomas, 106.

Fenicks, Marretje, 98.
Fenkenkar, Tinkenau, Jacob, 107, 108.
Ferguson, Patty, 89.
Fernow, B, 99.
Ferris, Farres, Jane, 148.
Josia, 148.
Feure, This, 93.
Filkins, Jacobus, 129.
Flagler, Flaglor, Fleger, John, 189, 192, 196.
Flucwelling, Fluellen, Flewilling, Phebe, Phoebe, 233, 235, 239.
Forgenson, Forgeson, George, 102, 109.
Forman, Furman, Caty, 88.
Howell, Noel, Nowell, 184, 188, 198.
Sally, 87.
Forster, Sheffield, 197.
Forsyth, William, 91.
Fort, Debora, 101.
Frederick, 101.
Johannes, 120.
Forter, Step, 60.
Forthum, Clarissa, 178.
France, John, 189.
Frederick, Rachel, 217, 222, 227.
Freeligh, Daniel, 229.
Jane, 91.
Moses, 70.
Peter, Petrus, 79, 88, 100, 223.
Frelinghuisen, Eva, 163, 171, 181, 185.
Theodorus, 97, 100.
Freyer, Frere,—, 91, 92.
Aart, Art, 90, 229, 236.
Abraham, 2, 3, 60, 63, 64.
Agetta, Eggie, 41, 100, 102, 118, 201, 206, 209, 217.
Alida, 196.
Anne, Anny, Antje, Hannah, 87, 89, 90, 92, 98, 100, 102, 104, 105, 106, 108, 111, 160, 162, 181, 182, 190, 195, 203, 215, 220, 224, 226, 229, 230, 236, 239.
Antonie, 138, 142.
Benjamin, Benyamen, 41, 42, 47, 50, 51, 52, 66, 67, 68, 69, 70, 74, 81, 100, 106, 107, 111, 112, 121, 123, 132, 135, 139, 147, 160, 162, 176, 182, 193, 195, 230.
Betsy, 89.
Bregje, Brachie, 151, 156, 168, 182, 194, 209, 212, 221.
Caty, Trina, Catharin, 58, 89, 94, 152, 168, 171, 172, 179, 187, 188, 192, 196, 202, 207, 211, 216, 220, 221, 223, 224, 234, 237, 239.
Christian, 87, 215, 220, 224, 229, 236, 239.
Cornelius, 186, 215.

Freyer (*Con.*).
Daniel, 41, 50, 54, 82, 83, 110,
112, 120, 121, 122, 124, 127,
128, 131, 133, 141, 150, 153,
158, 182.
Echje, Eghje, 100, 105, 110.
Elias, 58, 87, 208, 213, 219,
226, 234, 238.
Elisa, Elysa, 42, 69, 77, 84,
112, 124, 131, 135, 142, 148,
155, 164, 171, 177, 178, 188.
Elizabeth, 89, 91, 97, 104, 107,
108, 132, 147, 186, 197, 203,
207, 210, 212, 218, 220, 223,
226, 227, 228, 232, 234, 237.
Elsje, Elchie, 81, 90, 98, 104,
106, 127, 159, 166, 167, 198.
Ezechiel, 85, 154, 167, 185,
200, 211, 215, 220, 226.
Gerretje, 142, 155, 210.
Gerrit, 38, 39, 41, 46, 52, 53,
56, 66, 67, 70, 74, 77, 91, 98,
100, 103, 106, 109, 112, 121,
124, 125, 128, 131, 140, 156,
198, 201, 237.
Henry, 57, 92.
Hester, Ester, 175, 189, 194,
197, 208, 209, 215, 220, 228,
238.
Hetty, 93.
Hughe, Huge, Heuge, Hugo,
Hugue, Huwe, 2, 3, 5, 19,
38, 39, 41, 46, 47, 53, 60, 61,
62, 63, 64, 65, 66, 67, 68, 74,
75, 98, 100, 104, 106, 121,
126, 133, 140, 145, 150, 159,
162, 166, 210, 212, 220, 227,
234.
Isaac, Yzaak, 41, 48, 52, 54,
56, 65, 74, 93, 95, 96, 97, 99,
108, 110, 113, 122, 123, 125,
128, 143, 153, 170, 183, 187,
196, 205.
Isaiah, Jesaias, 222, 228, 238.
Jacob, Yacob, 2, 3, 18, 19,
41, 47, 48, 49, 54, 56, 64, 66,
67, 68, 74, 75, 84, 92, 101,
107, 125, 126, 127, 130, 132,
149, 151, 168, 173, 190, 208,
220, 228, 234, 238.
Jacomyntie, 228.
Jane, Jenny, Yanatje, 57, 74,
81, 93, 97, 106, 136, 138,
142, 148, 154, 167, 181, 210,
214.
Jemimah, 222, 238.
Jeremias, 68, 69, 70, 76, 92,
139, 145, 150, 155, 163, 172,
177, 187, 197, 199, 234.
Johannis, Joannis, 18, 41, 49,
66, 67, 68, 69, 74, 75, 100,
102, 107, 108, 110, 118, 121,
124, 126, 127, 135, 139, 154,
162.
John, Jan, 58, 77, 91, 120, 161,

Freyer, John, Jan, (*Con.*).
171, 183, 197, 204, 221, 227,
230.
Jonas, 5, 42, 49, 54, 66, 67, 68,
74, 76, 78, 84, 86, 94, 98,
108, 109, 121, 126, 127, 130,
131, 132, 137, 140, 143, 150,
152, 159, 166, 185, 188, 192,
201, 205, 207, 211, 217, 220,
227.
Jonathan, 58, 81, 88, 139, 151,
161, 173, 181, 187, 226, 231,
236.
Joseph, 41, 48, 64, 83, 104,
111, 121, 126, 129, 137.
Joshua, 58, 87, 204, 207, 216,
236.
Lidia, 105.
Lucy, 219, 225, 231.
M., 227.
Magdalina, Lena, 89, 140, 192.
Margriet, Margaret, 148, 191,
195, 202, 216, 220, 230, 234.
Maria, Mary, Marytje, 63, 64,
74, 78, 81, 82, 85, 86, 87, 88,
90, 93, 95, 96, 97, 98, 99, 100,
103, 104, 105, 106, 109, 110,
111, 112, 115, 119, 121, 125,
127, 128, 131, 133, 140, 143,
152, 153, 154, 156, 158, 166,
173, 174, 180, 186, 187, 188,
194, 196, 197, 198, 199, 201,
203, 204, 205, 207, 209, 210,
211, 219, 221, 225, 230, 237.
Martynes, 75, 85, 103, 152, 154,
173, 230, 234.
Maytje, 161.
Moses, 123, 181, 190, 195.
Paulus, 41, 75, 126, 131, 134,
139, 142, 154, 181, 189, 226,
229, 237.
Petrus, 42, 49, 54, 56, 67, 68,
75, 84, 105, 132, 174, 194.
Rachel, 91, 189, 193, 197, 201,
204, 205, 210, 218, 219, 228,
232, 234.
Rebecca, 74, 80, 94, 96, 98,
103, 106, 116.
Ruth, 234, 238.
Salomon, 154.
Sarah, 74, 86, 99, 101, 107, 126,
149, 151, 168, 173, 181, 204,
209, 219, 221, 226, 233.
Simon, 42, 49, 52, 54, 55, 56, 57,
91, 103, 118, 131, 133, 141,
147, 155, 164, 177, 181, 182,
188, 191, 195, 210, 234, 237.
Stephen, 58.
Thomas, 166, 174, 208.
Wyntie, Winche, 86, 104, 111,
112, 143, 202, 208, 213, 233.
Zacharias, 170, 188, 191, 196,
202, 208, 214, 221, 229.
Fryenmoet, Frymoet, J. C, 81, 96,
98, 100.

Frysiner, Vrysyn, Coenraed, 216, 220.

G

Galey, Daniel, 218.
Gallasbie, James, 177.
Garretson, Geritze, Gerrison, Lena, 172.
   Rachel, 117, 142, 148, 157.
Gasherie, Chasherje, Jan, 80.
   Mary, 81.
Gee, Molly, 162.
   Moses, 85.
   Uriah, 87.
Geer, Years, Dolly, Mary, 79, 210, 211, 213, 216, 222, 224, 231, 235, 238.
Gerow, Jerow, Elizabeth, Betsy, 86, 200, 204, 220.
Gilbert, Phebe, 169, 175, 181, 188.
Glaserin, Glaesing, An Marie, 111, 113, 129, 131.
Goetschius, Goetchius, Abraham, 146.
   Cathrina, 13.
   Do., 9, 98.
   Hendricus, Henry, 193, 205, 218, 226.
   Jacob, 211, 218.
   J. H. or Henry, 65, 66, 73, 75, 81, 96, 98, 99.
   Johannes Mauritius, J. M., 4, 5, 9, 10, 12, 13, 81, 120.
   Margrita, 176.
   Mauritius, 7.
   Rachel, 160, 172, 185, 197, 205, 216.
   Sally, 218.
   Salome, 87.
   Stephanus, Stephen, 16, 18, 19, 20, 59, 76, 84, 150, 160, 167, 176, 185.
Goff, David, 170, 184.
Graham, Andries, 95.
   Anne, 87.
   Beelletie, 95.
   Daniel, 55, 67, 75.
   Elisabeth, 83.
   Rachel, 165, 170, 176, 181.
Grame (Graham?), Jane, 100.
Granigje, Maria, 107.
Gray, Charles, 91.
Green, Christoffel, 179, 183, 190, 194, 199, 206, 214, 221, 230.
   Henry, 82, 112, 119, 122, 125, 127, 129, 131, 136, 164, 179.
   Jacob, 60, 167, 175, 180.
   Jane, 93.
Griffin, Anna, 104, 118.
   Caterine, 95.
   Charity, 145.
   Elanor, 133, 154, 162.
   Jean, John, 95, 97, 112, 133.
   Joh., 126.

Griffin (*Con.*).
   Joseph, 100, 102, 104, 107, 109, 112, 120.
   Louwerents, 104.
   Margarita, 100, 130, 144.
   Martynus, Martin, 120, 122, 125, 127, 129, 132, 136, 142, 148, 156.
   Nelly, 127, 130, 131, 136, 141, 145, 151.
   Rebecca, 100, 104.
   Seelitje, Sealy, Sile, 124, 126, 127, 130, 132, 136, 163.
Grootsch, Joh, 107.
   Maria, 107.
Gue, Henry Dickinson, 93.
Guimar, Quimar, Gemaar, Ester, 62, Pierre, 63.

H

Haarloo, William, 98.
Hais, James, 90.
Halstead, Halsted, Holstead, Abraham, 78, 218, 227.
   Isaac, 78, 220, 225, 232.
   Jacob, 78, 88, 221, 224, 235.
   John, 90, 93, 198, 205, 230.
   Smith, 192, 219, 224.
Handmor, Handmor, David, 177.
   Francis, 169, 175, 181, 188.
Hannyson, Richard, 104.
Hansz, Aart, 114.
Hardenberg, Hardenburgh, Hardenbergh, Abraham, 5, 66, 74, 81, 83, 97, 100, 101, 104, 106, 198, 204, 220, 236.
   Ann, 46.
   Catherine, 92.
   Charles, 74, 180, 186, 197.
   Cornelia, 133, 138, 147, 172.
   Elias, 133, 138, 147, 172.
   Gerardus, 116, 128, 134, 145.
   Hans, 74.
   Herman, 87.
   Isack, 59, 165, 170, 176, 181.
   Jacob, 74, 86, 105, 208.
   Jacobus, 45, 181.
   Jane, 79, 235.
   Johannes, 4, 12, 18, 41, 42, 48, 49, 51, 55, 65, 66, 67, 68, 73, 75, 81, 93, 94, 104, 105, 108, 110, 112, 121, 126, 140.
   John, 57, 59, 60, 97, 133, 153, 162, 167, 235.
   Lowis, 174, 177, 179, 183, 199, 222.
   Margrietje, 187.
   Mary, Polly, Maria, Maritje, 42, 73, 87, 90, 93, 94, 97, 101, 104, 105, 108, 124, 174, 179, 203, 218, 221, 222, 228, 230, 236.
   Myer, 209.
   Nelly, 92, 235.
   Peggy, 133.

Hardenberg (Con.).
Petrus, 190.
Rachel, 74, 187.
Richard, 90, 227, 239.
Sarah, 90, 164.
Thomas, 88.
Hardford, Hartford, Marybah, Moribah, 151, 155, 163, 168, 176.
Harding, George, 83.
Harp, Henry, 59, 108, 149, 162.
Harris, Herres, Abraham, 86, 206, 212, 225, 232.
Isack, 59, 136, 142, 148, 154, 160, 167.
Margaret, Margitje, 196, 200, 205.
Marretje, 181.
Hart, Hert, Lidia, 158, 165, 172, 184, 189, 193, 200, 213.
Paggy, 157.
Sara, 165.
Hasbrouck, Abraham, 2, 3, 34, 42, 48, 51, 53, 60, 61, 62, 63, 64, 89, 94, 95, 100, 106, 128, 227, 232, 233.
Altje, 91.
Anne, 63, 215.
Benjamin, 78, 81, 87, 93, 99, 112, 123, 129, 169, 176, 183, 187, 192, 200.
Catarina, 140.
Cornelia, 58.
Cornelius, 48, 55.
Daniel, 4, 65, 80, 81, 95, 96, 97, 171, 191, 195, 202, 204, 210, 211, 216, 220, 227.
David, 68, 75, 124, 125, 131, 134, 138, 143, 149, 155, 162.
Dievertje, 104.
Dinah, 90, 228, 234, 239.
Elias, 129.
Elizabeth, 88, 143, 166, 176, 184, 207, 213, 217, 222, 228.
Elsjie, Else, 84, 87, 94, 95, 112, 125, 128, 130, 132, 137, 143, 148, 149, 158, 209.
Ester, Hester, 62, 63, 76, 84, 94, 95, 129, 132, 137, 144, 154, 200.
Isaac, 41, 47, 48, 55, 64, 95, 97, 98, 100, 105, 220.
Jacob, 2, 3, 5, 18, 19, 38, 39, 40, 42, 47, 48, 49, 50, 51, 55, 57, 62, 65, 66, 67, 68, 69, 73, 74, 81, 85, 89, 94, 95, 96, 98, 100, 101, 104, 105, 106, 121, 129, 132, 187, 199, 204, 210, 215, 221, 230.
Jacobus, Kobus, 4, 12, 41, 50, 51, 54, 55, 66, 67, 68, 69, 73, 74, 77, 104, 106, 111, 113, 119, 122, 123, 166, 169.
Jane, Jannetje, 89, 100, 132, 226, 232.

Hasbrouck (Con.).
Jer., Jeremia, 60, 197.
Jesaias, 130, 140, 143, 149, 153, 160, 162, 166, 174, 179, 188.
Johannes, 167, 173, 183, 189, 193, 202.
John, Jan, Jean, Yan, 42, 49, 60, 61, 62, 63, 66, 74, 113, 120, 124, 234.
Jonas, 82, 140, 195.
Josaphat, 42, 49, 52, 75, 83, 121, 124, 127, 128, 131, 136, 144, 153, 202, 207.
Joseph, 2, 3, 42, 68, 74, 75, 76, 89, 128, 137, 143, 150, 158, 166, 226, 232.
Josiah, 70, 88, 157, 175, 194, 202, 211, 226, 237.
Josua, 220.
Lewis, 87.
Margaret, 58, 202.
Marie, Maria, 60, 61, 62, 80, 100, 101, 104, 105, 106, 137, 138, 188.
Methuselem, 212, 217, 224, 233, 237.
Noah, 93.
Petronella, Paternella, 80, 97, 100.
Petrus, Peter, 42, 46, 49, 50, 52, 68, 69, 75, 82, 90, 119, 123, 126, 129, 132, 136, 145, 151, 161, 168, 190, 226, 230.
Philip, 89.
Rachal, Rachel, 60, 63, 64, 84, 87, 88, 97, 222.
Rolof, 156, 169, 176, 181, 189, 229.
Salomon, 65, 88, 94, 95, 221, 226, 235, 238.
Samuel, 90, 228, 236.
Sara, Sally, Selly, 73, 90, 94, 95, 190, 196, 204, 212, 227, 232, 238.
Simon, 74.
Wilhelmus, William, 88, 196, 201, 206, 209, 217, 222.
Wyntje, Waantea, Wencha, Wyntie, 41, 46, 49, 55, 73, 86, 95, 96, 97, 124, 125, 130, 171, 195, 201, 207, 211, 217, 227, 229.
Zacharias, 85, 144, 153, 159, 165.
Haye, Marie, 62.
Haynes, (see Hyns), Hannah, 86.
Hefer, Elizabeth, 94.
Heffy, Peggy, 179.
Hegeman, Isack, 160.
Neltje, 160.
Heger, Catarina, 144, 154.
Hellebeeker, Grietje, 127.
Helm, Hellen, Abram, 98, 102, 110, 117.
Anna, 95, 100.

Helm (*Con.*).
　Catryna, 102, 104, 109, 125, 129.
　Elisabeth, Betje, Lisabeth, 74, 96, 98, 102, 103, 105, 109, 111, 120, 122, 154, 167.
　Eva, 131.
　Jacob, 100, 101, 102, 106, 107, 109, 124.
　Johanna, Hanna, 98, 102, 114, 187.
　Margrita, 107, 109.
　Maria, 83, 121, 124, 127, 133, 141, 150.
　Petrus, 187.
　Simon, Zymon, 60, 94, 95, 100, 167, 182.
　Hendricks, Arriantje, 160, 171, 180, 185.
　Jacob, 228.
　Lawrence, Lowrance, 59, 131, 138, 162, 172.
　Simon, 188.
Hennessey, Margriet, 137.
Hennisce, Richard, 100.
Hermanse, Heermance, Hermance, Edward, 182.
　Jacob, 219, 225, 232.
　Maretje, 182.
Hess, Abram, 59, 114, 157.
　Catrina, 117.
　Mary, 216.
　Matheus, 175, 180, 189.
　Robert, 175.
Heyms, Heems, Hyms, Frederick, 124, 126, 127, 130, 132, 136.
　Johan Frederick, 124.
Hill, Rachel, 88, 231.
Hoff, Huff, Margriet, 184, 188, 198.
Hofman, Hoffman, Adam, 126.
　Betsy, 90.
　Evert, 90, 125.
　Jacobus, 73.
　Johan Adam, 102.
　John, 59, 164.
　Zacharias, Sacharyas, 59, 81, 96, 98, 99, 163.
Hog, Hogg, Abram, 59, 158, 173.
　John, 88.
Hogelandt, Hogland, Hoogland, Maria, 75, 131, 134, 143, 149, 155, 162.
Holt, John, 8.
Hood, Hoed, Abraham, 192, 196, 208.
　Anny, 219, 223, 228.
　Elenor, 219, 236.
　Elizabeth, 156, 165, 175, 180, 186.
　Isaac, 91, 234.
　John, 91, 234.
　Laurence, 176, 180.
　Rachel, 186, 198, 203, 208.
　Robert, 86, 202, 208, 216.

Hood (*Con.*).
　William, 59, 78, 118, 128, 131, 188, 196, 200, 206, 212, 217, 223, 229, 237.
Hoogteling, Annatje, 76.
　Barbara, 170.
　Jannetje, 7, 74, 79.
　Jeremia, 155.
　John, 93.
　Margarita, 128.
!Ioornbeek, Garrit, 85.
　Gideon, 141, 146.
　Helen, 232.
　Jacob, 172.
　Jane, Yannetye, 131, 220, 225, 230, 237.
　Johannes, 137, 233.
　John, 91.
　Lany, 226.
Hopensted, Frederick, 59, 164.
Hoyt, Zachariah, 90.
Huber, Cathrina, 118.
　Georg, 75, 118.
Hubsch, Anna Maria, 105.
　Jacob, 105.
Huey, Ann, 79, 113.
　James, 22, 24, 25, 28, 44, 46, 58.
　Margarita, Margaretha, 76, 79, 116.
Hull, Laura, 91.
　Lucretia, 89.
Hunt, Henry, 88.
　Susan, 90.
Hunter, Thomas, 87.
Hutchins, Jacob, 90.
Hyns, (see Haynes), Anna, 163.
　Benjamin, 163.

I

Irwin, Ervin, Erwin, Allen, 200, 209, 216, 224, 231.
　Elizabeth, 85.
　George, 83.
　James, 85.
　John, 90.
　Margaret, 203, 208.
　William, 78, 88, 195, 199, 203, 214.

J

Jansen, Johnson, Abraham, 87, 138, 147.
　Anna, Antje, Hanah, 101, 108, 209.
　Catharina, Catrina, 134, 147.
　Dirk, 138, 142, 191.
　Elizabeth, 88, 221, 228, 236.
　Hester, Ester, 108, 110, 113, 123, 128, 153, 166, 168, 174.
　Isack, 134, 140.
　Jacob, 92.
　Johannes, 101, 225.
　John, 87, 209, 217.
　Jonathan, 87.

Jansen (Con.).
　Margaret, Margriet, 92, 104, 236.
　Maria, 217, 224, 232.
　Mathew, 88.
　Mercy, 87.
　Peter, 87, 195, 199, 205, 214.
　Rachel, 96, 102, 123, 179, 192, 196, 203, 209.
　Rebeccah, 89, 93, 224.
　Richard, 148.
　Simon, 219, 227.
　Thomas, 15.
　Zachary, 108, 123.
Jee, Maria, 75.
Jenkins, Jinkins, Jenkens, Albert, 92.
　Bridget, 215, 222, 227, 236, 239.
　Halen, 93.
　Hannah, 93.
　John, 86.
　Lambert, 181, 190.
　Magdalin, 239.
　Sally, 206.
　William, Wm., 77, 87, 206, 218.
Jeple, Yaple, etc., Adam, 160, 171, 180, 185, 214, 222, 231.
　Joseph, 238.
　Maria, 214.
Jerom, Eliphas, 161.
Johnston (see also Jansen), Jeremiah, 83.
　Peter, 206.
Jones, Henry, 89.
　Thomas, 157, 159, 168, 173.
Jumens, Lidia, 175.

K

Kain, Francis, 83.
Kalleheyn, Cornelius, 104.
Keen, Jimmy, 125.
Keesler, Sarah, 91.
Kelly, Killy, Celly, Margritt, 123, 151, 165.
　Paggy, 83.
Kerner, Kern, Cornelius, 102, 165, 176.
　Margrita, 165.
　Susanna, 165.
Kerny, Karney, Daniel, 59, 167.
Ketcham, Katcham, Kitcham, Phebe, 177, 181, 191, 195, 210.
Keter, Keeter, Cetur, Abraham, 131.
　Dirk, 131.
　Jacob, 131, 186.
　Janetje, 102.
　John, 182.
　Katrina, 102.
　Petrus, Peter, 159, 170, 186.
　Rachel, 131.
Keyser, Anatje, Hannah, 86, 173, 201.
　Andries, 141.
　Anganietje, 103.

Keyser (Con.).
　Charles, 176.
　Cornelius, 102, 134, 141, 149.
　Dirck, 95, 110, 126.
　Edward, 176.
　Elisabeth, Lisabeth, 102, 105, 111, 116, 119, 130, 135, 144, 149.
　Elsje, 176.
　Ephraim, 129, 139, 149, 166, 172, 178.
　Frederik, 136, 144.
　Isack, 154, 174.
　Jacob, 134. 139, 144, 146, 152, 178, 180.
　Johannes, 139.
　Lydia, Liedia, 97, 103, 113.
　Margaret, Grietje, 173, 222.
　Maria, 101, 103, 105, 141.
　Nicholaes, 102.
　Peter, 233.
　Rachel, 135.
　Sarah, 229.
Kidney, Gedney, James, 216, 221, 228, 234.
　Lany, 89, 224.
　Myndert, 91, 233.
　Robert, 91.
　William, 186, 191.
Kimbergh, George, 88.
　Mynje, 90.
　Susan, 89.
Kittle, Frederik, 148.
Klaarwaater, Abraham, 109, 115, 118, 123.
　Daniel, 59, 60, 165, 172.
　Edward, 89, 237.
　Elizabeth, 135.
　Ester, Hester, 115, 135.
　Eva, 115, 149.
　Frederik, 118.
　Jacob, 60.
　John, 92.
　Joseph, 59, 161, 179.
　Maria, Mareytie, Molly, 87, 118, 144, 162.
　Martynus, 85, 144, 157, 165.
　Peter, 91, 144, 151.
　Rachel, 233.
　Sacharias, 97.
　Thomas, 59, 60, 89, 149, 160, 167, 179.
　Wyntje, 163, 169.
Klein, Kleyn, Klyn, Annatje, 149, 151.
　Elizabeth, 107, 123, 129.
　Jacob, 139, 149, 151.
　Johannes, 102, 107, 111, 119, 123, 129, 130, 135, 149, 151.
　John, 105.
　Lena, 129, 139, 149, 166, 172, 178.
Knees, Margaret, 97.
Kniffins, Nathaniel, 88.
Koens, Joost, 129.

Kool, Cool, Abram, Abraham, 98, 103, 106, 108, 125.
Barent, 98, 99.
Cornelis, Cornelius, 98, 103, 115.
Geertje, 114.
Jennie, Jannatje, 163, 170, 182, 193.
Jesse, 181.
Marritje, 97.
Petrus, 97, 114.
Kortregt, Jannetjen, 62.
Kouwenover, Cowenover, Engeltie, 123, 129.
Hans, 123.
Kraig, Gordon, 217.
Reuben C., 90.
Kreig, James, 89.
Kritzinger, Catrina, 76, 153, 164, 169, 180, 186, 192, 199.
John, 161.
Polly, 161.
Sara, 178.
Susanna, 164, 173, 177, 199.
Krom, Crom, Bridget, 173.
Cornelius, 180.
Jane, 199.
Jonathan, 180.
Niekus, 27.
Sara, 171.
Wyntje, 92.
Kroos, Johannes, 107.
Merya, 107.
Kuykendal, Cuikendal, Sytje, 98, 103.

L

Lane, Anne, 132, 152, 160.
Elizabeth, 140.
Phebe, 85.
La Roy (see Leroy).
La Toynelle, Estel, Estere, 61, 62.
Lattin, Lea, 93.
Lawson, Robert, 89.
Le Blan, Marie, 61, 62.
Le Conte, Mary, 64, 80.
Lefever, Abraham, 4, 12, 19, 38, 39, 42, 49, 50, 53, 65, 66, 67, 68, 73, 89, 92, 98, 101, 102, 104, 106, 110, 122, 124, 126, 132, 218, 223, 227, 236.
Andries, Andreas, Andre, Andrew, 2, 3, 18, 40, 41, 47, 49, 50, 53, 65, 66, 67, 68, 69, 70, 73, 77, 81, 87, 99, 103, 106, 108, 112, 119, 123, 124, 132, 133, 145, 159, 178, 184, 186, 190, 217, 224, 233.
Annatje, Anne, 180, 186, 197, 219, 228, 235.
Catrina, Catreyntie, Tryntje, 81, 84, 92, 97, 100, 103, 110, 122, 129, 135, 143, 145, 153, 158, 159, 164, 172, 177, 179, 186, 187, 194, 238.
Christopher, 58, 93, 238.

Lefever (Con.).
Cornelia, 174.
Daniel, 19, 41, 50, 53, 67, 68, 69, 74, 81, 101, 106, 108, 113, 121, 126, 128, 142. 154, 155, 175.
Debora, 213.
Elizabeth, 76, 80, 94, 97, 128, 131, 133, 140, 148, 155, 159, 165, 175, 186, 201, 214, 218, 231.
Elsjie, 82, 119.
Gertruy, Guirtrey, 145, 148, 155, 168, 169, 175, 178, 185, 191.
Getty, Gitty, 58, 88.
Isaac, 2, 3, 42, 47, 53, 74, 77, 96, 133, 134, 137, 144, 150, 161, 168, 209, 212.
Jacob, 58, 69, 70, 71, 77, 156, 164, 174, 180, 192, 206.
James, Jacobus, 88, 221, 223, 228, 236.
Jean, John, Jan, 2, 3, 46, 50, 55, 64, 84, 129, 131, 133, 137, 146, 152, 162, 221, 232, 236.
Jenneke, Jane, 161, 166, 174, 193, 194, 200, 203.
Johannes, 66, 74, 75, 81, 86, 90, 100, 111, 132, 159, 166, 172, 179, 183, 190, 196, 202, 203.
Jonathan, 90, 179, 188, 196, 220, 228, 234, 239.
Josiah P., 57.
Louis, 58.
Magdalena, Madalena, Lena, 81, 88, 96, 97, 98, 99, 103, 106, 132, 184, 186, 190, 214, 221, 226, 235, 238.
Margrietje, Margaret, Margritt, 73, 75, 81, 96, 99, 100, 110, 113, 120, 122, 125, 128, 136, 137, 164, 214.
Maria, Marieka, 58, 77, 81, 93, 96, 97, 102, 103, 106, 108, 110, 121, 126, 129, 131, 132, 133, 134, 137, 140, 142, 144, 146, 148, 150, 154, 161, 168, 170, 180, 189, 202, 217, 238.
Matheus, Matthew, 42, 51, 56, 58, 68, 69, 70, 76, 80, 92, 96, 99, 112, 128, 129, 131, 133, 140, 148, 155, 165, 175, 201, 214, 218, 231.
Moses, 71, 78, 86, 201, 206, 214, 218, 231.
Nathaniel, Nath., 38, 39, 40, 47, 53, 66, 67, 73, 82, 84, 97, 103, 106, 112, 113, 124, 126, 128, 131, 134, 144, 147, 155, 159, 226, 232.
Noach, 85, 164, 177, 184, 191, 197.
Petronella, 34, 41, 49, 73, 95, 96.

17

Lefever (*Con.*).
  Petrus, Peter, 42, 47, 48, 50, 52, 53, 67, 68, 69, 70, 71, 75, 77, 100, 106, 108, 110, 111, 118, 120, 124, 131, 134, 137, 145, 158, 164, 165, 168, 174, 175, 179, 180, 184, 187, 190, 195, 201, 210, 214, 226.
  Philip, 69, 70, 71, 77, 78, 187, 192, 199, 207.
  Rachel, 58, 100, 103, 133, 164, 194, 197, 201, 208, 210, 215, 222, 227, 235.
  Salomon, 164, 199.
  Sara, 73, 74, 76, 77, 89, 92, 107, 113, 121, 158, 163, 170, 176, 178, 181, 183, 188, 192, 193, 199, 200, 206, 208, 211, 212, 218, 223, 225, 227.
  Symon, Simeon, 61, 69, 77, 80, 94, 95, 96, 97, 178, 210, 214, 218, 224, 231, 238.
Le Munyer, Lemonjon, Betsy, 88.
  Ester, 168, 173.
  Hannah, 134, 140.
  John, 59, 151, 161, 171, 185, 191.
  Joseph, 90.
  Margaret, 217.
  Mary, 157, 159, 168, 173.
  Philip, 168, 175, 180.
  Rachel, 93.
  Thomas, 88, 134.
Leroe, Larow, Le Rue, Polly, Mary, 190, 194, 199, 206, 213, 222, 233.
Leroy, La Roy, Le Rue, Betcy, Elizabeth, 186, 191.
  Hetty, 88.
  Marie, 62, 63, 64.
  Maryam, Marie Anne, Marian, 60, 63, 64.
  Pieter, 129, 144.
  Robert, 149, 169, 173, 184, 196, 201.
Lindebecker, Jeremias, 126.
Linkester, Caroline, 225.
Linus, Henry, 77.
Litz, Lits, Daniel, 161.
  Hilletje, 107, 111.
  Johannes, 140.
  Lea, 161.
  Lidia, 183.
  Martha, 107, 170, 175, 180, 189.
  Roeluf, Rulof, 107, 109, 112, 158.
  Williem, Willem, 82, 107, 111, 168, 189.
Lockwood, Henry, 91.
  Phabe, 88.
  Sarah, 171, 182, 192, 203, 212.
  Uriah, 90.
Longsberry, Abigael, 186.
Loundsbury, Richard, 86.
Lounsberry, Jesse, 93.

Louw, Low, etc., —90.
  Abraham, 6.
  Antje, Anne, 115, 130, 132, 138, 144, 197, 214.
  Catharine, Treyntje, 74, 77, 78, 86, 88, 107, 114, 117, 168, 171, 174, 178, 184, 191, 195, 223, 230.
  Caty, 163.
  Cornelius, 34, 58, 114, 115.
  Daniel, 86, 91, 200, 204, 214, 220.
  David, 25, 68, 76, 79, 80, 113, 116, 117, 141, 147, 155, 160, 171, 177, 190.
  Deborah, 78, 160, 215, 224, 231, 238.
  Elizabeth, 77, 79, 183, 192, 197, 206, 211, 214, 217.
  Ezechiel, Ez., 167, 174, 183, 197, 204, 209.
  Francisca, 169.
  Gideon, 102.
  Gitty, 93.
  Grittie, 109, 115.
  Hester, 174, 180, 184.
  I. C., 70.
  Isaac, 7, 15, 22, 24, 25, 26, 27, 29, 44, 45, 58, 72, 74, 79, 86, 115, 117, 145, 169, 174, 178, 201, 205, 209, 214, 218, 225, 231.
  Jacob, 68, 69, 70, 77, 85, 115, 130, 142, 175, 177, 200, 202, 203.
  Jannetje, Jane, Yanneke, 74, 86, 96, 117, 142, 202.
  Jehu, 85, 163, 171, 181.
  Jeremias, 139, 147, 167, 189.
  Johannis, 41, 47, 50, 66, 74, 80, 96, 98, 103, 106, 109.
  John, 70, 77.
  Jonathan, 74, 91, 106, 230.
  Judith, Judic, 90, 226, 230, 235, 239.
  Maria, 76, 79, 86, 103, 106, 114, 115, 116, 131, 165, 168, 174, 183, 190, 203, 206, 210, 221, 228.
  Petrus, 7, 22, 24, 31, 32, 44, 45, 58, 74, 79, 117.
  Rebecca, 96.
  Sara, 6, 74, 76, 79, 107, 114, 115, 116, 117, 138, 139, 178, 221, 232.
  Simeon, 42, 55, 56, 57, 69, 70, 76, 133, 138, 146, 152, 159, 168, 202, 204, 214, 220.
  Solomon, 7, 16, 22, 24, 25, 34, 44, 45, 46, 58, 68, 72, 76, 79, 80, 88, 96, 112, 114, 116, 138, 167, 174, 180, 184.
  William, 222.
Lucker, Luker, Hanyorg, Han-York, 109, 113.

Lucy, Margaretha, 79.

M

Maby, Mabee, Maybee, Fanny, 89.
  Rachel, 129, 144.
McAvey, McCaby, etc., Matthew,
  Matheus, 116, 130, 132, 134,
  138, 142, 146, 151, 156, 162.
McClaghley, James, 131.
McCollagh, McCollogh, McCullogh,
  James, 78, 88, 223, 230.
MacCollum, McCollum, Abraham,
  87.
  Eva, 86.
  Mathew, 89.
McCord, Robert, 92.
Maccy, Alexander, 144.
  David, 144.
McDonald, M'Danold, Caty, Kete,
  167, 173, 183, 189, 193, 202.
  Elisabeth, Betsy, 195, 215, 221,
  229.
  Levi, 169, 195, 202.
  Polly, 206.
  William, 60, 86, 173, 195, 201,
  206.
Mackey, Macky, Charles, 195.
  Susannah, 90.
McKinley, Elizabeth, 169, 176.
  Richard, 200, 207, 211, 215,
  233.
McMollin, Christina, 133, 138, 146,
  152, 159, 168, 202.
  Elsy, 84.
McNeel, John, 59, 160.
Mahony James, 180.
Manny, Sarah, 170,
Marinus, David, 12.
Masten, Anne, 197.
  Cornelius, 18, 127.
  Eliza, 86.
  Ezechiel, 19.
  Ida, 93.
  James, 92.
  Jeremiah, 93.
  Margriet, 193, 205, 218, 220,
  226.
  Matheus, 122, 127.
  Simon, 88.
  Stephan, 89.
  Tjatje, 186.
Masters, Robert, 128, 130, 137.
Mauses (see Moues), Magdalenah,
  96.
Meier, Annetje, 175.
  Arie, 182.
  Jacobus, 178.
  John H., 20, 85.
  Margaret, 85, 199.
  Sarah, 198, 205.
Merkil, Markel, Merkel, Benjamin,
  189.
  Cornelia, 189, 194, 200, 207,
  227.

Merrit, Meret, —— 93.
  Hannah, Annatye, 87, 207, 212.
Meynema, Do., Benjamin, 99, 100.
Michaels, Nancy, 86.
Middag, Margriet, 113.
Miller, Muller, —— 93.
  Helegond, 111.
  Pitter, 111.
  Rachel, 214, 223, 227, 231.
  Rebeccah, 89.
Minickhouse, Elener, 232.
Minten, Zara, 62.
Mitchell, Michel, Amassa, Amasy,
  193, 198, 202, 213, 217, 225,
  229.
  James, 87.
Mkel, Mckel, Haghe, Agaer, 61.
Montanye, George D. L., 93.
Moore, Hannah, 86, 204, 212, 216,
  222, 228, 232.
  Jane, 78.
Morris, Maria, 180.
Moues (see Mauses), Ury, 96.
Moul, Moule, Ann, 137.
  Maria, 184.
  Robert, 211.
Moulinars, J. J., 95.
Mounin, John, 81.
Mullen, Simon, 90.
Munson, Ira, 91.
Munster, John E., 58.
Myndard, Joseph, 90.

N

Newkerk, Adrian, 74, 96, 101.
  Anna, 95.
  Gerrit, 93, 95.
Nice, Neas, Annah, 96.
  Elisabeth, 191, 195, 200, 204,
  219.
  Hans Yory, 74.
  Jacob, 96.
  Johan George, 99.
  Johannes, 157.
  John, 87.
  Jurrie, Jury, 103, 140.
  Lourence, 143, 152.
  Magdalena, 140, 142, 157, 170.
  Margriet, 134, 167.
Niffins, —— 87.
North, S., 92.
Nostrand, Mary, 200.
Numan, Debora, 85.
Nyberg, Elizabeth, 150.

O

Odle, Jonathan, 85.
Oliver, Mary, 142, 156.
Oosterhoud, Oosterhoudt, Osterhout,
  Aplony, 211.
  Catrina, 160.
  Hermanus, 59, 160.
  Teunis, 114.
  Willem, 112.

Oostrander, Ostrander, —— 91.
   Ann, 91.
   Christophel, Stoffel, 41, 48, 52, 57, 120.
   Cornelius, 88, 220.
   David, 19, 41, 123, 129, 220, 226.
   Debora, 120.
   Dennis, 87.
   Elisa, 179, 188, 200.
   Elizabeth, 85, 204.
   Gideon, 125, 194.
   Henerik, Henry, 75, 88, 117.
   Hermanus, 4, 12, 18, 102, 104, 121.
   Jonathan, 84, 111, 123.
   Lambertha, 196.
   Laura, 77, 183, 191, 198, 207.
   Lea, 88.
   Lena, 86, 102, 113, 193.
   Lydia, 89.
   Marcus, 41, 66, 67, 75, 117, 119, 123.
   Maria, 88, 183.
   Petrus, 4, 12, 18, 41, 66, 74, 101, 103, 108, 109, 111, 113, 118, 120, 122, 125, 178.
   Rebeccah, 92.
   Reuben, 93.
   Sally, 92.
   Silvester, 92.
   Wilhelmus, Helmus, 41, 49, 84, 113, 127.
Ophrel, Michael, 137.
Owen, James, 91.
Owens, Thomas, 77, 193, 198, 204, 208, 213.

P

Pagh, John, 88.
Palmatier, Abraham, 140.
   Catryntje, Tryntje, 153, 188, 192.
   Dina, Blandina, Deana, Dintje, 149, 169, 173, 184, 196, 201.
   Elizabeth, 168, 189, 196.
   Isack, 147, 157.
   Johanna, Hannah, 85, 185, 192, 198.
   Neltje, Nele, 147, 153, 160, 168, 185.
   Sarah, Seletje, Sally, 86, 92, 143, 149, 157, 161, 184, 196, 202.
Pardee, —— 92.
   Elizabeth, 88.
Parker, Anna, 135.
   David, 238.
   John, 121.
   Mary, 128, 130, 137.
Parleman, Abraham, 91.
   Edward, 87.
   Johannes, 18, 130.
Parrine, Elisabeth, 187.

Parrine (*Con.*).
   James, 216, 223, 229, 237.
   John, 167.
   Nella, 167.
Patterson, Petterson, Enne, 171.
   William, 76.
Patty, Abby, 86.
Paulis, Mary, 93.
Pawling, Paling, Margrietje, 156, 166, 177, 194.
Peek, Phebe, 167.
Pekker, Catrina, 190.
Pennic, Elizabeth, 159.
Pennik, Sara, 99.
Penny, Anne, 84.
Perkens, Anna, 139.
Persen, Jannetje, 82.
Personius, Jacobus, 135.
Petilon, Petilion, Marie, 61, 62, 63.
Pettey, Lydia, 86.
Philips, David, 185, 191.
Phillips, Ellenor, 129.
Ploeg, Ploegh, Aldert, Albert, 101, 103, 109.
   Maretie, 112, 119.
Polhemus, Ame, 193.
   Cornelius, 84.
   Jane, 89.
   John, 222.
   Jordan, 140, 145, 149, 155, 161, 167, 174, 182, 186.
Poor, Robert, Robin, 132, 137.
Preskit, Anna, 96.
Preslar, Maria, 172.
Pride, Uriah, 87.
Purdee, Hannah, 228.

Q

Quantin, Quentin, Quntin, Moyse, 60, 63.
   Peronne, 62.
Quemby, James, 92.
Quick, Jacob, 87.
   Thomas, 99.
Quimar, see Guimaar.

R

Raiment, Samuel, 92.
Ralyea, Abraham, 90, 225, 234.
   Anatje, 185.
   Benjamin, 179.
   David, 69, 77, 183, 191, 198, 207.
   Debora, 164, 171, 186, 193, 201, 211.
   Dennee, Denis, Dinie, 41, 49, 63, 69, 75, 76, 92, 112, 119, 120, 122, 124, 127, 171, 172, 179, 185.
   Hendric, 158, 165, 172, 195.
   Hester, 181, 187, 193, 198, 205.
   Jacob, 58.
   Jerimie, 213.

Ralyea (Con.).
　Lena, 94.
　Maria, 124, 163.
　Rosina, 102.
　Saratje, 127.
　Simeon, 116, 127, 128 (Lenjee),
　　131, 134, 145, 160, 171, 188,
　　190.
　Willem, 193, 211.
Rang, Rauk, etc., Anna, 109, 122,
　125.
　Clarah, Claurah, Claatje, 96,
　　99.
　Christiana, Cristina, 108, 109,
　　111, 113, 120, 122, 125.
　Cornelia, 92.
　Cornelius, 88.
　Grittie, 109.
　Hans Jury, Johann George, etc.,
　　4, 65, 66, 73, 74, 99, 100, 102,
　　108, 111.
　John, 91.
　Lourentz, 109.
　Philip, 93.
　Sally, Saartje, 89, 108.
Ransom, Rensem, Smith, 93, 238.
Raymond, Polly, 90.
Rechtmeyer, George, 10.
Redmin, Redmen, Catherine, 92.
　Jane, 89.
　Meyndert, 89.
　Peter, 90.
Reediker, Cornelius, 93.
Repinbergh, Reydenberger, Maria
　L., Marieliss, 107, 108.
Replie, John, 60.
Réqua, Riqua, Daniel, 93.
　James, 86.
Revoe, Mary, 181.
Reynhart, Jacob, 80.
Richard, Margriet, 164.
Rim, John, 229.
Rippinghausen, Reppichausen, Rippighausen, Maria or Anna
　Maria, 75, 108, 122, 126.
Ripple, John, 170.
Ritzen, Anatje, 103.
Roberson, Robinson, Hulda, 157.
　William, Willem, 98, 101, 102,
　　103.
　Zebulon, 149.
Rogers, Thomas, 175.
Roggen, Johan Jacob, 73.
Romeyn, Romyn, Lammertje, 128,
　130, 132, 136, 143.
　Maria, 127.
Roose, ———— 92.
　Abram, Abraham, 96, 98, 102,
　　116.
　Aldert, 115.
　Daniel, 93, 239.
　Deborah, 200, 207, 211, 215,
　　233.
　Dirk, 15, 72.
　Geertje, Geertruy, 159, 170, 186.

Roose (Con.).
　Grietje, 190.
　Gysbert, 118.
　Isaac, 98.
　Jacob, 190.
　Jacobus, 18, 70, 71, 77, 84, 198,
　　203, 208, 215, 222, 230.
　Jane, 88.
　John, 85, 190.
　Lea, 197, 201, 205.
　Lena, 116, 118, 121, 123.
　Maria, 118.
　Nicolaas, 65, 94, 95.
　Peter, 216, 224.
　Sara, Saartje, 94, 95, 208, 215.
　Simeon, Simon, 69, 70, 71, 77,
　　78, 88, 191, 196, 202, 206,
　　210, 213, 222, 223, 229, 235.
　Tjatje, 85, 175, 188, 193.
Root, Maria, 127.
　Martin, 127.
Rosekrans, Rosekrantz, Roosekrans,
　Elizabeth, 92.
　Frederick, 137.
　Henricus, 124.
　Johannes, 59, 159.
　Maria, 92.
　Sara, 137.
　Wilhelmus, 117.
Rost, Simon, 87.
Russel, Ann, 88.
　James, 196.
Rutan, Abraham, 61, 62, 63, 65.
Ruth, Catherine, 62.
　Jacob, 62.
Rutsen, Rutse, Elizabeth, 96, 98,
　102.
　Marretje, Marytje, 96, 101.
Ryerson, Ryerse, Ann, 116, 134.
　Nancy, 116, 128, 145.
Rynes, Isack, 165.
Rysdyk, D^s., 18, 113.
　Isaac, 6, 7, 9, 72, 82.

S

Sahler, Hannah, 91.
Samaria, Samuel, 205.
Sammons, Samons, Jacob, 90.
　James, 89.
　Maria, 92.
　Matthew, 91.
　Nella, 187.
　Rachel, 102, 167, 175, 180.
　Sampson, Sem, 4, 12, 123.
　Teunis, 59, 156.
　Thomas, 90, 230.
Sax, Jacob, 109, 121.
　Michel, Michael, 74, 105, 107.
Saxton, Saxon, Sexton, Aaron, 91.
　Betsy, 88.
　Freelove, 208, 210.
　Gilbert, 141, 149, 153.
　Jane, 90, 93, 239.
　John, 90, 230, 233.

Saxton (*Con.*).
  Justus, 93.
  Nancy, 195, 199, 206, 214.
  Sarah, Sally, 86, 171, 179, 201, 206, 210, 219, 225, 233.
Schooncher, John W., 58.
Schoonmaker, Schonmaker, Schoonmaeker, Abraham, 92, 187, 192, 196, 202, 207, 211, 216, 221, 234.
  Anne, 198, 202, 212, 217, 225.
  Arriantje, Arntie, 193, 211, 213, 217, 218, 224.
  Benjamin, 87, 210, 217.
  Cornelius, 15, 97.
  Edward Edmundus, 197, 201, 205.
  Elias, 58.
  Elizabeth, 97, 114, 115, 118.
  Eva, 159.
  Fredric, 59, 159.
  Henry, 220, 225, 230, 237.
  Hester, 99.
  Isack, 161.
  Jacob, 91, 213, 217, 224, 231, 237.
  Jacob De Wit, 83.
  John, 58, 91, 236, 239.
  Lewis, 92.
  Lidia, Elidia, 81, 99, 112, 129.
  Margaret, 204, 211.
  Maria, Polly, 115, 167, 182, 194.
  Peter, Petrus, 41, 51, 56, 84, 86, 114, 125, 126, 128, 130, 133, 139, 189, 202, 204, 210, 216, 225.
  Philippus, 189, 193, 197, 201, 205, 210, 215, 218, 232.
  Rachel, 87, 123, 187, 207, 215, 216, 236.
  Samuel, 27, 31, 48, 58, 134.
  Thomas, 30.
  Wilhelmus, 31, 42, 48, 58, 77, 86, 117.
  Wyntje, 162.
Schryver, Annatje, Anna, 148, 169.
  Cornelius, 89.
  Emerich, 112, 157.
  Magdalanah, 78, 218, 227.
  Maria, Mary, 192, 219, 224.
  Martynus, 170.
  Osseltje, 157, 183, 192, 198.
  Steps, Stephanus, 60, 76, 169, 184, 192, 228.
Schut, —— 45 (see also Scott).
  Abraham, 85, 199.
  Anetie, 84.
  Jannetie, 124, 127.
  Madelin, 60.
  Willem, 97, 104, 108.
Scott, Scat, Seat, James, 86, 147, 201.
  Susanna, 99, 100.
Seaman, Abraham, 88.

Seaman (*Con.*).
  Ambrose, 205.
  Anny, 229.
  Catherine, 91.
  Esther, 91.
  Joseph, 85.
Selks, Amy, 91.
Serjent, Mary, Polly, 132, 137.
Ses, Henerik, 109.
Shaw, Nella, 175.
Shearman, John, 88.
  Michael, 86.
Shely, Jacob, 135.
Sherad, Phebe, 84.
Shurager, Skurigan, Lea, 90.
  Simeon, 60, 191, 196, 222.
Silie, Sielie, Maria, 165, 172.
Silkworth, William, 92.
Simmons, Simons, Symonsz, Abram, 162.
  Ambrose, 223, 235.
  Anny, 78, 196, 200, 206, 212, 217, 223, 237.
  Caleb, 91, 233.
  Edward, 162.
  Esther, 88, 233.
  Joseph, 175.
  Pieter, 73.
  Rebeccah, 93.
Simson, Simpson, Sally, Sary, 179, 188, 200.
Sinsapagh, —— 93.
  Elizabeth, 93.
  Margaret, 93.
Sleght, Slecht, Elizabeth, 129.
  Hend., 6.
  Rachel, 106.
Slott, Slotte, Daniel, 88.
  John, 89, 176, 186.
  Jonas, 186.
  Polly, 88.
Sluyter, Abram, 129, 130, 133, 141, 168, 178, 188.
  Albartus, 125, 129.
  Amelena, 131, 139, 146, 152, 178, 180.
  Anna, Anny, 85, 89, 97, 102, 103, 108, 117, 121, 125, 128, 129, 131, 169, 182.
  Benjamin, 84, 112, 125, 128, 139, 191, 195, 200, 219.
  Catharina, 87.
  Corneles, 118.
  Cornelia, Neeltje, 98, 101, 103, 108, 109, 110, 136, 144.
  Daniel, 85, 163, 169, 175, 181, 187.
  Dirk, 103, 105.
  Eduwaard, 99.
  Elizabeth, 85, 154, 167, 185, 200, 211, 220, 226.
  Evert, 86, 102, 109, 113, 117, 118, 124, 149, 173.
  Hugo, 86, 181.
  Isack, 178.

Sluyter (Con.).
Jacob, 97, 98, 103, 110, 113, 176.
Jesaias, 183.
Johanna, Jannetie, 100, 108, 128, 132, 135, 141, 144, 146, 165.
Johannes, Hannes, 100, 101, 102, 103, 108, 116, 117, 119, 121.
Jonathan, 86.
Lea, 85, 102, 157, 165, 188.
Lena, 105, 108, 111, 118, 121, 124, 129, 141, 144.
Lydia, 97.
Marghriet, Maragrieta, Grietye, 95, 100, 103, 105, 109, 110, 118, 141, 149, 211.
Maria, 98, 101, 102, 103, 109, 110, 112, 176, 185, 189, 226, 231.
Nicolaas, 118.
Rebeccah, 89.
Sarah, 92, 98, 103, 106, 107, 108, 109, 112, 118, 124, 125, 144, 151, 158, 166, 186, 236.
Willem, Wilhelmus, 95, 101, 103, 105, 125, 128, 132, 135, 141, 144, 146, 165.
Wouter, 103, 126, 132, 136, 140, 149, 156, 164, 169, 176.
Zacharias, 77, 82, 97, 108, 112, 119, 125, 127, 130, 134, 141, 147, 150, 151, 158, 197, 203, 207, 212, 218, 226.
Smedes, Abraham, 115.
Beletje, 115.
Benjamin, 4, 12, 96, 102.
Cathrina, 110, 117, 160.
Elizabeth, 137.
Jacob, 15, 128.
Josua, 115.
Mattheus, 102.
Petrus, 42, 49, 55, 84, 125, 128, 130, 132, 137, 143, 148, 149, 158.
Rachel, 102.
Smith, —— 91.
Abel, 91.
Anny, Annatje, Hannah, 92, 102, 130, 234, 238.
Catherine, 92, 95, 154, 169, 173, 184.
Cornelius, 173.
Deborah, 82, 111.
Eliphas, 87, 173, 182.
Elizabeth, 94, 96, 98, 99, 101, 103, 112, 152, 166, 176, 179.
Eva, 94, 163, 173, 179, 185, 198, 205, 209, 227, 236.
Hendrick, 48, 56, 69, 76, 77, 98, 101, 119, 162, 173.
Johannes, 102, 111, 119, 121, 129, 132, 147, 166.
Jonas, 176, 181, 187.

Smith.
Lea, 98, 99, 101.
Magdaline, 92.
Margarita, Margrietje, Margrit, 100, 101, 102, 106, 107.
Maria, 87, 90, 236.
Oliver, 89.
Peggy, 171.
Philippus, 95.
Phoebe, 93.
Rachel, 112.
Sarah, 119, 163, 173, 182.
Syntje, 166.
Thomas, 94.
Willem, William, 59, 60, 94, 152, 162, 169, 182, 185, 203, Wyntje, 91, 238.
Snediker, Arriantje, 154.
Sarah, 154.
Snese, Snies, Margaret, Maragrieta, 97, 130.
Snyder, Schneyder, Anganitta, 110.
Anny, Ann, 88, 234.
Catrina, 178.
Charles, 88.
Christoffel, 160.
Elizabeth, 85, 90, 163, 171, 181.
Hendric, Henry, 59, 90, 160.
Jacob, 163, 171.
John, 88.
Mary, 90.
Pieter, 10.
Sarah, 110.
Wouter, 110.
Soper, David, 58, 117, 127, 132, 136, 139, 146.
James, 196, 201.
Lea, 216, 220.
Rachel, Ragel, 120, 122, 125, 127, 129, 132, 136, 142, 148, 156.
Sort, John, 59, 166.
Sparks, Sparreks, Catherine, 89, 114.
Ezzekiel, 88, 218, 224, 229, 236.
Spenieneck, Geessie, 94.
Jeames, 94.
Spineks, Spinnik, Lena, 98.
Rebecka, 129.
Sara, 98.
Spriggs, —— 27.
Squire, Isaac, 87.
Stawbridge, Betty, 154.
Steel, Matthew, 104.
Steen, Abraham, 58, 218, 223, 228, 234.
Steenbrinck, Clara, 100, 102.
Stevans, Stevens, Stephens, Betsy, 88.
John, 161.
Peleg, 71, 78, 86, 204, 212, 216, 222, 228, 232, 237.
Steveson, Catrina, 185.
Stilwell, Stephen, 58.
Stips, Hans Jacob, 197.
Stokes, Antje, 167.

Stokes (Con.).
Ephraim, 92.
Frederick, 222, 229.
John, 59, 165.
Margriet, 167, 173.
Nelly, 92.
Rachel, 176.
Richard, 60, 169.
Sally, Sara, 222, 238.
Stokraed, Catryna, Catrina, 74, 98, 130.
Clara, 74.
Maria, 94.
Storm, Lena, 144.
Stratton, William, 88.
Strawbridge, Jackemyntje, 180.
Strickland, Syntje, 77, 84.
Stryker, Eva, 167, 174, 183, 197, 204, 209.
Peter, 90, 228, 235.
Sturn, Santje, 182.
Suert, Suart, Shuart, Johannis, 117, 142, 148, 157.
Swam, Cornelius, 168.
Swart, John, 86.
Lena, 87.
Peter, 82.
Swarthout, Swartwout, Polly, 185, 191.

T

Tak, Geertje, 99.
Tank, David, 90.
Jane, 90.
Maria, 88.
Tapper, Tappen, Tappan, Cornelia, 108.
Yannetje, Jane, 116, 130, 132, 134, 138, 142, 146, 151, 156, 162.
Tebenin, Yan, 64.
Teerpenning, Boudeweyn, Bodewyn, 104, 107, 110, 112, 118, 138, 177.
Cathrina, 208, 213, 226, 234, 238.
Caty, 86, 87, 219.
David, 87.
Deborah, 90.
Dirk, 18.
Elias, 170.
Elizabeth, 104, 107, 110, 112, 118, 138.
Greatje, 170,
Henry, 89, 128.
Jacob, 100, 101, 104.
Jan, John, 18, 81, 102, 105, 107, 111, 119, 123.
Johannis, 106.
Maria, 101, 195, 171, 212.
Marynus, 193, 211.
Noah, 88.
Rachel, 75.
Samuel, 131.

Teerpenning (Con.).
Simeon, 171.
Sophia, 42, 50, 51, 92.
Teunis, 18.
Teers, Sally, 93.
Telson, see Tilson.
Ten Eyck, Mattheus, 115.
Terbos, Terbush, Catarina, 141, 150.
Terwilger, Abraham, 99.
Alida, 111, 118, 122, 125, 127, 132, 141, 170, 177.
Ari, 97.
Art, 171, 179.
Barbara, 102, 104, 121.
Benjamin, 15, 77, 81, 86, 98, 104, 106, 107, 127, 182, 187, 194, 197, 198, 201, 203, 206, 207, 210, 214, 215, 219, 225, 233.
Catrina, 183, 213, 221, 233.
Caty, 85.
Charity, 90.
Cornelius, 99, 103, 239.
Daniel, 89.
David, 87, 197, 202, 208, 212, 224, 230.
E., 60.
Elizabeth, 81, 90, 147, 160, 178, 186, 195, 197, 202, 212, 230, 237.
Else, Elsje, 86, 107, 121, 202, 204, 210, 216, 225.
Evert, Evardt, 65, 73, 93, 98, 99, 137, 151, 158, 174, 180, 186, 198, 211.
Georgius Wilhelm, 102.
Gertrude, 87.
Hannah, Annatje, 91, 174, 186.
Henry, 217, 222, 227.
Hugo, 4, 12, 73, 81, 97.
I., 60.
Isaac, 129.
Isaiah, 208, 210.
J., 231.
Jacob, 19, 88.
Jacobus, James, 85, 223, 235, 239.
Jane, Joanna, Jannetje, Annatje, Anny, 91, 93, 151, 158, 171, 174, 175, 186, 219.
Johannes, 77, 102, 104, 186.
John, Jan, 18, 41, 52, 54, 58, 66, 67, 74, 98, 99, 102, 107, 108, 109, 111, 112, 119, 123, 124, 126, 127, 136, 142, 146, 151, 158, 171, 175.
Jonathan, 29, 41, 51, 81, 82, 110, 111, 113, 119, 121, 122, 126, 127, 134, 139, 189, 194, 198, 205, 207, 212.
Joseph, 42, 50, 118, 120, 122, 125.
Josia, 144.
Laura, 162.
Lucas, 158, 175.

Terwilger (Con.).
Lydia, 84.
Margaretha, 94.
Maria, Mary, 77, 80, 90, 93, 96,
    97, 98, 99, 102, 108, 126, 134,
    137, 139, 142, 160, 163, 166,
    172, 179, 182, 183, 185, 189,
    193, 194, 197, 198, 199, 202,
    207, 212, 214, 215, 230.
Matheus, 4, 12.
Obadiah, 92.
Petrus, 77, 94.
Rachel, 103, 156, 177.
Ruth, 78, 87, 210, 213, 223,
    229, 235.
Samuel, 186, 209, 213.
Sara, Saartie, Sally, 83, 89, 90,
    91, 93, 97, 121, 126, 129, 137,
    151, 158, 170, 187, 205, 209,
    214.
Stephen, 86, 202, 208, 213, 233.
Teunis, 214.
William, 90.
Thaller, Lucas, 154.
Thomson, Sally, 172.
Thorn, Zadok, 89.
Tice, Hendric, 133.
Tilson, Telson, Job, 189, 194, 197,
    209.
Tinkenau, see Fenkenkar.
Titesorte, Elisabet, 64.
    Exgye, 64.
    Haiquiez, 63, 64.
Titus, James, 89.
Todd, Robert, 89.
Tomas, Maria, 100.
Tompkins, Tamkins, Jonathan, 179.
    Thomas, 87.
Torner, Tornar, Margaretha, 114,
    138.
Totton, Tatton, Rebecca, 173, 178.
Townsend, Townsand, Ester, 200,
    209, 216, 224, 231.
Traphagen, Trophagen, Abraham,
    89, 224, 230, 237.
    Hannah, 89.
    Jonathan, 166, 172, 179, 185,
        197, 202, 207.
    Maria, 219, 227.
    Rachel, 216, 224.
    Tyny, 88, 93.
    William, 86, 166, 219, 228.
Tremper, William, 92.
Troies (see Twies), Jurian, 98.
Troup, John, 92.
Trowbridge, Trubridge, Elizabeth,
    174.
    Jemima, Jackemyntje, 78, 174,
        188, 192, 204, 225.
Turk, Anny, 78, 229, 235, 237.
Tuttle, Thankfull, 144.
Twies, see Troies, Jurri, 96.

U

Underhill, John, 91.

Upright, Upregt, Benjamin, 93.
    Sophia, 92.
Urien, Ury, Honnes, Johans, 96.

V

Van Aken Abraham, 86.
    Annatje, 130.
    Charity, 88, 221, 224, 235.
    Eliza, 128.
    Elizabeth, 238.
    Gideon, 78.
    Grittie, 109.
    Isack, 147.
    Jan, 109.
    Jesyntje, 129.
    Judic, 123, 147.
    Maria, 109, 112, 127, 128, 130,
        135, 144, 171, 178.
    Marynis, 98.
    Roseyntje, 119, 121, 132, 147.
    Sophia, 128.
Van Alst, Alida, 148.
Van Bergh, Dina, 105.
Van Berk, Frederick, 105.
Van Bommel, Christoffel, 209.
    Elizabeth, 75.
    Maria, 87, 217.
    Nelly, 89, 225, 232.
    Sally, 210.
Van Bunschoten, Bunschooten, Van
    Buntschooter, Gerret, 173,
    178.
    Jane, 87.
    Malle, 105.
Vandebogert, Charity, 192.
Van de Keyk, Lea, 101.
Vandelyn, Vanderlyn, Abraham, 92.
    Jacobus, 25, 26, 80.
Vandemark ―― 92, 93.
    Abraham, 41, 49, 51, 66, 68,
        73, 99, 101, 107.
    Annetje, 171.
    Catrina, Catarina, 73, 75, 81,
        99, 101, 103, 104, 105, 106,
        107, 108, 110, 112, 118, 122,
        125, 127, 130, 139, 151.
    Freer, 99.
    Henderik, 73.
    Jacob, 89.
    Jakomyntje, Jaquemeytie, 73,
        99, 101, 102, 107.
    Jane, 86, 89.
    Lea, 73, 83, 105, 111, 129.
    Maria, Mary, 87, 89, 208, 224,
        230, 234.
    Petrus, 41, 47, 66, 67, 73, 103,
        107, 109, 111, 119, 123. 128.
    Rachel, 73.
Van der Schuyven, Lea, 95.
Van Deusen, Catrina, 179.
    Jan, 25.
Van Driessen, Johannes, 3, 4, 80.
Van Garden, John, 212, 216.
Van Hoovenberg, Jane, 218.

Van Husen, David, 163.
Van Kampen, I., 29.
Van Keure, Van Keuren, Benjamin,
  15, 105.
  Jacob, 178, 186.
  Jannetje, Yanneke, 85, 117.
  Maria, 218, 226, 234.
  Sherk, 105.
  Tryntje, 140.
Van Kleek, Johannes, 155.
Van Leuwe, Daniel, 136.
  Jacob, 166.
  John, 163.
  Lena, 166.
  Majerie, 74.
  Margriet, 135, 147, 154, 163, 191.
  Maria, 232, 237.
  Mesjel, 100.
  Petrus, 135, 136.
  Rachel, 160.
  Samuel, 233.
Van Nest, Rynier, 13, 15, 18, 72, 144.
Van Nette, V. Netta, Van Natten,
  Catrina, 99, 103.
  Lisabeth, 99.
  Rachel, 92.
Van Ostrant, Van Ostrand, Casparus, 163, 171, 185.
  Dina, 176, 181, 187.
  Frederick, 218.
  Guirtry, 183.
  Jacobus, James, 88, 231.
  Jenny, 169, 172, 178.
  John, 181.
  Laura, 217, 223, 227, 235.
  Rachel, 91.
Van Schuyve, Lea, 99.
Vansile, Van Zyl, Vansyl, Caty, 87.
  George, 182, 190.
  Hennah, 175.
Van Steenberg, Abram, 19, 130.
  Catharina, 130.
  Caty, 89.
  Ezekiel, 91.
  John, Jan, 91, 98.
  Lidia, 130.
  Margaret, Margrietje, Grietje, 78, 138, 142, 148, 191, 234.
  Maria, 98.
  Rachel, 91, 101.
  Sara, Sally, 76, 87, 169, 184, 192.
  Themotheus, 101.
  Theunis, 98, 101.
Van Tessel, Catarina, 133.
Van Valkenburg, Valkenburg, Lidia, 149, 151.
Van Vliet, Van Fleet, Agnes, 216.
  Anatje, 76, 172, 179, 185.
  Catharina, 114, 237.
  Cornelis, 172.
  Debora, 7, 74, 79, 103, 105, 112, 120, 156, 178.

Van Vliet (Con.).
  Dirk, 185.
  Elisabeth, 179.
  Frederick, 143.
  Geertruy, Gertje, 176, 186.
  Jan, 108.
  Jannetje, Janneca, Jenneke, 74, 102, 105, 108, 122, 135, 184.
  Judith, Judic, 79, 114.
  Maria, Mareytie, 75, 112, 120, 127, 171.
  Neelye, 212.
  Sary, Sally, 92, 108.
  Teunis, 41, 52, 56, 128, 130, 132, 136, 143.
Van Voorhees, John, 233, 235, 239.
Van Wagenen, Abraham, 104, 120.
  Aert, Ardt, 28, 30, 116, 118, 120, 123.
  Annatie, 120, 134.
  Archa, 86, 199, 204, 211.
  Benjamin, 89, 111, 130.
  Catharine, Tryntie, Caty, 77, 78, 114, 124, 128, 131, 133, 145, 163, 176, 178, 187, 189, 193, 195, 198, 204, 208, 213.
  Charles, 236.
  Cornelius, 92.
  Daniel, 57, 77, 163, 168, 174, 178, 184, 191, 195, 215.
  Divertje, 74, 106, 111, 122, 166, 169.
  Elizabeth, Lizabeth, 75, 111, 123, 126, 131, 134, 139, 142, 144, 154, 181, 189.
  Ezechiel, 179, 192, 196, 203, 209.
  Gerrit, 113, 115.
  Henrick, 97, 189.
  Hester, Esther, 215, 220, 226.
  Isack I., 59, 60, 87, 109, 159, 166, 167, 198.
  Jacomeyntie, 83.
  James, 113.
  Jan, John, 115, 141.
  Jane, 92.
  Johannes, 154, 199.
  Jonathan 54, 57, 69, 70, 71, 77, 168, 215.
  Levi, 77, 183, 192, 197, 206, 211, 217.
  Lucas, 54, 56, 57, 189, 194, 200, 207, 227.
  Margriet, 141.
  Maria, 77, 107, 109, 112, 119, 120, 123, 127, 136, 146, 191, 196, 202.
  Petrus, 6, 7, 22, 24, 25, 26, 29, 33, 44, 58, 72, 76, 79, 107, 110, 114, 115, 116, 117, 139.
  Rachel, 109, 113, 114, 120, 126, 128, 130, 133, 139, 189.
  Rebecka, 6, 76, 79, 82, 85, 114, 115, 116, 117, 150, 154, 164, 175, 177, 200, 202, 203, 216.

Van Wagenen (*Con.*).
Sally, Sara, 76, 77, 104, 107,
111, 120, 130, 139, 145, 150,
155, 162, 163, 172, 177, 187,
197, 198, 199, 203, 215, 222,
230.
Solomon, 47.
Van Wyen, Henry, 90.
Velten, Regina, 135, 136.
Vernoy, Vanoy, Andrew, 86.
Annaetje, 105.
Catriena, 215.
Charles, 87.
Coenraet, 100.
Cornelius, 19, 120, 123, 153, 206, 218.
Elizabeth, Lizabeth, 75, 100, 108, 111, 118, 120, 124, 131, 134, 137, 145, 158, 164, 174, 180, 206, 218.
Jenneke, 150, 152.
Jonathan, 75 137.
Margaret, 78, 86, 201, 206, 218, 231.
Maria, 111, 137, 138.
Nathan, 131.
Sara, 81, 100.
Simon, 215.
Viele, Ann, 220, 226, 237.
Elizabeth, 88.
Jacobus, 153, 188, 192.
Jannetje, 155.
Johannes, 168.
Maria, 130.
Mynert, 185, 192, 198.
Petrus, 127, 130, 142, 155.
Rachel, 192, 196, 211.
Simon, 147, 153, 160, 168, 185.
Vinnik Grietje, 97.
Volk, Vol, Johannes, Hans, 116, 118, 121, 123.
Vredenbergh, Vreedenburgh, John, 58.
Mary, 58.
William, 90.
Vroom, Catrina, 160.
Vrooman, B., Barend, 4, 10, 12, 99.
Vybau, or Vylar, Genne, 61.
Vylar, or Vybau, Genne, 61.

W

Wackman, Werkman—etc., 93.
Gitty, 92.
Henry, Hendric, 59, 158, 165, 172, 184, 189, 193, 200, 213.
Janetje, 180.
Laura, 214.
Marcus, 59, 107, 163, 170, 182, 193, 214, 217, 223, 227, 235.
Martha, 86, 202, 208, 216.
Sarah, 86.
Wagener, Elizabeth, 113.
Waldron, Johannis, 42, 52, 83, 120, 124, 129, 132, 176, 181, 212.

Waldron (*Con.*).
Maria, Mary, 86, 91, 206 212, 225, 232, 237.
Sara, 176, 180.
Waring, Wering, Israel, 59, 153, 158.
James, 218.
Newman, Numan, 59, 159, 164.
Rebecca, 85, 153, 159, 165.
Salomon, 59, 154.
Warner, John, 88.
Watch, Jacob, 94.
Waters, Catarina, 143.
Weast, Weest, Mary, Polly, 226, 237.
William, 93.
Weaver, Wever, Betsy, 157.
David, 157.
Sally, 157.
Webb, Web, Wheb, Nathaniel, 84, 147, 151, 163.
Peggy, 91.
Weerts, Cornelius, 58.
Maria, 58.
Weldin, Elijah, 210.
Weldon, James, 183.
Weller, Annatie, 118, 125.
Johannes, 186.
Lodewyk, 86.
Margaritt, 122, 127, 186.
Mary, Maria, 93, 125.
Rachel, 91, 215.
Willem, 118.
Wells, Charles, 219, 223, 228.
Elizabeth, 151, 161, 171, 185, 191.
Joseph, 148.
Maria, 76, 93, 148, 168, 175, 180.
Miles, 93.
Nath., 59.
Peter, 148, 157, 169, 183, 192, 198.
Wesmiller—92.
Abram, 181, 187, 193, 198, 205.
Elizabeth, 158, 165, 172, 195.
Hendrick, Henerich, 85, 109, 111, 122, 126.
Jeremia, 77, 84.
Joh. Heinerich, 108.
Maria, 109, 111.
Wessey, George, 146.
Westbroeck, Aaltie, 93.
Anthony, 93.
Westervelt, Martyntje, 166.
Westluck, Ann, Enne, 139, 146, 152, 162, 170, 179, 185.
Weynant, Jannetje, 101.
Jurry, 101.
Maria, 101.
Weyt, Maria, 129.
Wheeler, Anna, 102.
Edward, 94.
Margarita, Margrith, 102, 104, 107, 109, 112, 120, 126.

Wheeler (Con.).
　Neeltie, 118.
　Sara, 94.
　Timothy, 200.
　Willem, William, 83, 123, 151, 165.
　Wyntje, 139, 147, 167, 189.
Whelpley, Maria, 92.
Whitaker, Witaker, John, 215, 221, 229.
Wickam, Wikem, Mary, 83, 160.
Wiept, Jacob, 87.
Wiesst, Wiest, Jacob, 87.
　Johannes, 170.
　Marinus, 87.
Wilkenlow, Antoney Lepold Friderich, or simply Friderich, 111, 113, 129, 131.
　Catrien, 182, 190.
　Daniel, 86, 202.
　Jacob, 156, 165, 175, 180, 186, 196, 200, 205.
　Jacomyntye, 211.
　Johannes, 174, 180, 188, 192, 211.
　John, 78, 204, 225.
　Polly, 91, 239.
　Sarah, 220, 232.
Williams, Icabod, 144.
Williger, Ruth, 206.
Wilson, Wilzon, Catharine, 94.
　David, 116.
　Elizabeth, 88.
　John, 94.
　Rachel, 91.
Wilsy, Catarina, 157.
Wind, Lisabet, 109.
Windfield, Benjamen, 130, 143, 158, 169.
　Bridget, 228.
　Catrina, Tryntje, 107, 131, 138.
　Daniel, 138.
　Elizabeth, 162, 181, 188.
　Eve, 87.
　Hanna, Johanna, 131, 138, 162, 172.
　Isaak, 112.
　Jacob, 102, 104, 107, 109, 125, 129, 131.
　Jan, John, 98, 101, 105, 112, 121, 169, 172, 178.
　Josiah, 91.
　Lany, Leentje, 88, 125.
　Lea, 209, 230, 235.
　Maria, 78, 80, 112.
　Richard, 60.
Wirtz, Caty, 89.
　George, 19, 42, 47, 56, 67, 68, 69, 75, 76, 84, 129, 132, 137, 144, 154, 200.
　Jacob, 78, 86, 200, 207, 213, 219, 233, 238.
　Jane, Jenny, Jannetje, 190, 194, 204, 208, 212, 221.
　Mauritius, 154, 217, 224, 232.

Woester, Cathrina, 129.
Wood, Woed, Woodt, Abraham, 150, 211.
　Anne, Hanna, Antje, 107, 160, 166, 195, 202.
　Benjamin, 59, 163, 173, 185, 234.
　Catarina, 146, 158, 170.
　Daniel, 105, 114, 138.
　Edward, 59, 81, 99, 100, 101, 103, 105, 107, 109, 118, 139, 146, 152, 162, 170, 179, 185.
　Eleanor, 74.
　Helena, Lena, 103, 107, 109, 111, 119, 123, 128.
　Jesse, 57.
　Lea, 149, 160, 167, 179.
　Lidia, 108, 161, 179.
　Margaret, 224, 231.
　Maria, 100.
　Nancy, 169.
　Peter, 60, 163, 169.
　Rachel, 57, 194.
　Rhoda, 90.
　Timothy, 160.
　William, 59, 107, 108, 152, 159, 172, 182, 188.
Woolsy, Wolsy, Daniel, 93.
　Phebe, 155, 161.
Wooly, Abraham, 92.
Wyant, Wygant, Jane, Jenny, 153, 158.
Wynkoop, Wynkop, Winckoop, Adriaan, 114.
　Cornelia, 77, 115, 191, 195, 199, 203, 208, 213, 219, 225.
　Dirk, Derick or D., 6, 7, 9, 15, 19, 28, 45, 68, 70, 72, 76, 79, 80, 114, 115, 165, 199, 203, 204.
　Geertje, 165, 195.
　John, 27.

Y

Yelverton, Selly, 190.
Yendell, Yandel, Jane, 91, 230.
　Mary, 204, 208, 216, 222.
York, Anna, Antje, 86, 130, 143, 150, 158, 169, 201, 205, 209, 218, 225, 231.
　Bridget, Breche, Breggie, 82, 112, 119, 125, 127, 130, 134, 141, 147, 150, 151, 158, 223, 231, 235, 239.
　Catharine, Caty, 90, 230, 233.
　Daniel, 109, 112, 119, 127, 130, 135, 144, 171, 178.
　Deborah, 88, 218, 224, 229, 236.
　Dolly, 208.
　Elias, 79, 208, 210, 213, 224, 231.
　Elizabeth, 86, 87.
　Johannes, 48, 54, 57, 69, 76, 135, 140, 146, 151, 157, 165, 188, 197.

York (*Con.*).
  John, 41, 53, 56.
  Margriet, 189.
  Mary, Maria, Polly, 79, 87, 127, 130, 131, 132, 135, 139, 145, 152, 159, 168, 174, 177, 178, 183, 184, 189, 194, 198, 207, 209, 210, 219, 222, 225, 229, 232, 236.
  Moses, 74, 100, 104, 112, 119, 131, 132, 171.
  Petrus, Peter, Poetrik, 60, 74, 86, 88, 100, 127, 135, 147, 154, 163, 191, 204.

York (*Con.*).
  Rachel, 147.
  Zacariah, 79, 211, 216, 222, 229, 235, 238.
  Youngs, Richard, 87.

Z

Zwart (see also Swart), Egje, 152, 162.
  Geertje, 115.
  Jenneke, 178.

ERRATA.

Page		for		read	
"	61	for	Lymon,	read	Symon.
"	100	"	Andies,	"	Andries.
"	139	"	Duand,	"	Dubois.
"	143	"	Van Viet,	"	Van Vliet.
"	155	"	Mararita,	"	Margrita.
"	159	"	Hood,	"	Wood.
"	182	"	Hood,	"	Wood.
"	182	"	Connency,	"	Conneway.
"	188	"	Hood,	"	Wood.

www.ingramcontent.com/pod-product-compliance
Lightning Source LLC
Chambersburg PA
CBHW050843230426
43667CB00012B/2120